W9-DDH-787

FEMINIST HOLLYWOOD

FEMINIST HOLLYWOOD

FROM
Born in Flames
TO
Point Break

CHRISTINA LANE

WAYNE STATE UNIVERSITY PRESS

DETROIT

Library of Congress Cataloging-in-Publication Data

Lane, Christina.
    Feminist Hollywood : from Born in flames to Point break / Christina Lane.
      p. cm.—(Contemporary film and television series)
    Includes bibliographical references and index.
    ISBN 0-8143-2922-5 (pbk: alk. paper)   ISBN 0-8143-2799-0 (alk. paper)
    1. Women motion picture producers and directors—United States—Interviews.
  2. Motion pictures—Production and direction.   3. Feminism and motion pictures.
I. Title. II. Series.
PN1998.2.L35   2000
791.43′0233′0820973—dc21   99-053522

Parts of chapter 2 appeared in a
slightly different version in
Cinema Journal 37 (Summer 1998): 59–81.

*For Neil
and Gretchen
and Ken
and Deborah*

CONTENTS

ACKNOWLEDGMENTS

LIKE SO MANY BOOKS that have inspired it, this project has been a labor of love, a labor made easier and more rewarding by a number of people. First and foremost, I would like to thank Judith Mayne for planting the seeds of this project and Janet Staiger and Sabrina Barton for nurturing its growth. Not only have their individual pieces of scholarship served as excellent examples, but they have functioned as mentors whose guidance and intellectual enthusiasm I will always hold dear. To Judith, I owe an additional debt of gratitude because she helped me come up with this book's title. I also extend my sincere appreciation to Thomas Schatz, Lisa Lewis, Laurie Schultz, Alisa Perren, Walter Metz, and Linda Mizejewski for reading various parts of this manuscript at a number of different stages. Their willingness to engage in conversation, often over and over again, about the issues raised by this project made the work much easier.

I wish to thank the women directors featured in this book, who offered up their valuable time and resources in order to provide me with important insight into their experiences: Susan Seidelman, Martha Coolidge, Kathryn Bigelow, Lizzie Borden, Darnell Martin, and Tamra Davis. A special thanks goes to Lizzie Borden and Tamra Davis for generously tracking down materials that aided my writing and for offering incredible encouragement along the way.

This book might not have been completed if it were not for the friendly support and confidence of Susan Murray, Alison Macor, and Michael DeAngelis. They have proven to be excellent comrades and

9

great friends. I also thank Jeffrey Bullock and Barb Davidson for daily inspiration.

My deepest appreciation goes to my editor, Jennifer Backer. She has been a pure joy to work with. Series editor Patricia Erens has also provided invaluable advice and support, continually helping me to think about this project in new ways. I additionally thank the anonymous readers at Wayne State University Press for their comments.

In closing, I thank my mother, Gretchen Gaines, for her unrelenting confidence and her openness to jump onto this carpet-ride adventure into women's filmmaking at various points of its incarnation. I thank my father, Ken Lane, and my "other mother," Deborah Lane—their sense of humor and wonderful ability to philosophize about the writing process got me through the book a little easier. Lastly, I thank Neil Pollner, whose support never faltered and who was always willing, when the work became too heavy, to drop everything and journey out to a matinee movie.

INTRODUCTION

In her book *Technologies of Gender: Essays on Theory, Film, and Fiction*, Teresa de Lauretis highlights the act of revision in relation to women directors. According to de Lauretis, revision "refers to the project of reclaiming vision, of 'seeing difference differently'" (1987: 136).[1] Women directors who enter the Hollywood industry, which has traditionally functioned as a male institution, inevitably (though sometimes subconsciously) confront the question of whether or not to reclaim that supposedly male vision. Revision seems even more pressing for independent directors who gain entrance into Hollywood by virtue of challenging its dominant cinematic codes.

Judith Mayne further grapples with the issues at stake in feminist film revision, pointing to the example of the female protagonist in the 1903 film, *A Search for the Evidence*. The woman, accompanied by a male detective, travels down a hotel corridor peeking into keyholes in search of her adulterous husband. Mayne reports that the climax of the film occurs when the detective's point-of-view shot ushers the spectator into the hotel room where the husband dallies with his lover. With this early silent, Mayne makes the case that women (such as the protagonist, in this example) have often held the power of vision in cinema but not without deep ambivalence nor without having to negotiate the authority of masculinist power (1990: 170–71).

This book examines the career trajectories of women directors who have left the world of independent cinema to enter contemporary mainstream Hollywood over the last two decades. I interrogate the relationship between counter cinema and mainstream film through the work of six women directors: Susan Seidelman, Martha Coolidge, Kathryn Bigelow, Lizzie Borden, Darnell Martin, and Tamra Davis. What is the kinship between their independent cinema (my umbrella term for their various counter-cinema films or alternative work), which resists mainstream cinematic codes, and the films they direct in Hollywood? How might a feminist consciousness, a "revision," be articulated in their later work—films that are not exclusively designed and marketed as feminist? Do women directors find a space to comment on that feminist consciousness, or on their own difficult position within the industry, in the films they direct? What is the dialectical relationship between women's alternative and mainstream representations?

Filmmaker and feminist theorist Michelle Citron remarks that many women directors are forced to make a choice: either they maintain control over production of their films and settle for smaller audiences, or they relinquish a degree of control to establishment forces in order to reach a wider audience. In her attempt to understand that decision-mak-

Director Susan Seidelman prepares to shoot a scene for
Desperately Seeking Susan (1986). (Orion Pictures)

12

ing process as a cultural phenomenon, Citron asks: "What does it mean for women to decide to enter the production of mainstream popular culture?" (1990: 45). Before the 1970s, when access to commercial production opened up slightly, women had only two avenues for becoming Hollywood directors: as film actresses or as secretaries/production assistants who worked their way up through the ranks of the system.[2] Only recently have women been hired as directors on the basis of their independent films.[3]

In an attempt to answer Citron's question, I concentrate on a selection of women's films that includes Susan Seidelman's *Smithereens* (1982), *Desperately Seeking Susan* (1985), and *She-Devil* (1989); Martha Coolidge's *Not a Pretty Picture* (1974), *Valley Girl* (1984), *Rambling Rose* (1991), and *Angie* (1994); Kathryn Bigelow's *Near Dark* (1987), *Blue Steel* (1990), and *Point Break* (1991); Lizzie Borden's *Born in Flames* (1983), *Working Girls* (1986), and *Love Crimes* (1991); Darnell Martin's *Suspect* (1991) and *I Like It Like That* (1994); and Tamra Davis's *Guncrazy* (1993), *CB4* (1993), *Bad Girls* (1994, a production from which Davis was fired), and her short *No Alternative* (1994). Although all of these selections may not be easily identified as "feminist films," they enter into what Christine Gledhill calls a "feminist orbit," making themselves accessible to feminist debates and critical readings (1994: 121). (The case of Darnell Martin is the most tenuous of this bunch because her independent film, *Suspect*, was only a student short. However, her status as an African American woman makes her transition particularly significant, especially considering how this status was handled by Columbia Pictures when it released her commercial feature. Arguably, Martin's early associations with the Sundance Institute positioned her as an "indie" as she knocked on studio doors, and her experiences speak volumes about the situation of independent filmmaking in the early 1990s.)

Even though their careers are not examined in detail in this book, a handful of other women directors who moved from American independent cinema to Hollywood also deserve mention. These women include Joyce Chopra, Claudia Weill, and Penelope Spheeris. Chopra and Weill are well known for *Joyce at 34* (1974), the documentary they co-directed about the psychological and social obstacles Chopra faced as she gave birth to her first baby. Chopra went from feminist documentaries to the narrative feature films *Smooth Talk* (1986), which examines a teenage girl's experience of rape, and *The Lemon Sisters* (1989), a studio film that explores the long-term female friendships of characters played by Diane Keaton, Carol Kane, and Kathryn Grody. Weill directed the film *Girlfriends* (distributed by Warner Bros.) in 1978, which garnered critical attention for its experimental approach to the story of a woman photographer who explores her sexuality (Foster 368). Weill also helmed the more mainstream film *It's My Turn* (1980) starring Jill Clayburgh and Michael Douglas. In the 1980s and 1990s she went on to direct television episodes of *thirtysomething* and *NYPD Blue*.

Like Chopra and Weill, Penelope Spheeris honed her craft in documentary cinema. She then made a lasting impression in the independent world with her 1982 exploitation film *Suburbia*, which she says reflects her personal interest in "outcasts from society" (Cole and Dale 224). Spheeris is known for her oddball sensibility and comedic appeal more than for any alignment with feminist politics, but she has made a significant mark as an independent filmmaker who parlayed her craft into enormous commercial success. Her films *Wayne's World* (1992) and *The Beverly Hillbillies* (1993) have earned very high returns, with the former grossing more than $100 million (Foster 346).

The films of these directors certainly deserve more scholarly attention; this study, though it does not explore them in depth, nonetheless points to ways in which their work might be examined and contextualized. Also of interest are women directors such as Allison Anders (*Gas Food Lodging* [1991], *Mi Vida Loca* [1993]) and Nancy Savoca (*True Love* [1989], *Dogfight* [1991], *Household Saints* [1993]) who have opted *not* to move out of the independent realm. Anders and Savoca seem to enjoy a higher degree of autonomy as independent directors—they also apparently have more control over defining their target audience. Julie Dash (*Illusions* [1982], *Daughters of the Dust* [1991]) and Rose Troche (*Go Fish* [1994]) represent another camp of women filmmakers who, though they have so far directed only independent films, have negotiated with the major studios to do more mainstream work.

In an effort to limit the scope of this project, I focus on American directors. However, a number of women have made the transition into Hollywood after directing alternative films in other countries. These directors include Sally Potter (*Thriller* [U.K., 1979], *The Golddiggers* [U.K., 1983], *Orlando* [U.S., 1993]), Euzhan Palcy (*Sugar Cane Alley* [Martinique, 1983], *A Dry, White Season* [U.S., 1989]), and Jane Campion (*Sweetie* [Australia, 1989], *The Piano* [Australia, 1993], *Portrait of a Lady* [U.S., 1996]). An examination of their career trajectories and a consideration of how their films have changed as they have crossed international boundaries would prove quite fruitful.

Crucial to this book is the question of authorship, particularly the extent to which these directors have agency and authority over their own cultural representation. In the rest of this introduction I re-visit theories of auteurism because this grouping of films represents an intersection of "art cinema," where the singular, visionary author is presumed, and the commercial mainstream, where authorship is considered problematic, if not non-existent. Moreover, the deepening entrenchment of the New

Hollywood—governed by high-budget blockbusters, new technologies, and multi-media synergy—affects the debate about auteurism on a multitude of levels, engaging industrial and institutional issues as well as theoretical ones. As a result, the bodies of work produced by these directors need to be considered in relation to their historical moment, in which questions about commerce and art, politics and ideology, and text and reception are growing increasingly more complex and relative with each new film. So before turning to the case studies of directors in the following chapters, it will be worthwhile to address theories of identification, feminist aesthetics, the status of the New Hollywood, and questions of authorship and genre. Susan Seidelman's career then provides an entryway into discussions of the case studies.

CINEMATIC IDENTIFICATION AND THE "GAZE"

For the past several decades, a debate has been carried on within feminist film theory regarding the properties of the Hollywood cinematic apparatus and the complexities of spectator identification. Much of this debate represents a response to Laura Mulvey's seminal essay "Visual Pleasure and Narrative Cinema" (1975). In this essay, Mulvey argues that the textual systems of classical cinema fix a particular kind of viewing process, most specifically a "male gaze" that positions men as active subjects and women as passive objects (1989: 16–21). Using psychoanalytic theory, Mulvey postulates that women have traditionally been denied "the look" because "the female image as a castration threat constantly endangers the unity of the diegesis and bursts through the world of illusion as an intrusive, static, one-dimensional fetish" (25–26). In her original essay, Mulvey suggested that classical Hollywood films offer no position for female or feminist spectators. If Hollywood cinema is governed by a patriarchal system of operations, Mulvey argues that women would do better to challenge mainstream representations from an avantgarde perspective rather than from within the Hollywood industrial complex (26).

Mulvey's essay has had an extremely wide influence on cinema studies but it has also elicited challenges from a number of theoretical vantage points. A number of feminist scholars reacted against her depiction of spectatorship as fixed, universal, and monolithic. Although Mulvey's essay initiated the project of studying the ways in which formal operations such as camera positioning, editing, and lighting contribute to the articulation of gendered power relations, further examinations of these processes have suggested that Hollywood films address spectators in complex and multiple ways. There are many exceptions to the "rule" of the male gaze, to the status women are conventionally assigned in point-

15

of-view shots, reaction close-ups, or placement in the frame. In addition, the different parts that make up a film may work against each other in a way that complicates a spectator's identification with characters or with "the look" of the camera—a contradiction may occur, for example, between the script and the camera work. Moreover, the assumption that editing inevitably implies viewer manipulation seems too simplistic to account for the number of ways in which a film might be cut or paced, not to mention understood by a viewer; poststructuralist theory has compellingly critiqued the notion that camera positionings or editing techniques can fix a particular response on the part of a spectator.

While a great many important pieces of scholarship regarding the "gaze," spectatorship, and identification have emerged over the years, a brief look at the work of Jackie Stacey, Linda Williams, Tania Modleski, and Carol Clover should bring some of the major concerns to the foreground. In a relatively early critique of Mulvey's assumptions, Julia Lesage, Michelle Citron, Judith Mayne, B. Ruby Rich, and Anna Marie Taylor discuss the "bisexuality" of the female spectator in a *New German Critique* article (1978). They proffer that, given the Pre-Oedipal ties between mother and daughter, looking relations between women need to be considered in the context of the gaze. Making this exploration more concrete, Jackie Stacey examines Susan Seidelman's *Desperately Seeking Susan* in her article "Desperately Seeking Difference." She proposes that the film is structured by female desire, most specifically, the desire to "be like" another woman (128–29). Not the same as a lesbian desire, though not exclusive of it, this mode of feminine spectatorship *within* the film points to the progressive possibilities of women looking at other women.[4] Stacey's argument illuminates the problems associated with a binary model in which an active male looks and a passive female can only be looked at.

Other scholars have challenged Mulvey not because her formulation is strictly binary regarding the economy of gazing within a classical Hollywood narrative film, but because she posits a monolithic spectator. Using examples from King Vidor's *Stella Dallas* (1936), Williams argues that any female spectatorial position must be fraught with contradiction because it involves "both a *knowing* recognition of the limitation of women's representation in patriarchal language and a contrary *belief* in the illusion of a preoedipal space between women free of the mastery and control of the male look" (1990: 156). The ambivalence described by Williams suggests that female identification is often encouraged by formal textual systems, but that it becomes a matter of "juggling" many positions at once (155). Similarly, Tania Modleski, in her examination of Hitchcock's films, understands spectatorship to be ambivalent as well as heterogeneous. Modleski remarks that "if the films do indeed invoke typical patterns of male and female socialization . . . they do so only to reveal the difficulties inherent in these processes—and to implicate the spectator in these difficulties as well" (13). As much as classical Hollywood films might cater to a fixed male (white, heterosexual) subject, they also imply the vulnerability and instability in such a subjectivity, which can only dominate by continually displacing and projecting its own fears and weaknesses (14–15).

Along the lines of Modleski's formulations, Carol Clover proposes that any spectatorial positions constructed by filmic discourses are unfixed and marked by a certain "doubleness." In her analysis of horror films, Clover asserts that any gaze consists of both "assaultive" and "reactive" elements that reveal the ultimate vulnerability of the subject who is looking (175). In addition, Clover refutes the assumption that identification is only possible in relations of male spectator/male character or female spectator/female character (61–63), meaning that women may identify with male protagonists and vice versa. It also means that even though the active, agency-oriented protagonist may be played by a man, male or female spectators might be identifying with secondary or peripheral characters. Furthermore, while formal elements such as point-of-view shots or editing might encourage identification with a specific character, spectators may resist those elements in favor of another character or choose not to identify at all.[5]

Looking relations work in complex and multiple ways in the Hollywood films under consideration here. Films such as *Angie* (Coolidge), *Desperately Seeking Susan* (Seidelman), *Blue Steel* (Bigelow), *Love Crimes* (Borden), and *I Like It Like That* (Martin) privilege the subjectivities of their female protagonists through various devices such as point-of-view shots, reaction close-ups, placement within the frame (foreground versus background), sound, lighting, and editing. *Blue Steel* and *Love Crimes*, for example, feature an economy of gazes controlled by female protagonists who are, somewhat ironically, involved in investigations that highlight their own disenfranchised positions within a patriarchal order. However, these devices do not necessarily function in the same way for all spectators, especially when spectatorship is broken down along lines of gender, race, class, and sexual orientation.

The above four films are further governed by a narrative trajectory based, at least in part, on female agency. Drawing on the work of Louis Althusser, Suzanna Danuta Walters asserts that narrative structure needs to be considered alongside the "gaze." Walters states, "In Althusserian and post-Althusserian film theory, the subject is defined, even constructed, *as* a (fictive) subject. In this structuralist sense, narrative is not simply 'the story,' but the vehicle through which the processes of identification and the construction of subjectivity occur" (68). *I Like It Like*

That is driven by a series of narrative beats, all of which are moments in which the female protagonist furthers her quest for self-discovery and empowerment. However, her agency does not guarantee spectatorial identification with a "female subjectivity" any more than her point-of-view shots do.

Seidelman, Coolidge, Bigelow, Borden, Martin, and Davis come out of a tradition of counter cinema that challenges the supposed mastery and coherence of any spectatorial position. This tradition, which will be outlined further in the next section, has been geared toward destabilizing subjectivity and making spectators feel uncomfortable. As might be suspected, these directors' films often complicate easy identifications, making the problems of "the gaze" and its agency explicit almost as often as they encourage the viewer's identification with a female protagonist or the cinematic system. The sections of textual analysis in this book represent attempts to understand, at a material level, the ways in which identification is reinforced or troubled, how a gaze might be constructed or usurped, and how agency might be structured or questioned. But, because spectatorship is undeniably complex, the textual analysis sections are not meant to provide authoritative conclusions about how these films are, or should be, read.

FEMINIST COUNTER CINEMA: AESTHETIC PRINCIPLES

The New Left and art cinemas that emerged in Europe after World War II became formative influences on American filmmakers who resisted commercial Hollywood in the 1960s. During this decade, New York City became an international center for foreign imports, and the American Co-op Movement (a vanguard influenced by the German and French fine arts of the 1920s) opened up independent distribution outlets. As a result, various forms of counter-culture resistance took hold. Influenced by this European movement, New York avant-gardists (e.g., Jonas Mekas, Kenneth Anger, John Cassavetes) focused increasing attention on the spectator, particularly in terms of the deployment of cinematic techniques intended to make the spectator more conscious of filmic processes, and therefore called attention to the constructed nature of film. So avant-garde film has generally been defined in relation to the notion of self-reflexivity, which Constance Penley described as that sense of critical judgment that sometimes enters our dreams: "In *Interpretation of Dreams* Freud offers an answer to the enigma of critical feelings in dreams, that is, the moment when the thought 'this is only a dream' occurs in a dream" (1989: 18). This analogy of cinema and dreams demonstrates how the interruption of a narrative with the intrusion of "real-

18

ity" potentially operates as a distancing technique, breaking the suture of a cinematic text.

Regardless of whether the motivation for encouraging self-consciousness—and film-consciousness—in the spectator lies in artistic or political intentions (or both), the awareness that film holds reflexive possibilities arose indirectly from Saussurian theories of semiotics. Ferdinand de Saussure's explanation of the sign as an arbitrary relationship between the signifier and signified stands as an argument against the camera as a tool that grasps "essential truths or shared experiences" (Lapsley and Westlake 1988: 29). French intellectuals and filmmakers of the 1960s engaged in intense debates about the mediation of language and ideology in representation. Since the 1960s, counter cinema has emphasized the inherent constructedness of so-called essential truths and attempted to coach the spectator toward reflexivity and critical awareness.

Bertolt Brecht also offered insight into avant-garde practices through his notions of distanciation and defamiliarization. Brecht opposed the idea that art should be a mimetic process that copies the psychology of the individual (182). Avant-garde filmmakers of the 1960s and 1970s often used cinematic techniques, such as direct address or desynchronization of sound and image, in order to "make strange" the experience of watching film. The process of distanciation is meant to construct a critical distance between spectator and image, one that de-emphasizes pleasure and escapism and tries instead to tap into cognitive and intellectual practices. Take, for example, Laura Mulvey and Peter Wollen's *Riddles of the Sphinx* (1977), whose circular camera pans presumably "make strange" the close-up shot and conventional editing techniques.

As new ideas about filmic codes and conventions were explored during the 1970s, postmodern theories about the subject also gained increased circulation. For instance, Michel Foucault posited identity as an effect of discursive practices that lacks any singular definitive "core" (1990). In this sense, various aspects of subjectivity are in intense and continuous conflict. From another perspective, Lacanian theory destabilizes subjectivity by focusing on the gap between "self" and image, emphasizing the fragmentation and incompleteness of identity. Christian Metz has drawn on Lacan to argue that film, like the "mirror phase" of psychological development, operates on the principle of the simultaneous presence and absence of that ideal image; thus, cinematic processes have the potential to either efface or foreground the "lack-in-being" that defines the viewing subject (1975). If, as these theorists suggest, identity is essentially fictive (a process that attempts to unify that which is fragmented and incoherent) then reflexive or Brechtian devices play on and exacerbate inherent tensions, unsettling the viewer rather than centering her at the focal point of a narrative universe.

As will become evident, these theories of text and spectator have proven very promising for feminists interested in interrogating mono-lithic notions of identity and text-spectator relations. Initially, however, the more powerful filmmakers in the avant-garde movement, and those with the most financial resources, tended to be men whose creative agendas often questioned the ideological status quo, but very rarely ad-dressed gender politics (Penley 27).

It took feminists to move the interrogation forward, beyond the in-dividual spectator who might experience these critical perceptual and cognitive responses. Taking a cue from alternative women directors such as Germaine Dulac (in the 1920s) and Maya Deren (in the 1940s), sec-ond-wave feminist directors aimed toward a re-working of subjectivity; they were also concerned with collectively mobilizing spectators.[6] Penley claims, "The recent work of several women filmmakers focusing on fem-inist concerns is less work on 'codes' and 'perceptual processes' than it is on narrative, fiction, and the construction of another subject-relation to the screen" (27). Penley problematizes the "tunnel vision" that looks only toward visual aesthetics for oppositional strategies instead of, more broadly, to the possibilities of self-conscious devices at the level of genre, ideological thematics, and textuality. Robert Lapsley and Michael West-lake echo Penley's critique of male filmmakers in their book *Film Theory: An Introduction*. They argue that, although the avant-garde movement has generally lost its steam, it has maintained a crucial role in the wom-en's movement, where "utopic expectations for the future" frame oppo-sitional film as a move toward progress (210).

Women who took up avant-garde conventions in the 1970s were heavily influenced by counter cinema's goals of interrupting the realism of Hollywood films and rejecting the sense of closure traditionally pro-vided by classically structured narratives (Kuhn 166). They were also drawn to documentary approaches, especially cinema verité because the relatively accessible and inexpensive technology of 16mm film enabled women to "document" their lived experiences (147). Documentary prac-tices allowed women to uncover past and present female "realities," a task that corresponded to the political goals of the feminist movement and its "positive images" approach. Women's documentary was typically organized around autobiography or oral history and was therefore struc-tured through the consciousness-raising rhetoric of 1970s feminist poli-tics (155).

To some extent, the conventions of women's counter cinema and documentary overlapped because both modes paid close attention to minute detail (presumably to match women's everyday experiences, espe-

20

cially those of housework and child care) and both relied on a relatively static camera (to avoid overt "manipulation" of the audience and to keep costs down). Martha Coolidge's *Old-Fashioned Woman* and *Not a Pretty Picture*, Kathryn Bigelow's *The Loveless*, and Lizzie Borden's *Born in Flames* and *Working Girls* clearly reflect the conventions of both cinema verité and the feminist avant-garde. As we will see, however, none of these directors fully subscribes to the belief that documentary brings undisputed "truths" to light, a philosophy that has been roundly critiqued since the 1970s.[7]

The terms "feminist documentary," "art cinema," "avant-garde," "experimental," "counter cinema," and "independent cinema" have long and complex histories. For the sake of simplicity, I have chosen to employ "counter cinema" when referring to issues of style, and "independent cinema" when referring to issues of economy. These labels are meant to describe the early films of each director, works made with a limited number of commercial goals and distributed outside of studio territory. In the following section on feminist aesthetics I attempt to achieve consensus about the stylistic definition of women's counter cinema. Then, in my discussion of New Hollywood, I define independent films as those that are not distributed by the major studios or their related subsidiaries. The early films of Seidelman, Coolidge, Bigelow, Borden, Martin, and Davis meet these two (stylistic and economic) definitions, although some fit more easily than others.

As women gained more access to film equipment and resources in the 1970s, independent counter cinema served them as a useful tool for social commentary and change. The relation between counter cinema and feminism, however, is more complicated than it may appear at first glance. As Annette Kuhn points out in *Women's Pictures*, not all attempts to critique commercial Hollywood cinema do so with feminist goals (158). At what points do the two movements intersect? Is there anything inherently progressive in the work of women filmmakers?

Sylvia Bovenschen addresses concerns over sexual difference in a 1977 article, "Is There a Feminine Aesthetic?," in which she argues that women's art has traditionally been produced in the "private," domestic sphere. Therefore, according to Bovenschen, a re-definition of aesthetics is necessary in order to appreciate women's artistic contributions. Her re-definition holds that women's films are inherently different from those produced by men working in male-dominated institutions. Judith Mayne extends Bovenschen's argument, re-organizing it to imply a socially constructed or ideologically imposed difference rather than an essentialist one. Mayne suggests that certain women filmmakers (such as Germaine Dulac, Chantal Ackerman, and Dorothy Arzner) attempt to transform the space in front of the camera by interrogating divisions

Wren (Susan Berman) exudes hostility toward her
unwelcoming surroundings in *Smithereens* (1982). (Courtesy of
New Line Cinema)

between public and private space and ambitiously investigating private,
"female" space (1984: 53–55). She also posits that women who question
dominant cinematic models tend to demonstrate an awareness of their
female spectators; more specifically, they reveal an understanding of the
simultaneous "disavowal" and "embrace" that many feminists experience
when watching Hollywood films (1990: 62).

Mayne points out that a reclamation of women filmmakers should
not result in a romanticization of difference, however. Acknowledging
that certain racist stereotypes exist in Arzner's work despite the director's
many intriguing feminist signatures, Mayne cautions critics against asserting that any director's work is ideologically "perfect" or problem-
free (117). Other pitfalls deserve consideration as well, such as the tendency to use an author's work to lay down corrective "prescriptions" that
might ignore industrial or social context; or the danger of universalizing
women's experiences and thereby denying important differences. Relatedly, every director's identity is determined by more than gender. Race,

class, sexual orientation, and age make gender just one of several influences on an author's work.

Current discussions of aesthetics tend to move away from the notion of a specifically "feminine" medium, focusing instead on how individual films may be considered *feminist*, given the context of a film's release and the ways in which an author's identity is constructed through various social discourses. Kuhn hypothesizes that such a mode of inquiry depends on consideration of three central factors: female spectatorship, feminist address, and feminist intention on the part of the filmmaker. She concentrates on how a "female subject might negotiate her own space within a text," claiming that "a feminist deconstructive cinema is possible: feminist, that is in its textual operations and matters of expression, and also feminist in intent" (175). Kuhn's description of the negotiation of cinematic space on the part of the female spectator echoes Mayne's discussion; spectatorship is examined briefly at the end of this chapter. The notion that feminist aesthetics rely on feminist intent, however, becomes difficult to apply. First, the social construction of feminism changes over time and geography, presenting problems for the critic who wants to work historically. Secondly, the backlash against feminism in the United States may cause some contemporary women directors to avoid identifying themselves as feminists for fear of being outcast by industry insiders. They may have internalized a value system that may not be anti-feminist, per se, but is certainly governed by ambivalence. A director's identification with feminism may also change in degree or shape over time.

In terms of "feminist address," the works of Teresa de Lauretis and Claire Johnston have proven central to scholarship on women directors. Describing the intersection between counter cinema and feminism, de Lauretis distinguishes the generic avant-garde film from feminist avant-garde in that the former usually "decenters the bourgeois subject" and destroys narrative coherence, but maintains the norm as male (122–23). In contrast, feminist cinema begins with an understanding that the spectator is gendered, "and then essays to fashion narrative strategies, points of identification, and places of the look that may address, engage, and construct the spectator as gendered subject" (123). This address is threaded through the filmmaker's selection of shots, sequencing, pace, and so on.

In her discussion of gendered subjectivity, de Lauretis teases out three distinctions, including a film's address to 1) the female ("a biological fact"), 2) femininity ("a positionality of desire") and 3) feminism ("a critical reading of culture, a political interpretation of the social text and the social subject, and a re-writing of our culture's 'master narratives' ") (113). Counter cinema and feminist strategies intersect, then, in this third node by emphasizing critical awareness and self-reflexivity through the lens of the construct "gender." In an argument that informs both Mayne and Kuhn's work, de Lauretis notes that an "aesthetic of reception" has become inscribed into women's avant-garde film—the directors imply, through their work, that they are already conscious of possible interpretations on the part of female spectators as they construct the film (141). An example offered by de Lauretis is Lizzie Borden's *Born in Flames* (discussed in chapter 4), a film that presupposes a female spectator through its unusual juxtaposition of women's interactions and layering of political images and sounds. De Lauretis ties feminist intent to a concern about a particular kind of spectator.

De Lauretis's argument helps to differentiate between a feminine aesthetic and a feminist one. In *Technologies of Gender*, she moves from Bovenschen's notion of a feminine aesthetic to a "feminist de-aesthetic," a process of "destructuring" conventional codes by way of "the de-aestheticization of the female body, the de-sexualization of violence, the de-Oedipalization of narrative and so forth" (146).

Even here such definitions of female / feminine / feminist are hard to pin down. When is a subject being addressed from a position of feminine desire, and when is she being engaged through the terms of her feminist critical awareness? Do filmmakers make that distinction as they construct a film, and even if so, aren't these definitions to some extent unknowable? Still, de Lauretis undoubtedly contributes to the description of an interpretive process based on both feminist subjectivities and an understanding of the address that deconstructs both cinematic processes and definitions of gender.

One of de Lauretis's claims about feminist address involves its focus on "revision," mentioned earlier. Drawing on Adrienne Rich's formulation, de Lauretis notes that re-vision:

> refers to the project of reclaiming vision, of "seeing difference differently," of displacing the critical emphasis from "images of" women "to the axis of vision itself—to the critical modes of organizing vision and hearing which result in the production of that 'image.' " (136; the words in quotations are Rich's)

In other words, feminist counter cinema appropriates dominant codes in order to attend to female subjectivities and modes of seeing—female spectacle becomes female point of view. This definition, with its critical emphasis on "the axis of vision itself," is quite productive because it can also be applied to the representations of women in mainstream, mass culture. For example, we will see how the female protagonists in *Love Crimes* and *Blue Steel* assume an investigative gaze that encourages its spectators to "see difference differently."

24

Mayne makes a similar case for understanding that women's counter cinema springs from multiple locations. She asserts that although feminist theory has relied on a division between dominant and alternative forms, such an opposition needs to be questioned. For Mayne, "the claims that can be made for an alternative vision that exists within and alongside the dominant cinema" will prove to be extremely important for studies of feminist counter cinema. Her decision to discuss Dorothy Arzner's classical Hollywood films in relation to those of contemporary experimental directors such as Chantal Ackerman and Ulrike Ottinger bears this argument out (see *The Woman at the Keyhole*).

Even de Lauretis, who restricts her discussion of address to avant-garde films, notes the ways in which strategies of "revision" are developing in mainstream films as feminist discourse and self-conscious filmmaking have been appropriated. She has commented on the movement of alternative filmmakers into more narrative conventions, offering up the example of Yvonne Rainer who, though she has not engaged with mainstream narrative techniques, has become more concerned with narrativity. De Lauretis asserts that "feminist work in film should not be anti-narrative, or anti-Oedipal, but quite the opposite. It should be narrative and Oedipal with a vengeance" (108). This notion of "vengeance," of recuperative attack, will become an important part of the process of understanding revision. Here, "vengeance" functions as a wedge between conservative narratives and progressive ones.

De Lauretis also parallels this increasing interest in pushing the limits of narrative with a growing investment in feminism, in Rainer's case, which suggests a provocative relationship between women's processes of consciousness-raising and their desire to tell stories. Likewise, Patricia Mellencamp posits Rainer's return to narrative (as well as that of Sally Potter) as a shift in lenses that adds a "third knowledge"—from alternative to commercial back to alternative—to her stories (1990).

Historically, then, directors like those in this study were engaging with feminist filmmaking at a time when women were opening themselves up to the possibilities of narrative conventions, especially the oedipal narrative, "with a vengeance." How does this extra force work ideologically? What are the limitations of vengeance in Hollywood film? Can we distinguish between "ordinary" narratives and avenging ones? The question of vengeance is crucial to the examination of women directors who critique mainstream film "from within."

Feminist scholar Claire Johnston explored this theoretical question as far back as 1973, laying the groundwork for a consideration of "women's cinema as counter cinema" within Hollywood narrative and visual conventions. Johnston argues that the mythic qualities of mainstream cinema, which ahistorically and eternally naturalize stereotypes of women, end up normalizing dominant ideology. However, drawing on semiotic theory, Johnston proposes that a signifier and signified may be detached and re-configured, creating a new signified within which meaning is usurped and ideology challenged (210).

Johnston criticizes the feminist documentary movement of the 1960s and 1970s for its reliance on the concept of realism, pointing out the ways in which all representations are ideologically constructed products (214). Instead, Johnston proposes, why not deploy documentary and counter cinema in a way that acknowledges its own "manufacturedness"? This proposition coincides with the more general tenets of 1970s counter cinema that held up techniques of self-reflexivity and distanciation as ways of rejecting the supposed "essentialized truths" of realist cinema. Martha Coolidge's pseudo-documentary *Not a Pretty Picture* (analyzed in chapter 2) represents an extension of Johnston's argument because it points to the constructedness of documentary codes by stressing the presence of the director and the labor of the performers.

Johnston also argues that if ideologies are manufactured, feminist ideologies could be fashioned and deployed within Hollywood in an effort to denaturalize dominant myths about gender. She cites strategies of interruption and distanciation in the work of Dorothy Arzner or the narrative distortions in female perspectives within Ida Lupino's work as examples of this critique "from within." By advancing examples of Hollywood cinema that interrogate dominant ideology, and by simultaneously arguing that art cinema can promote sexist iconography just as easily as commercial film, Johnston insists that film can serve as a political tool and an entertainment form at the same time (217).[8] If we remember de Lauretis's contention that Borden's *Born in Flames* functions as a feminist tract, we might support a Johnstonian argument that Borden's mainstream film, *Love Crimes*, reflects an attempt to de-naturalize female fantasy and, therefore, extends her earlier political interests.

The search for cinematic reflexivity and feminist address presents many problems, especially at the level of definition. In an effort to get beyond very narrow and text-based arguments about feminist aesthetics, Christine Gledhill remarks that, at its best, feminist criticism can "enter the polemics of cultural negotiation by drawing the text into a female or feminist orbit. Such cultural criticism is not concerned with the progressiveness or reactionariness of the text, but with tapping its cultural energy, making it productive for feminist debate and practice" (1994: 121). While it may be difficult to locate all of the films under consideration here as inherently "feminine" or "female-addressed," they each lend themselves easily to this feminist orbit. Although this book may implicitly (sometimes subconsciously) argue for the "progressiveness" of women's mainstream films, my main reason for including the films discussed

26

here (both counter cinema and mainstream) is that they centrally engage feminist issues.

Gledhill's "feminist orbit" offers promise because it refuses to stall out at the imaginary counter cinema/mainstream Hollywood "divide," emphasizing instead the continuities between films. As we will see, such a division has become increasingly blurred, especially in the period of so-called New Hollywood. Films conceived as alternative projects often end up being bought for distribution by studios or large companies. Kaja Silverman attempts to chip away at this mainstream/counter-cinema division in *The Acoustic Mirror*. She laments that feminist film theory, especially scholarship that focuses exclusively on cinematic specificity and textual analysis, assumes that a female authorial voice is only detectable in women's experimental work and cannot be spoken through the apparatus of Hollywood cinema. She is troubled by de Lauretis's tendency to privilege avant-garde filmmakers (such as Chantal Ackerman and Lizzie Borden).

Silverman discusses the example of Jacqueline Suter's article "Christopher Strong and Feminine Discourse," in which Suter all but ignores Dorothy Arzner's role in the film. Suter elevates *Jeanne Dielman, Quai du Commerce, 1080 Bruxelles* (1975) over *Christopher Strong* because, Silverman relates, it does not recuperate its own progressive elements. Silverman suggests that a female author may well be difficult to locate in Hollywood texts, especially given the collaborative nature of the studio production mode; she argues, however, that the project to find female authors will simply require feminist theorists to devise new and alternative strategies of analysis for women's mainstream cinema. Methods of textual analysis—which have yet to fully address the tensions between feminism and auteurism—might be stretched in order to read these films in all of their complexity. This means incorporating visual considerations with thematic, generic, and ideological strategies of subversion—in other words, re-situating auteurism beyond visual terms.

This is to say that textual analysis offers the most value when it relies on an industrial language that accommodates both the existing studio system and women's role in that system. The upcoming pages depend on a vocabulary that takes into account the specificity of the director's role, considers the particular circumstances of the director in question, and acknowledges the collaborative nature of mainstream production. For example, Tamra Davis's contribution to the development of *Bad Girls* underwent a major overhaul when she was replaced with director Jonathan Kaplan, but it would be a mistake to attribute the entire film to him. In chapter 6, the Davis version (as relayed through the original screenplay) is examined in relation to the Kaplan film in an effort to explore the possibility of her remaining authorial presence.

27

An understanding of counter cinema and mainstream film as two sides of one coin helps facilitate the necessary work of locating women's alternative voices within Hollywood cinema. Additional insight can be gained by recognizing the way that Hollywood works as a cultural power center. Michel Foucault's formulations regarding how knowledge is conveyed through discourses of power are particularly useful. Foucault proposes that power does not operate repressively and hierarchically from the top down. In other words, dominant meanings are not singularly controlled by an elite few at the top of "the" Hollywood power structure. Instead, power is "continuous, subtle, [and] productive" because it flows from multiple and local power centers (Davis and Fisher 8).

According to Foucault, sites of power "should be seen rather as a dispersion of centers from which discourses emanated, a diversification of their forms, and complex deployment of the network connecting them" (1990: 34). Drawing on Foucault's characterization of the "capillary movement" of dominant discourses, Nancy Davis and Susan Fisher understand power as "circulating through the social body and exerting its authority through self-surveillance and everyday, disciplinary micropractices—practices more fundamental than beliefs (ideology)" (8). An application of these observations to the situation of women directors suggests that these women should be seen as part of the power system of Hollywood industries, not outside of it. Their individual "micro-practices" help to produce filmic discourses as they respond to those already in circulation. In this way, all subjects operating within the radius of Hollywood engage in multiple positions of power. Many discourses permeate films, and women emphasize certain ideological themes over others; it isn't the case that a particular film or director embodies one unified theme to the exclusion of all others, as in either "patriarchy" or "feminism" (Hayward 113).

This means that any manifestations of resistance to dominant Hollywood discourses become "disorganized and fragmentary" because those discourses are already multiple and sometimes incoherent (Davis and Fisher 8).[9] If individuals can be said to embody both dominant and resistant discourses, then everyone, at least potentially, has power. This model facilitates an understanding of how oppressive belief systems can be simultaneously internalized and challenged by the same individual, especially considering how self-surveillance and self-discipline operate in institutions such as the Hollywood complex (Bartky 79). It is easy to see, then, how a single film by a woman (or any) director might contradict itself, or how her body of work might display multiple messages about gender, race, or class. One important aspect of the Foucauldian model is its refusal to dismiss these processes as mere co-optation or internalization of dominant discourses. As Jana Sawicki interprets Foucault's work,

28

the spiraling circulation of power means that power can attach itself to strategies of resistance as well as to those of domination, insinuating that social subjects continually engage in the process of negotiating *both* of these strategies (185).

These important advances in discourse theory more adequately explain the relationship between counter cinema and Hollywood. Embodied in a series of local power centers that traditionally resist the commercial discourses of Hollywood industries, counter cinema has served as an outlet for articulating resistance and struggle. As Susan Hayward puts it, "women's counter-cinema is about discursive disclosure, that is, the expression of other knowledges passed over in silence" (113). In other words, women's independent films have the potential to expose the dominant ideologies that have traditionally been naturalized and reinforced through classical Hollywood conventions. Counter cinema stands in dialectical relation to studio production; however, it is not wholly "independent" of it. No matter how much the director of an independent film might be romanticized via auteurism's "cult of the artist," her film is always a product of a broader economic and ideological context.

As Foucault's model of power implies, the production and reception of independent films occur in active relation to Hollywood finance. Moreover, because of the capillary movement of knowledge and power, the visual techniques, narrative patterns, thematic concerns, and ideological messages of counter cinema are rather easily recuperated into mainstream cinema (113). As we will see in the next section, this makes the relationship between Hollywood studio films and independent counter cinema increasingly complex and difficult to define.

THE NEW HOLLYWOOD: MAINSTREAM VS. INDEPENDENT

Since the mid 1970s, in response to the upheaval caused by the decline of the studio system in the 1950s and 1960s, the mainstream film industry has developed into what is now often described as the "New Hollywood." In the last two decades, Hollywood has increasingly become controlled by conglomerates and multinational corporations, with the result that high concept films, or "blockbusters," have governed the decision-making processes of the major studios. As Thomas Schatz has pointed out, film production and distribution are now related to an entire entertainment industry, which includes franchising, merchandising, and the synergistic interaction between all of these industrial appendages (1993). Increased importance is placed on pre-sold properties that are easily identifiable to audiences and comfortably carry over to areas such as fast food promotions, computer games, and theme park rides (not to mention sequels). In addition, the industry has become more agency-

29

controlled as "packaging" of talent and projects has emerged as the norm. The current arrangement of the New Hollywood has also meant that mainstream productions depend on bankable stars and global appeal, given that international profits are necessary to pull a high-budget film out of the red.

In fact, Jim Hillier suggests that by the middle 1980s, the majors had practically re-instated the studio system, which had been undone by the Paramount Decree of 1948 (1993). The effect of Japanese takeovers, conglomeration, and the buying up of theater chains (after a 1985 reversal of certain exhibition legalities, helped along by Reaganomics) is that Hollywood institutions are just as oligopolistic and vertically integrated as they were fifty years ago (17). According to Hillier, the monolithic economy of the New Hollywood offers little room for variation among studios, independent production companies, promotion departments, franchises, and stars.

Taking a more optimistic view, however, Schatz explains that a system of conglomerates may not function as monolithically as we might assume: "In one sense the mid 1970s' ascent of the New Hollywood marks the studios' eventual coming-to-terms with an increasingly fragmented entertainment industry—with its demographics and target audiences, its diversified 'multi-media' conglomerates, its global(ized) markets and new delivery systems." (9) The fragmented industry, which depends on the synergy of many parts to run the "whole," Schatz says, parallels an increasingly fragmented audience whose demographics are difficult to determine and forecast. More specifically, Hollywood of the 1990s targets a variety of audiences—categorized by gender, age, race, even sexual orientation—in quite complex ways. Jim Hillier notes an inclination among the studios to "narrowcast" for women and children in ways we did not see in the 1970s (31).[10] I would also highlight the narrowcasting aimed at African Americans and gay men and lesbians.

In terms of age demographics, it may be incorrect to presume that the average movie-goers have been and will continue to be males aged eighteen to twenty-four. Statistics from 1990 demonstrate otherwise. Only 56 percent of movie-goers were twelve to twenty-nine years of age (36 percent of whom were twelve to twenty), which leaves 44 percent of movie-goers outside that age bracket. Significantly, the percentage of film audiences in their forties has increased from 15 percent in the 1960s to 24 percent in 1990 (Hillier 31). Formerly of Fine Line Features, Ira Deutchman points to middle-aged audiences as a target market whose presence could tremendously alter the current landscape of New Hollywood product (Deutchman 327).

These industrial and economic structures have profound implications for filmmakers in the independent sphere. The result of narrower targeting is that studios concentrate their resources on two types of films—the high-budget/high-concept film and the low-budget or first-time director/first-time star film. As Hillier points out, the "event movies" act as tent poles to the industry, but they do not expand the audience. Major studios have found that low-budget, more experimental productions do broaden their audience; and as low risks, these films compensate for failed blockbusters (Hillier 30). Schatz agrees with Hillier, stating that "one crucial dimension of the New Hollywood is the 'space' that has been opened for independent and alternative cinema" (Schatz 10). According to Schatz, at the end of the 1980s, independent "niche" companies such as Miramax and New Line Cinema were finding ways to exploit the market fragmentation that resulted from an overwhelming number of high concept blockbusters, successfully promoting crossover films such as *sex, lies and videotape* (1989) and *My Left Foot* (1990) (Schatz 34). The industrial approaches of Hillier and Schatz appear to match the theoretical assumptions made by Scott MacDonald. He argues that mainstream film and counter cinema are inextricably connected because the latter is always a response to the former, and the former often appropriates the latter (1988: 1–2).

The map of counter cinema has undergone considerable change over the past decade. The success of Spike Lee's *She's Gotta Have It* and Lizzie Borden's *Working Girls* at the 1986 Cannes festival revived possibilities for American low-budget filmmaking, which had a very low profile in comparison with European independent films. But it was the "landmark" event of Stephen Soderburgh's sweep of the Cannes Film Festival with *sex, lies and videotape*—and the fact that the film eventually earned $25 million—that caused a major shift in the boundary between commercial and counter cinema (Ferncase 1996: 116). Its success at Robert Redford's Sundance Institute also helped American independent festivals gain more attention (123). Lizzie Borden observes, "I think *sex, lies and videotape* basically changed the world for all independents. When I was at Sundance, *Working Girls* had won the feature prize but it wasn't even noticed by Hollywood, basically because it was still a counter cultural festival. Independent filmmaking started to mean something else with Soderburgh's film" (author's interview, 7 Aug. 1996). Borden, whose *Working Girls* helped forge crucial links between American independent industries and the European Cannes Festival, had earned only minimal visibility through Sundance.

Although it is hard to underestimate the impact of *sex, lies and videotape*, its oft-obscured production history points to the underlying connections between contemporary independent cinema and studio filmmaking. Before the film's domestic theatrical rights were purchased by Miramax following Cannes, it had been co-financed by Columbia Pictures and European investor Virgin Films. (Columbia had American distribution while Virgin held on to foreign rights.) Columbia, in the midst of upheaval, saw little profit in Soderburgh's first feature, so the studio proceeded to sell its domestic distribution rights to the highest bidder, Miramax, and retain only the rights to video distribution (Perren 65). This means that the film's billing as "independent" effaced its studio origins.

As the tale of *sex, lies and videotape* demonstrates, the independent world became increasingly industrialized in the late 1980s and 1990s as small companies began making distribution deals with major studios, with advantages for both entities. Only the major studios held the financial resources to spend as much money on promotion as on production, and only they had gained a global foothold (Hillier 16). However, when "mini-majors" such as Vestron and Lorimar collapsed in the late 1980s by trying too hard to compete with the majors, new independents Miramax, New Line Cinema, and Largo came in to fill their niche (21–22). The demand for product created by the expansion of new technologies such as cable, video, and pay television, was a primary reason for the financial success of both of these kinds of companies, the mini-majors and the new independent companies. But organizations such as Miramax and New Line—what Justin Wyatt calls the "major independents"—outdistanced their predecessors by working with studios rather than against them.

This new breed of independent financed some of its own production, but in many cases it acquired already produced films that could be well marketed. The company would bear the brunt of costs associated with designing a marketing plan and with releasing prints and advertising, but it reaped the benefits of hands-on control with fewer projects. Studios found that although this partnership garnered them fewer profits than their own higher-budget films, this kind of venture exposed them to very little risk. In the early 1990s, "major independents" were dependent on the studios in many ways; however, they were often able to foster a degree of autonomy because their films did not seem, on the surface, to threaten studio product.

The strategies cultivated by Miramax and New Line are critical to understanding the climate of 1990s independent cinema. They turned off-beat, non-traditional narrative formulas into commercially lucrative films by focusing their primary attention on marketing and promotion. For example, Harvey and Bob Weinstein transformed Miramax into a "giant" through the creation of controversy around films. They followed in the "exploitation" tradition of New York City theater-owner Michael Rugoff, who transformed counter cinema into a force studios had to reckon with in the 1950s and 1960s (Wyatt 1998: 68–69). Whether they were publicly rebelling against the Motion Picture Association of America's X or NC17 ratings of films such as *Scandal* (1989), or creating hype about the "secret" of *The Crying Game* (1992), Miramax executives attracted audiences by producing "buzz" about relatively "small" pictures (Wyatt 1996: 62–63). Justin Wyatt attributes the success of major independents "to their aggressive marketing approach of art house films," making the important point that part of this approach involved a return to a "romantic discourse of authorship," which turns a directorial debut or follow-up into an "event" (61).

Another reason that these companies prospered was their decision to divide product into two brands, genre films and more quirky, experimental fare. For example, after the triumphs of the franchises *Teenage Mutant Ninja Turtles* and *House Party*, the well-established New Line formed its Fine Line Cinema division in 1991, through which it eventually distributed the less commercial *Barcelona* (1994) and *Mrs. Parker and the Vicious Circle* (1995) (Deutchman 326–27; Wyatt 61–62). Miramax operated through a similar split by producing their genre films, specifically horror films, through Dimension Films. This arrangement allowed the company to establish separate marketing identities and to experiment with untried ideas while maintaining control over their budgets according to individual film proceeds (Wyatt 62). Wyatt likens the low-risk genre film/high-risk alternative film division to the high-budget blockbuster/low-budget "edgy" film split that structures New Hollywood studios (61).

The definition of "independent" became even more complicated in the middle 1990s when studios began to purchase the major independents (Disney bought Miramax, Time Warner acquired New Line) or investing in their own "independent" branches (Sony launched Sony Pictures Classics for foreign or alternative product and, soon afterward, Screen Gems to focus on teen-oriented genre films). The heightened studio involvement stood as evidence that films bucking conventional formulas and including aesthetically jarring visuals, even films that contain politically leftist themes, were commercially viable. Major independents claimed that they maintained their creative autonomy, defending their new direction as a logical move toward increased distribution.

What was clear, however, from the studios' acquisitions of independent companies was that the "difference" provided by quirky characters, anti-realist techniques, overlapping story lines, or feminist/queer/non-Eurocentric commentary served as a primary selling point for low-budget films (Perren 210–11). It was now commercial to take on unconventional, experimental film projects, or to promote relatively traditional films as such (196–98). The line between counter cinema and commercial Hollywood was beyond blurry—it was practically moot. In addition, because of the importance of genre to these major independents, narrative counter cinema increasingly began to override experimental forms.

Although "independent" executives such as the Weinstein brothers insist that their control has not changed with the studio buy-out of their companies, the degree of their autonomy remains in constant question. The 1995 controversy surrounding Miramax's pseudo-documentary *Kids* offers a case in point—Disney balked at distributing the film, forcing Miramax to form a separate company, Shining Excalibur, for the film's release. The problem was also faced by October Films when its parent company, Universal, reneged on its agreement to distribute *Happiness* (1998), a film that incorporated complex themes concerning pedophilia and masturbation. Despite the fact that *Happiness* was performing extremely well at festivals, October had no choice but to sell it back to its producers, who distributed it through their own production company (Pener 20–21). These kinds of incidents have been, to date, isolated, but they function as reminders that the independence boasted by major independents remains precarious.

Furthermore, questions of autonomy and agency at the sub-conscious level—particularly in the development stage of film production—have gone unexplored by trade press and film scholarship. Considering that junior and senior executives are forced to think pragmatically and opportunistically when working within commercial industries, they may be inclined to avoid an idea that they deem too risky to earn them a promotion or keep them in their present position.

Even if a questionable project makes it through development, executives may decide (consciously or subconsciously) to drop it mid-stream for fear of losing approval from those in power above them. Since the major independents and low-budget studio divisions base much of their activity on acquiring already-completed product, the consequences of such commercially based decision-making obviously affect how counter-cinema producers and directors go about choosing material and launching films. Very few measures currently exist for gauging the processes of projection, speculation, and second-guessing on the part of independent directors hoping to gain distribution once their films are complete, although these processes are certainly important considerations. They decidedly help create a climate in which output by the extreme avant-garde seems to shrink as more mainstream independents continue to grow.

As the boundaries between independent companies and studios become more indefinite, the division between film criticism and film promotion also becomes less certain. The momentum of independent films has traditionally been driven by reviews that spur word-of-mouth notoriety. In the 1970s, Pauline Kael "rescued" a number of non-commercial

34

films from obscurity, most notably Robert Altman's *M*A*S*H* (1970) and *Nashville* (1975) (Wyatt 1996: 53–55). The role of reviewers has slowly been colonized by studio marketing departments. This phenomenon means that the ability to shift a negative tide surrounding a particular film is now, more and more, out of the hands of Kael-style critics. Considering that major independents such as Miramax have mastered the techniques of promotion and publicity to an even greater degree than many studios, reviews have become increasingly corporatized, often looking more like advertisements than evaluation.

The commercialization of the film criticism field provides only one example of the many ways in which the entire apparatus of independent filmmaking has evolved since the 1970s. The growth of "indie" film festivals, cable channels, screenwriting contests, and trade periodicals aimed at hopeful independent filmmakers has been incredible. Considering the increasing likelihood that films that would have been considered "anti-Hollywood" a decade or two ago will be screened in multiplex theaters, independent filmmaking and film-going have been transformed into popular pastimes.

Another important factor involves the contemporary commodification of the first-time director. In the 1970s, many feminist filmmakers who embarked on their first features did so based on political motivations, or in the spirit of exploring cinematic territory in innovative and rebellious ways. In the 1990s, a number of them have done so with the goal of gaining a foothold in Hollywood. The growth of film schools and the explosion of the festival circuit has meant that the arena of counter cinema offers an opportunity to garner the visibility and marketability that will launch a blockbuster career. This is encouraged by the fact that major independents often exploit the artisinal philosophy of auteur theory and the capitalist discourses of the American Dream to advertise lesser-known films.

Although nostalgic reminiscences about 1970s avant-garde filmmaking should be avoided, it is important to acknowledge the practical, economic considerations of the current industrial climate. Contemporary counter cinema has changed from the days when Lizzie Borden made *Working Girls*, when her primary goal seemed based on her personal desire to bring a feminist representation of middle-class prostitution to the screen and her political aspirations of attracting an adult female audience, no matter how small. Borden's film would eventually be picked up for distribution by Miramax and it would earn her the chance to direct a feature for that company, but she did not launch *Working Girls* as a means of gaining entry into the Miramax stable—in fact, there was no stable.

In comparison, the early careers of Darnell Martin and Tamra Davis played out quite differently from Borden's, primarily because the world of independent cinema has been remarkably altered. The "buzz" created by the success of Martin's short film at Sundance, in conjunction with the strength of her spec script (a screenplay written on pure speculation, with no financial investment from an outside party), earned her the chance to direct a studio film. Davis's first feature, *Guncrazy*, became a viable commodity only after the film garnered critical attention at festivals; but, in all likelihood, the music video director saw the debut as an avenue toward more commercial endeavors. Whether or not she was particularly calculating about the project, *Guncrazy* did ultimately serve that purpose, offering up feminist elements without "pigeon-holing" Davis as a non-commercial, feminist filmmaker.

It should be obvious by now that contemporary modes of independent distribution were not available to most women directors who got their start in 1970s or early 1980s counter cinema. Nor is it likely that if major independents had in the 1970s the power they do now (how could they?) that they would have distributed, acquired, or financed the kinds of "marginal" works these women made, which were blatantly feminist (*Not a Pretty Picture, Born in Flames*) or boldly defiant of generic codes (*The Loveless*). However, these corporate structures have now made it possible for women outside the commercial mainstream to enter "Hollywood" and reach a wider audience. Two obvious downsides of this phenomenon exist. First, films that lean more toward the avant-garde than to the crossover independent hold little promise for the marketing departments of major independent companies. Second, with independent output having doubled over the past decade, competition among counter-cinema directors is much greater (Garvin 80).

On the upside, because of the interconnectedness of studio and independent films, it has perhaps never before been more economically viable to critique the dominant ideologies of the studios from within. The blurred boundaries and constantly negotiated relations between truly independent companies (which distribute independently of majors), major independents, and studios are at the center of any discussion of how one goes about critiquing status quo power relations. The relational position of the individual director within these complex power structures obviously determines how her films are produced, packaged, and distributed.

For what it's worth, my own distinction between counter cinema and mainstream film hinges on distribution and is, therefore, at one level, an economic distinction. Of course, a line is also drawn according to the aesthetic and political strategies that resonate within specific films. But, when I discuss each woman director's "entrance" into Hollywood, my definition of "Hollywood" depends on whether or not her films are being distributed commercially, most often by a major studio.

If the New Hollywood privileges high-budget blockbusters and, to a lesser extent, low-budget "smaller" pictures, then it is the middle range ($25–$30 million) films that tend to suffer. These "non-event" movies also tend to be the projects assigned to women directors struggling in Hollywood, which impedes their access to the industry somewhat. Although Kathryn Bigelow has built her career on relatively high-grossing action thrillers (*Blue Steel, Point Break, Strange Days* [1995]), most women directors, even those who want to foray into such films, find themselves "pigeon-holed" into either the "teen-film" or relationship-oriented/family projects.[11] For example, Martha Coolidge made a name for herself with films aimed at a teenage market, including *Valley Girl* and *Real Genius*; more recently she has directed *Angie*, about a woman facing single motherhood, and *Three Wishes* (1995), featuring a troubled boy and his single mother whose lives are touched by a strange outcast. The financial impetus behind, and the later response to, mid-range films such as Coolidge's *Angie*, Martin's *I Like It Like That*, or Borden's *Love Crimes* will always depend on the status of the New Hollywood blockbuster. Their financing and reception are inevitably determined by the number of blockbusters being produced and the success of those higher-budget films at the box office. In other words, mid-range films represent risky investments and are less likely to be financed in years when high-budget films yield low returns. Their success is also based on their release date in relation to event movies—if scheduled during holidays or summer seasons, these films are often destined to "fail" commercially.

Even if most women directors are relegated to mid-range, non-event movies, the New Hollywood has seen a massive entrance of women and minorities into powerful roles within the world of commercial cinema. This change is due in part to an affirmative action agreement negotiated by the Directors Guild of America in 1981 that promised "good-faith" efforts to hire women and minorities (Corliss 1986: 83). Such reparation has proven sorely needed: *Time* magazine reports that of 7,332 feature films made between 1949 and 1979, 14 were directed by women—and it was only 7 women who directed those (Schickel 1991: 78)! This means that one-fifth of 1 percent of all Hollywood films were directed by women during that time span.

Over the last decade or so, the population of women directors in Hollywood has greatly increased. As of 1993, 565 women belonged to the Directors Guild (Cordero 1993: 3). (However, only 23 out of the 406 features made in 1990 were directed by women [Acker 1992: 64].) One result of the increase is that women directors' movies and mainstream films with feminist points of view are being distributed at a higher rate than twenty years ago. Take, for example, the increased number of screens reached by *Rambling Rose* (1990), *The Piano* (1992), *Orlando*

(1993), and *The Incredibly True Adventures of Two Girls in Love* (1995)—films that lend themselves well to feminist readings and yet go beyond art-house distribution.

One of the most disturbing phenomenons of Hollywood in recent years, however, is that, as women directors increase in numbers, the number of desirable acting roles for women has decreased. Susan Faludi relates a Screen Actors Guild study that found that, between 1988 and 1990, the number of women's roles had sharply dropped while men's roles doubled (1991: 138). These findings correspond with Susan Jeffords's argument that the 1980s saw an escalation of "hard body" films—action adventure "narratives of heroism, success, achievement, toughness, strength, and 'good old Americanness' " (1994: 15). The box office hits such as the *Rambo* series (1982, 1985, 1988), *Lethal Weapon* (1987), and *Robocop* (1987), Jeffords contends, promoted the militaristic and populist discourses of President Reagan, leaving very little room for major female roles, let alone rhetoric supporting collective feminism. Indeed, this trend, which shored up conservative and static versions of masculinity, appears most likely a reaction against the strides made by the second-wave feminist movement.

As further evidence of the ramifications of the New Hollywood for women, a 1990 *Los Angeles Times* article reported a rumor about a memo that supposedly circulated through a major studio in 1989. This memo indicated that all "female-driven" projects were to be put on hold until further notice. While this rumor was never substantiated, the climate for such a message certainly existed. Mainstream film representations of women in the late 1980s and 1990s often featured women as either peripheral sex objects, threats to the social order, or as nostalgic about a time during which they had less power (Faludi 1991). Recall also the shabby "Year of the Woman" response of the Academy of Motion Picture Arts and Sciences in 1993 after a general outcry from women in the industry.

Regarding this phenomenon, Susan Faludi declared that a "female backlash" has been waged against women in their efforts to gain economic and political power over the last two decades. Citing films such as *Fatal Attraction* (1987) and *Baby Boom* (1987), Faludi contends that women were often pitted against women in the 1980s, that their lives were frequently de-politicized (through the erasure or distortion of feminist discourse), and their narratives tended to take the form of morality tales in which powerful or transgressive women must be punished (113).

These concerns need to be examined contextually, of course, taking into account the ways in which dominant ideology is negotiated through visual and narrative techniques in individual films. However, the onslaught of such female-protagonist films as *Fatal Attraction* (1987), *Pre-*

sumed Innocent (1990), *The Hand That Rocks the Cradle* (1992), *Basic Instinct* (1992), *Single White Female* (1992), and *Body of Evidence* (1993) does indicate a cultural backlash against women that positions them as social threats that need to be contained by male authority. When seen in conjunction with the "hard body" movies, this trend of female psychokillers relates rather undeniable backlash imagery. This is especially true considering that these films distort the reality that women are much more likely to fall victim to male violence than to be perpetrators of violence against men.

The Hollywood female-psychothriller trend has not occurred in a vacuum. Suzanna Danuta Walters compares the historical moment of the early 1990s to that of the late 1940s, during which, as feminist historians have demonstrated, the government-sponsored propaganda that encouraged women to return to the home once they were no longer needed in the workforce. Walters argues that contemporary government, corporate, and media propaganda is much more subtle and nefarious because it responds directly to the threatening forces of the feminist movement (1995: 139). In her definition of a backlash film, Walters highlights the prevalence of "postfeminism," noting the ways that Hollywood films, such as *Fatal Attraction*, *The Hand That Rocks the Cradle*, and *Pretty Woman*, simultaneously incorporate and de-politicize feminism. These films, she explains, acknowledge feminism and often appear to present progressive discourse, but result in a reactionary, defensive processing of feminist politics.

How do we manage the paradox that women's more powerful presence in Hollywood coincides with increasingly distorted and disturbing representations of them? The backlash against feminist values in Hollywood suggests that women's power over female representation is still restricted, as it is under continual contestation via hiring and contract agreements, executive decisions, attitudes of cast and crew, and publicity and marketing measures. Many of these restrictions and negotiations will be attended to in the following pages. The paradox of women's growing presence in Hollywood also serves as a reminder that not all women, whether producers, directors, or development executives, choose to or have the ability to activate a feminist consciousness in their work. According to the Foucauldian model of power described earlier, dominant ideologies can be internalized by those invested in resisting them— individuals are almost always both subjects and objects within institutions of power (Foucault 1977: 194).[12]

Due to the cultural backlash against feminism, women who enter Hollywood from counter cinema might be viewed as a threat, resulting in a circular pattern in which even more "hard body" films centered on male fantasy are produced. Insight from directors will also shed light on the specificity of their own perceptions of their creative control within the industry. For example, Seidelman claims that, in the early 1980s, she deliberately avoided commercial filmmaking because she knew her gender would present an obstacle. She explains, "I came up through the independent route . . . [because] you generate your own opportunities, you're not depending on somebody to hire you. I just instinctually knew coming out of film school that if I went out to L.A. to any of the kind of 'institutions' of filmmaking and said, 'I want to be a director,' they'd laugh" (Robinson 5).

AUTEURISM AND AUTHORSHIP

Any study that examines a director's body of film work obviously holds some stake in theories of auteurism. In line with auteurist tenets, this book first links each director to her own films—an approach that has typically been facilitated through biographical information or industry anecdotes—and then relates each film to the others in her oeuvre by searching out recurring motifs, narrative strategies, and politics. In order to position my work within the various discourses of auteurism, what follows is a brief summary of the debates over film authorship.

The 1950s and 1960s saw the emergence of auteur theory in Europe, especially in the work of Francois Truffaut and the *Cahiers du Cinema* journal. The *Cahiers* movement needed to defend film as a high art form in order to position it alongside the more valued cultural products of theater and literature. In safeguarding cinema, the editors of *Cahiers du Cinema* took an elitist tack, differentiating auteurs (great visionaries) from *metteurs en scène* (average "establishment" filmmakers). They touted the value of filmic representation by conferring status on authored texts over non-authored ones (Lapsley and Westlake 127). As Andre Bazin explained at the time, "[the politiques des auteurs] has to discern the contribution of the artist as such, quite apart from the qualities of the subject or the technique, i.e. the man behind the style" (1963: 152). In addition to their elitism, advocates of auteurism might be criticized for engaging in self-involved projection. Lapsley and Westlake suggest that Truffaut and his peers identified "real artists" as those who reflected the critics' own ideological preferences (106). However, the contribution of this movement needs to be acknowledged because its novel focus on the mise-en-scène put the director into the limelight (a relatively new, although not exclusively original, idea), raising important questions about how to pinpoint producers of meaning within the filmic text. The development of auteurism was particularly ironic given that this group of French intellectuals was valorizing "low culture" Hollywood films and hence directors with relatively little creative control were celebrated as aesthetic visionaries in need of critical attention.[13]

In the 1960s, Andrew Sarris picked up the auteurist discourse based in Europe and Americanized it, singling out his own "pantheon" of visionary directors.[14] In the United States, auteurism functioned not only to liken film to other forms of high art, but also to differentiate it from television (a new "low art"), which was gaining increased popularity. Peter Wollen, although British, is also associated with this Americanized brand of auteurism. His "first wave" of theories on authorship is based on structuralism and attempts to identify certain recurring motifs (of binary oppositions) on a scientific basis (Wollen 1972). For example, Wollen hones in on a certain system of oppositions and differences in the work of John Ford and Howard Hawks, claiming that these oppositions (e.g., civilization/wilderness) serve to unify their work.

In his early work, Wollen assumes this oeuvre stems from the conscious efforts of certain "genius" directors. However in his 1972 postscript to *Signs and Meaning in the Cinema, Rev. Ed.*, he argues that theorizing the effects of the director's unconscious helps solve the problem of authorial intent. Rather than claim, for instance, that Ford's name represents an identifiable individual who consciously plants certain motifs in his films, Wollen proposes that we can only refer to "Ford"—a structure traced through a series of films. According to Lapsley and Westlake, Wollen's argument is pivotal in representing a movement from "pre-structuralism" (where the author creates meaning) to post-structuralism (where the author is a construct of the reader) (111).

Wollen's argument links certain directors with their bodies of work and problematizes the notion of authorial intent. A "second wave" of auteurist discourse, however, occurred in the 1970s and 1980s in which a historical materialist approach was put forth. Here, directors are considered in light of the fact that films are commodities determined by technical, economic, and political factors. The editors of *Cahiers* began to be criticized for the ideological approach they took in their essay on Ford's *Young Mr. Lincoln*, which detected important inconsistencies in the text but was deemed flawed because of its assertion that the film is primarily a reflection of the ideological biases of studio head Darryl Zanuck (Lapsley and Westlake 116). *The Classical Hollywood Cinema* refutes traditional auteurism by emphasizing the industrial mode of film production—"a characteristic ensemble of economic aims, a specific division of labor, and particular ways of conceiving and executing the work of filmmaking" (Bordwell, Staiger, and Thompson 1985: xiv). The authors implicitly contend that films are not products of single visionaries; they represent, instead, a combination of specific production practices, demonstrated, if for no other reason, by the similar "look" of most classical films (87). While *Classical Hollywood Cinema* functions as a major intervention into auteur theory, the book also implicitly lays the groundwork for new directions in author studies, so that scholars might develop an alternative understanding of the auteur (as writer, producer, star, etc.) or examine a single director while taking into account the collaborative nature of Hollywood film. Attention to industrial and economic influences underscores the collaborative nature of Hollywood film, supplying alternative ways to theorize the auteur (as writer, producer, star, etc.).[15]

Along with the transition to historical materialism, a growing trend in criticism has been the emphasis on auteurs not as "great geniuses" but rather as artists who seem especially in touch with the "collective unconscious" of their own historical and social moment. In this way, they represent not visionaries in a vacuum, but voices of their culture (Lapsley and Westlake 118). For example, Bazin asks, "And what is genius anyway if not a certain combination of unquestionable personal talents, a gift from the fairies, and a moment in history?" (144). In a polemic move toward questioning auteurist assumptions, he reminds his readers that "the individual transcends society, but society is also and above all *within* him [sic]" (142). Bazin's emphasis on the social and historical forces that shape filmmakers suggests that an "auteur" might be defined less in individual terms and more as someone whose work happens to address the convergence of highly charged cultural issues at an opportune historical moment.[16]

This notion of "progressive" auteur challenges monolithic assumptions about the ideology of Hollywood studios and at the same time broadens the construct of "aesthetic genius" to include possibilities of political messenger. But questions about authorial intent remain. For example, in his study of Douglas Sirk, Paul Willeman sometimes suggests that the director dramatized unconscious ideological contradictions and, at others, intentionally subverted the dominant order with its own tools (Lapsley and Westlake 119). Is the author a "conscious originator of the text" or is he/she "its structural effect" (119)? Most theorists would argue that both processes are engaged; however, detecting and detailing the difference between the two in a text, or even in public discourse surrounding the author, proves quite problematic.

The directors in this book fall into the category of "progressive" author because their films can be classified in the *Cahiers du Cinema* catalog as "E" films—ones that appear to fit into dominant ideology but nevertheless ambiguously subvert certain aspects of it (see Comolli and Narboni, 1977).[17] (Similarly, Tom Schatz has labeled certain directors "genre auteurs," arguing that a few Hollywood players such as Jonathan Demme, Martin Scorsese, and David Lynch have maneuvered their way through the complex systems of the New Hollywood in a way that still allows them to critique the very genres that govern their work [1993: 35]. Women are rarely associated with this camp. In suggesting that certain women's films fall into the "E" category, my project is not meant to get tied up in claims of authorial intent. The dialectic between "author as originator" and "author as structural effect" is crucial. Throughout this work, the director's name should be considered to be in quotation marks, connoting her *partial* status as a social construct, even though I do not go to the confusing trouble of using these marks at each mentioning.

There are several obvious problems with assuming that a director consciously structures her films in certain ways—problems having to do with politics, psychoanalytic quandaries, and postmodernism. As far as political considerations, some critics have argued that a focus on individual authorship distracts theorists from contemplating ideology. Stephen Heath, for instance, criticizes auteurism for blocking thinking about political effectiveness—he argues that the theory itself represents an ideological construct (Caughie 1981). In other words, hermeneutic debates about who is the "real" author and what is the "real" meaning of a film can end up going in circles, without regard for political ramifications. With such concerns in mind, this project activates broader ideological debates, insisting on moving beyond the lone individual in the director's chair.

Secondly, in psychoanalytic terms, Lapsley and Westlake complain that auteurism often becomes a projection mechanism whereby the critic-subject is driven by a desire to identify with the director when searching out an author's identity within a text (127). Because of this, I have tried to remain aware of my own desires and identifications—I attempt to keep my own curiosity about the position of women directors from becoming an unproblematized search for feminist role models.

Thirdly, postmodernism has highlighted the ways in which identity and subjectivity are unstable, incoherent entities. Knowing that identity is fragmented—that it changes from day to day and can rarely be known even by the individual who assumes it—how do we define films through a director's identity? It seems futile to argue unabashedly for the intention of the author in the production of ideological and political subversion when such intentions are only partially knowable to the critic, let alone the author.

Auteurism has been historicized by Janet Staiger in *Interpreting Films: Studies in the Historical Reception of American Cinema* (1993). As she examines the ways in which American critics perceived the importation of foreign films and the growing role of art cinema in the 1960s, Staiger draws compelling conclusions about how "spectators use authorship to make the experience coherent" (180). She suggests that, in the 1950s and 1960s, critics differentiated art cinema as separate from Hollywood fare because it was more "realistic" and its subject matter was "considered 'serious' or socially conscious. Consequently, a 'message' was inferred which, logically, had to come from somewhere, that somewhere being the traditional pre-structuralist source: an 'author' " (181).

So American auteurism grew out of the rationale that if a film had a message, there must be a source transmitting that message. And, of course, the more a film lacks coherence and narrative logic, the harder spectators work to detect or believe in a message, and hence an author. The auteur then became a central aspect of the development of counter cinema. Staiger's postulation, which supports the theory that the author is an effect of the text, complicates the intersection of counter cinema and mainstream film. How are directors situated in the inter-textual discourse surrounding their films both before they enter the mainstream and after? Is the role viewed more crucially when it is presumed their films (outside and inside of Hollywood) have a message to send? Once a counter-cinema director begins making commercial films, how is that authorial presence managed?

Staiger's focus on the author as a construction follows Foucault's argument in "What Is an Author?" Foucault contends, "Undoubtedly, this construction is assigned a 'realistic' dimension as we speak of an individual's 'profundity' or 'creative' power, his [sic] intentions, or the original intention manifested in the writing. Nevertheless, these aspects of an individual, which we designate as an author . . . are projections" (Rabinow 116). He insists that the author be considered within the context of institutional systems that dictate that no message is articulated in a "uniform manner in all discourses, at all times, and in any given culture" (119).

Auteurism faced its first major threat when Roland Barthes pronounced the death of the author in 1973. Influenced by political and social upheaval, particularly the events of May 1968 in France, Barthes argued (like Foucault after him) that the director should not be seen as the source of meaning: culture produces meaning. This polemic initiated a shift from auteurism toward theories of readership that presumed that the author cannot always control her/his own reception. Barthes's assessment carried important implications for feminism, primarily because it coincided with a realization that a stake in auteurism possibly paralleled an investment in patriarchal authority. As Mayne points out, any mode of inquiry into authorship "risks appropriating, for women, an extremely patriarchal notion of cinematic creation" (1990: 95).

Mayne insists, however, that an inquiry into female authorship is "not simply a useful political strategy; it is crucial to the reinvention of the cinema as it has been undertaken by women filmmakers and feminist spectators" (1990: 97). Whatever progressive consequences Barthes's proclamation of the reader had for feminists, the "birth of the reader" came at a very inopportune time. Just as women were gaining increased access to the commercial film industry, not to mention experimenting with the transcription of their own experiences in other ways, auteurism became an outdated tool with which to theorize meaning and ideology. Andy Medhurst makes this point regarding gay perspectives on authorship, arguing that marginal groups continue to have a political stake in auteurist theories (207). Foucault strove to problematize auteurism because it privileges the humanist subject. But feminism and gay studies, with their investment in political agency and mission to represent marginal subjectivities, cannot fully accept poststructuralist edicts. Foucault looked to the day when, "Behind all these questions we would hear little more than the murmur of indifference: 'What difference does it make who is speaking?' " (120). Those who have little access to representation argue that it makes a lot of difference. And, as Medhurst explains, "I might even want to take the step of putting quotation marks around the word 'gay'—but the man who queerbashed me some years ago did not put quotation marks around his fists" (208). The discussion of authors (and spectators for that matter) as constructions or projections cannot fully exclude their existence as flesh-and-blood individuals. My goal is to hold these two positions in tension through the provision of both textual analysis and primary interviews.

Since the proclamation of the death of the author, feminist scholars have experienced considerable difficulties theorizing the role of the female author, as much as they might want to grant her power and agency over her own cultural representation. Claire Johnston initiated a recuperation of auteurism by lobbying for textual analysts to highlight women's strategic critiques within Hollywood (1976). However, female authorship continues to present a major obstacle for feminist theorists. In this study, I find it useful to incorporate some aspects of auteurism while enforcing major revisions at the same time. For example, because none of the women in my study stands out discursively as a Hollywood auteur in the 1990s, I recuperate the notion of the "metteur en scène"—the talented but not genius filmmaker who supposedly does not instill her or his films with visionary meaning; I argue that, though they are not "auteurs," they are primary makers of meaning who deserve attention. The evaluative standards inherited from the classical Hollywood industry have been constructed in such a way that most of their mainstream films go unappreciated. Aesthetic criteria of excellence are culturally determined in a direction that excludes female authors. For example, films that correspond to the generic codes of the so-called woman's picture, which women are more likely to be hired to write or direct, have been left out of most film canons when they have not been downright demeaned. Indeed, I wonder if standards of auteurist excellence are not in and of themselves based on a "male" logic of visual and generic rigor.

In this book, a concerted effort is made to avoid the elitism typically associated with auteurism—its arguments are built on the notion that these directors are unique artistic "geniuses." In fact, unlike the French auteurist school, I do not attempt to detect "the man behind the style," or even the woman behind the style. Instead, I search out the political or ideological impetus, and implications, behind the style, proffering that even metteurs en scène can be—indeed, often are—motivated by such an impetus.

I have selected Seidelman, Coolidge, Bigelow, Borden, Martin, and Davis because their film careers originated on the political margins. By positioning their works of counter cinema as platform texts, so to speak, I will argue that these directors are developing or responding to certain oppositional ideologies central to their formative work. In an attempt to be dialectical, though not teleological, I foreground the intricacies and complexities of the relationship between their earlier and later works.

One other pitfall of auteurism deserves consideration. A focus on women directors runs the risk of conforming to another form of elitism, the possibility of erasing the work of others involved in the collaborative process of film production. The labor of less powerful industry players such as writers, editors, and even costumers—which have always been the roles most likely to be assumed by women—tends to be effaced due to the overemphasis on the director as author (Mayne 1984: 66). Andy Medhurst points out that the erasure of certain types of authors, such as writers, from film production remains part of a process of privileging masculinist, heterosexist texts (201).

Take, for example, Dudley Andrew's essay, "The Unauthorized Auteur Today." In his determination to pronounce the "rebirth" of the director, Andrew suggests that directors have agency to revise genres and challenge dominant discourse. He provides Ridley Scott's rendering of *Thelma and Louise* (1991) as evidence that auteurism lives in contemporary Hollywood cinema. However, especially given the content of various feminist discourses in the film, shouldn't we also consider the ways in which the co-producer (Mimi Polk), the screenwriter (Callie Khouri), and the stars (Susan Sarandon and Geena Davis) also contribute to the critique in that film?

Seidelman's *Desperately Seeking Susan* presents a similar dilemma. The director deserves credit for her "imprint," a system of visual and thematic preoccupations that is evident in much of her work, not just that particular film. At the same time, the contributions of the female producing team, Midge Sanford and Sarah Pillsbury—and screenwriter Leora Barish, who reportedly based the Roberta character on her friend

Pillsbury—cannot be underestimated ("Desperately Seeking Susan" 1986). The stars, Rosanna Arquette and rising pop star Madonna, provided ingredients that were crucial to the film's overall look and feel. The linkages between these factors are indeed complex, as the producers claim they hired Seidelman because they were impressed by her idea to hire Madonna for the part of Susan ("Desperately Seeking Susan"). In addition to these production considerations, the historical context of the film helped to create a climate in which women in their thirties who had come of age during the second-wave feminist movement and teenage girls immersed in a nascent "girl culture" could converge at the movie theater.

One of the most important aspects in addressing female authorship involves situating each director within a series of complex discourses, not in a vacuum. This means understanding that the director often has access to multiple forums through which to shape the reception of her own works—direct interviews in journalistic or academic publications, press releases and publicity stills, television appearances, and so on. It becomes confusing when, within these kinds of public discourses, the author claims a certain intent or strategy. In foregrounding her extra-textual information, one runs the risk of locating a single "truth" or knowledge about the film with only one of its producers of meaning. Conversely, in choosing to ignore or complicate details provided by the director, that woman's authority and agency over her own avenues of meaning production become effaced.

My inclusion of primary interviews with directors represents an attempt to locate the ways in which their material, financial, and creative control (including their own sense of what kind of meanings they can produce) appear to change (or not) as they enter commercial film production. I also incorporate biographical information and interview material from secondary sources to accompany my textual analysis of films. In doing so, I am very careful to negotiate this dilemma of female director as producer of meaning: she needs to be understood not only as an individual we can interview and learn from, but also as a discursive figure who continually mediates and is mediated by her films, her publicity, and her own public articulations.

Along similar lines, the director is generally assumed to be less "mediated" within the context of low-budget, counter cinema. We need to recognize the ways in which avant-garde and oppositional cinemas are no less discursive than Hollywood productions—there is no such thing as a "pure" art form. And directors outside the mainstream are no more immediately accessible "real" people than Hollywood directors. In *Points of Resistance*, Lauren Rabinovitz takes issue with how the artist-centered system of the avant-garde tends to view the director as a "free agent," with more autonomy and authority over her films, and with a stronger biographical relationship to her work (1991:19). Women have also always been more associated with the personal and private anyway, which further explains the tendency to closely attach them to their less mainstream work.

Rabinovitz cites a passage by Kaja Silverman that is worth repeating here:

> The author often emerges within the context of these discussions [of feminist theory and female authorship] as a largely untheorized category, placed definitely "outside" the text, and assumed to be the punctual source of its sounds and images. . . . There is no sense in which the feminist author, like her phallic counterpart, might be constructed in and through discourse. (Silverman 1988: 209 in Rabinovitz 22)

In revising auteurism for women authors, it is important to see the ways in which both genders are situated within myriad institutional discourses. Furthermore, oppositional cinemas are governed by historical and economic discursive practices just as mainstream, commercial cinemas are. Those practices can only be scrutinized when the figure of the counter-cinema director as the (knowing) origin of meaning is problematized.

In understanding the author as a discursive figure, as I have suggested, the interviews she gives and film publicity she initiates need to be viewed as a partially manufactured construct, part of a larger "author-function." Timothy Corrigan, in *A Cinema without Walls*, proposes that the New Hollywood auteur differs from previous manifestations in terms of her or his promotion of a "self." Corrigan states that "the commercial dramatization of self [is often] the motivating agent of textuality" (1991: 108). Subscribing to a postmodern philosophy of New Hollywood, he posits that the auteur "has rematerialized in the eighties and nineties as a commercial performance of *the business of being an auteur*" (104).

If directors are currently distinguished less for their artistic genius than for their financial prowess (especially with regard to publicity and advertising), how do we relate their presence to their texts? Furthermore, what counts as a text? Corrigan's argument suggests that the contemporary auteur emerges as a star, another kind of text to be read alongside the film(s). He sees "a marked shift in emphasis on auteurism as a way of viewing and receiving movies, rather than as a mode of production" (116). With this shift, audiences know what films mean before they even see them—through the performance of the director and the publicity produced therein (106). Corrigan's focus remains on a handful of (male) directors, such as Francis Ford Coppola and Alexander Kluge, who have tactfully navigated the commercial institutions of mainstream cinema. However, his work applies to the women directors in this book in that their own navigations through the economy of the industry and various publicity outlets shape the reception of their personas and their films. These directors have not necessarily mastered the "commercial performance" side of the industry (perhaps because they are less invested in it). But the ways in which they are struggling to survive within such an industry via economic resourcefulness or press publicity prove quite provocative.

Corrigan's position also highlights the extra-textual discourse of the director in terms of reading strategies—whether those take the form of "auteur as star" or "auteur as political spokesperson"—which provide pleasure for audiences. Kathryn Bigelow comes the closest to achieving a star persona—she is often positioned by the popular press according to her model-like appearance and "larger than life" status (see chapter 3). She has also been extremely adept at handling big-budget films and producing major box-office returns. Hence, she could possibly be read within the context of Corrigan's definition of the commercial auteur.

Meanwhile, the personas of directors such as Susan Seidelman, Lizzie Borden, or Martha Coolidge may not attract wide general public attention; however, many within the feminist community may read them extra-textually as political or public spokespeople. Because there are so few women (especially those with a history of feminist involvement) in Hollywood, the publicity and promotion of these directors may produce a more intense following based on the way their gendered personas relate to their films. They may also be more likely to present their films through the lens of politics (whether gendered or not) because of their following. For example, Martha Coolidge's promotion of her 1995 film *Three Wishes* included a full page advertisement in *The Washington Post* promising to donate $100,000 to the Make-a-Wish foundation in the names of President Bill Clinton and presidential candidate Bob Dole if the two political leaders watched this film together (26 Oct. 1995: C9). Coolidge's summons embodies a response to both politicians' criticism of Hollywood for discouraging "family values": her promotional strategy includes a political agenda whereby the film can unify two opposing parties and redeem Hollywood at the same time. In this vein, her public persona is governed by a political identity.

While Martin and Davis cannot be categorized as stars or spokespeople per se, their individual personas have been shaped via their management of scandal—Martin in terms of her public disgruntlement with Columbia over its *I Like It Like That* publicity campaign and Davis in regards to her termination from *Bad Girls*. These scandals resulted in press coverage that allowed each director to address an audience by "speaking her piece." The fact that they voiced a set of intentions about a film means that they provided a lens through which to interpret their work.

As we have seen, the difficulties involved in contemplating a female author are numerous. However, the productiveness of looking for the "woman behind the camera" should not be overlooked. Feminist works such as Rabinovitz's *Points of Resistance*, Sandy Flitterman-Lewis's *To Desire Differently* (1990), Judith Mayne's *Woman at the Keyhole* (1990), and Lucy Fischer's *Shot/Countershot* (1990) have contributed to the debate about how women's world views and experiences are inscribed into cinematic representation; at the same time, these books have complicated the very notion of essentialized femininity and unproblematized authorship.[18] I think the most effective way to address, and revise, contemporary problems posed by the concept of the female author—in addition to attention to industrial factors and extra-filmic discourse—is by privileging the process of reading and interpreting the films explored in the upcoming pages. Corrigan's conclusion that the concentration on auteurism has shifted from the mode of production to "a way of viewing and receiving movies" points to the ways in which a feminist reading, which emphasizes key moments and themes in a text, can re-conceptualize current theories of authorship.

These theories will be challenged if for no other reason than because they are being applied to women's work in Hollywood. As Mayne argues:

> The analysis of female authorship in the cinema raises somewhat different questions than does the analysis of male authorship, not only for the obvious reasons that women have not had the same relationship to the institutions of the cinema as men have, but also because the articulation of female authorship threatens to upset the erasure of "women" which is central to the articulation of "woman" in the cinema. (1990: 97)

In other words, the insistence on a female authorial presence disturbs the narrative economy of mainstream cinema. Because so few female voices seem apparent throughout the history of Hollywood, a feminist re-reading presents a crucial key to unlocking the various positions and contributions of women directors. In her discussion of Lea Jacobs's article on *Now, Voyager* (1942), Silverman calls for feminists to "reauthor" classical texts. She explains, "rather than working to disclose the chorus of cultural voices within the text, it [feminist criticism] strives to install the female voice at the site of a very qualified and provisional origin . . . the voice, that is, of the female critic or theorist" (211). The study of women's work at the intersection of counter cinema and Hollywood yields even more evidence that production and reception are truly interrelated: a re-vision of auteurism can only be performed through an act of re-reading.

At the same time, feminist theorists should not posit some kind of idealized reading that overrides other meanings in the text or ignores industrial factors that surround the text. As Mayne explains, "But if a feminist reading against the grain does not take into account the ways in which female audiences have been constructed in the course of film history, then we risk developing a kind of tunnel vision that never sees much beyond the living rooms of contemporary feminist critics watching 1930s and 1940s movies on TV" (1985: 28). Feminist readings against the grain have empowered critics and audiences as well as women who have made somewhat invisible contributions to the commercial industry. However, one danger in developing a single reading and "running with it" is that we might completely rewrite popular culture, wearing blinders all the way. Suzanna Danuta Walters cautions critics "not to find ideological slippage under every hegemonic rock" (78). The process of feminist analysis, which fortunately liberates certain locked positions of classical narrative, also needs to keep itself in check, with an implicit understanding that further historical and sociological research will better inform textual analysis.

The possibilities suggested by the meeting of feminist readings and theories of authorship are encouraging because they require a multi-vocal model of cinematic enunciation. Tania Modleski delineates the heterogeneity of authorship in her contention that Alfred Hitchcock's *Rebecca* (1940) contains dual logics—one masculine and one feminine. She argues that the director was at times forced to identify with a female character in order to represent her victimization (1988: 55). Following Modleski, I would argue that most often there are multiple logics at work in the cinema of these women directors. As Mayne puts it in *The Woman at the Keyhole*, a "both/and" logic seems more productive than a "neither/nor" approach to the question of whether a film is feminist or misogynistic (1990: 102). Because women from counter cinema access Hollywood narrative from a position that accentuates the alternative logics of counter cinema, their more commercial films stress contradiction, ideological fissures, and the impossibility of a unified voice. Their marginal origins encourage heterogeneity and multiplicity in the mainstream work.

One of the central governing presuppositions of classical film studies, embodied for example by formalism or strict French auteurism, is that Hollywood films contain a uni-vocal and uni-directional logic. Like Modleski and Mayne, Rick Altman has proposed a "tension-based," dialogical approach to mainstream films, one that views films as multi-vocal and contradictory. He writes in terms of searching out the excesses of a text, honing in on instances of resistance to dominant ideology (1989: 342). This approach facilitates a deeper understanding of all the various contributions to Hollywood films, emphasizing the ways in which the values and biases promoted by particular studios, as well as the personal ideologies of producers, directors, writers, actors, editors, and even lower-level crew members all contribute to the narrative and ideological makeup of a single film. In this way, the debate about whether counter-cinema filmmakers "sell out" when they enter the mainstream becomes more complicated, allowing their mainstream texts to be probed for multiple meanings, many of which relate to their earlier, more "political" work. Once it is assumed that a film is produced by many makers of meaning, that it is "fractured" with multiple meanings, and that a reading is never singular or unified, the meeting of the female author and the feminist critic becomes an event of dialectic and revision.

GENRE

Debates about auteurism have included on-going questions about how Hollywood genres can be developed and revised by well-known directors. In the early 1980s, scholarship on genre served as an intervention into auteurism by illuminating influences other than the director. But genre and authorship intersect at a crucial point because they suggest one way in which an individual, if given the opportunity, might make a mark on a highly commercial system by understanding its conventions and formulas well enough to manipulate them. Alfred Hitchcock gained his commercial reputation, in part, because of his critical role in cultivating, and then reshaping, the thriller (Kapsis 1992: 21–25). John Ford has been celebrated by auteurist scholars for, first, honing the Western and then, later, exposing its ideological excesses in such films as *The Searchers* (1956) and *The Man Who Shot Liberty Valence* (1962) (Wollen 96–102).

It is, no doubt, important to keep in mind that the problems of auteurism—granting a director too much agency, romanticizing his or her relation to the production process, etc.—carry over to the discussion of genre. However, genre represents one of the major sites explored by these women directors. The complicated relationships between gender and genre prove to be especially ripe for revision and exploitation. Schatz's application of Saussurian theory to genre is particularly relevant to an examination of women directors. Here the "film genre" is analogous to Saussure's *langue* and the "genre film" to *parole* (1996: 96).[19] In this formulation, the directors' individual films, especially those that might be considered "genre films" (e.g., *Desperately Seeking Susan* as a screwball comedy, *Angie* as a "woman's picture," *Blue Steel* and *Love Crimes* as thrillers), represent particular utterances that attempt to critique, re-design, or disarm both their own purported genres as well as the broader ideological systems inherent in them.

52

Cataloging films by genre is a process that involves a kind of contract between industry members and audiences. This process allows product to be standardized, and sometimes differentiated, and it provides spectators with concrete ways of selecting and interpreting films. Steve Neale understands genres to be "systems of orientations, expectations, and conventions that circulate between industry, text, and subject" (1980: 20). However, genres are by no means static; they continue to change, grow, and interact with one another, especially in response to their socio-historic contexts. Although the ideological nature of genre remains in dispute, Schatz makes a strong case for the progressive potential of genres by framing them as ritualistic forms of "cultural problem-solving" (Feuer 144–45; Schatz 1981: 261).

The various "systems of orientations, expectations, and conventions" of specific genres tend to be engendered as "masculine" or "feminine." Not only are "action films," for example, associated with maleness, but they also typically articulate certain patriarchal ideologies that reflect negatively on their female characters and on femininity in general. While it is important to acknowledge the gendered connotations of various genres, Linda Williams has suggested that it is important to examine specific genres, and individual films, for the very complex ways in which they figure woman as "enigma," rather than simply assuming that they convey "evidence of a monolithic and unchanging misogyny" (1996: 156).

The genres most often invoked by the women directors featured here include the "woman's picture," film noir, psychothriller, Western, and action buddy film. A great deal of theoretical work on the "woman's picture," the psychothriller, and the action film suggests that women's experiences and feminist politics are often positioned in ambivalent and ambiguous ways in even the most apparently homogeneous or transparent films. Films in these three genres—regardless of the gender of their directors—often expose dominant ideologies and reveal the difficult positions of their female characters.

While the melodramatic "woman's picture" has historically been degraded and trivialized, many feminist scholars contend that this genre has the potential to explore women's experiences in ways that other genres do not, precisely because of its confinement to the "low," feminine sphere. Williams advances the argument that the "woman's picture" foregrounds the contradictions of lived experience faced by women who move through a "male" world they cannot fully control (1990: 152). Likewise, Tania Modleski asserts that "mass-produced fantasies" provide women with plots that help them work through their own vulnerabilities and obstacles (1984: 18–19). As chapter 2 demonstrates, Martha Coolidge utilizes melodramatic female friendships and parent/child relation-

53

ships to explore her characters' ambivalence about being female within a larger patriarchal society.

As for the psychothriller genre, the Gothic novels examined by Modleski and the 1940 "paranoid woman's film" analyzed by Mary Ann Doane should be seen as precursors for the cycle of women's investigative psychothrillers that include Kathryn Bigelow's *Blue Steel* and Lizzie Borden's *Love Crimes*. Modleski indicates that nineteenth-century Gothic novels work through intense female anxieties about marriage and family, expressing women's "fears about intimacy—and the exceedingly private, even claustrophobic nature of their existence" (20). Mary Ann Doane formulates a similar argument about films such as *Rebecca* and *Jane Eyre* (1944) by suggesting that their protagonists are investigating an "institution of marriage [that] is haunted by murder" only to be punished for that investigation in the end (1987: 123).

The more recent cycle of the women's psychothriller, which includes *Silence of the Lambs* (1991) and *Sleeping with the Enemy* (1991), registers a female search toward understanding women's position in social worlds marked by male resistance to the 1970s feminist movement (Barton 1998). Bigelow's *Blue Steel* subverts the conventions of the psychothriller (as well as the film noir and cop film) by making her police-officer protagonist a woman. The main character in Borden's *Love Crimes* embarks on a quest for sexual identity that involves her playing out the positions of both victim and master through a series of games with a psychopath. These films challenge some of the gender assumptions that underpinned the male-dominated thrillers of the 1930s and 1940s (e.g., *Foreign Correspondent*, 1940; *The Maltese Falcon*, 1941); they also extend and update some of the conventions of the 1930s and 1940s thrillers that starred women, like *Rebecca* and *Suspicion* (1941).

The action buddy film has been discussed for the ways its generic conventions express 1980s and 1990s versions of masculinity. As mentioned, Susan Jeffords's examination of "hard body" films represents one particularly formative analysis of this genre in relation to the socio-political context of the Reagan-Bush era (1994). Alexander Doty and Cynthia Fuchs, separately, have focused more specifically on how the action buddy genre plays out tensions of homosocial desire in its representations of male-male friendships (Doty 1993; Fuchs 1993). Bigelow's *Point Break* engages both of these issues of contemporary action-film masculinity and homoerotic relations as it follows an evolving relationship between its two main characters, Johnny (Keanu Reeves) and Bodhi (Patrick Swayze). Secondarily, *Point Break* offers a commentary on the inevitable subjugation of female characters when male buddies focus their repressed erotic energies onto each other. While these tensions and problems exist in almost any action film, Bigelow draws them out and

54

exploits their presence even as she caters to a young male audience. Her work points to the value of focusing attention on issues of masculinity in conjunction with those of femininity in order to better make connections about how gender is ideologically enforced.

Most of these women directors demonstrate an elaborate understanding of certain genres and their links with gender structures (and, often, those of class or sexual orientation). Their films indicate that genre formulas change in response to the social and historical concerns of their audiences (Braudy 1985: 414; Hayward 162). It is fairly obvious that films such as *Rambling Rose*, *Angie*, *Blue Steel*, *Love Crimes*, and *Point Break* (in addition to Tamra Davis's version of the Western, *Bad Girls*) respond to various genres in ways that reflect the cultural changes and social concerns raised by the 1970s feminist movement. Of particular interest are the issues raised in and by these films regarding female agency, women's status as victim, women's relations to other women, and women's various positions within a male-dominated society that defines "law and order" in gendered terms. I propose that these women directors' connections to the feminist movement and independent film industries allow them to revise specific genres in ways that reflect and illuminate historical and social anxieties in contemporary culture.

Let us return for a moment to Michelle Citron's question: "What does it mean for women to decide to enter the production of mainstream popular culture?" Citron ends her essay by suggesting that feminists entering mainstream Hollywood will need to take risks, maybe even make disreputable (poorly received or flash in the pan) films. But "what we need now are narrative films made by as many women as possible in as many ways as possible about as many things as possible" (62–63). The films of Davis, Martin, Borden, Bigelow, Seidelman, and Coolidge offer a number of these possibilities. In examining them, hopefully two major questions will be answered: How have women directors subverted, revised, or exaggerated patriarchal codes of cinema from within Hollywood? And to what extent have their oppositional discourses been betrayed, negotiated, uncontained (not recuperated by the status quo), or embraced by mainstream, commercial production?

SUSAN SEIDELMAN'S FILMS: A POINT OF DEPARTURE

As mentioned, feminist critics have celebrated Susan Seidelman's *Desperately Seeking Susan* for its centralization of feminist themes around identification, desire, and fantasy. That film reflects the visual and thematic preoccupations of her earlier film, *Smithereens*, which earned Seidelman the notoriety of becoming the first woman and the first independent American filmmaker to compete in the Cannes film festival

(Ferncase 44). She was hired to direct *Desperately Seeking Susan* by Orion Pictures, a "mini-major" with studio distribution connections. On the basis of that film, which grossed $27.5 million while costing only $5 million, she signed a three-picture contract with Orion (Corliss 1986: 82).

One of those three projects was *She-Devil*, which cost $60 million at a time when the average budget was $25 million. Based on the Fay Weldon novel, *The Life and Loves of a She-Devil*, the film starred Meryl Streep and Roseanne Barr. After a brief hiatus, Seidelman directed the independent short film *The Dutchmaster* (1994), an exploration of a young woman's budding sexual desires spurred on by a seventeenth-century painting; this film was part of the European-financed compilation *Tales of Erotica*. She also directed several episodes of HBO's experimental, female-centered sitcom, *Sex in the City*, in 1998. Her brief return to independent film and her entrance into cable television indicate that the rejuvenated independent industry and the expanding "niche" possibilities of television provide Seidelman with increased options outside of commercial Hollywood.

From *Smithereens* to *Sex in the City*, Seidelman registers a preoccupation with female fantasy and with women's relationships with other women; she is especially interested in the ways in which these areas of women's lives interact. For example, Wren (Susan Berman), the female protagonist in *Smithereens*, weaves a distorted narrative web about herself, engaging in delusions about her own popularity and her potential rise within the punk music scene. As the film opens, Wren pastes fliers of her own image next to the question "Who is this girl?" on the walls of a subway car. This flier re-surfaces throughout the film (on a building wall, on a telephone pole) along with other images of her, such as a portrait drawn by one of her love interests, Paul (Bard Rijn). But Wren has difficulty maintaining relationships with men—relationships, that is, that are devoid of illusion and deceit—and she loses the only promising connection she has in Paul by obsessing over punk singer Eric (Richard Hell).

Toward the end of *Smithereens*, Wren encounters an unnamed blonde woman in the stairwell outside of Eric's apartment. What seems like an inconsequential meeting might also be understood as the endpoint of Wren's journey. For it is here that she begins to realize that her yearning for Eric is a lost cause—she discovers that the woman is Eric's wife, and she is as unimportant to him as Wren herself. This scene also offers up a rare glimpse of one direction of hope for Wren, the possibility of connection and growth through female friendship. The recurring reference to Wren's troubled yet compelling relationship to her own image finds an answer in an alternative female-female representation, the feminist bond of friendship.

The two women are linked by a sudden mutual understanding of Eric's misogyny. Wren tells the woman, "I was gonna manage his group." The woman responds, "I was going to do that once too." Wren asks, "So what happened?" The woman answers, "Same thing that happened to you." The film ends without following up the theme of friendship, closing with a rather bleak and unoptimistic picture of Wren's future. But her conversation with the anonymous woman reverberates as an important missed opportunity, a promising moment that is further explored in Seidelman's later work.

Smithereens has many of the characteristics of independent counter cinema, including low production values (based on an $80,000 budget), stationary camera work, a protagonist who does not invite intense identification, minimal momentum, and an ambiguous ending. With *Desperately Seeking Susan*, Seidelman shifted into conventional narrative as she told the story of a disenchanted housewife, Roberta (Rosanna Arquette), who becomes fixated on the flamboyant title character played by Madonna. Roberta leaves behind her safe, suburban life when she embarks on a journey into the trendy New York underground. Her identity quest leads her to learn more about her sexual desires and long-term life goals, but it also enables her to achieve a more liberated perspective regarding how she might enact her femininity.

The relationship between Roberta and Susan becomes foregrounded through subjective camera work, shot/reverse shots, and parallel editing, all of which are bolstered by the star presence of both Arquette and Madonna. Within the light comedic formula of the screwball comedy genre, the theme of female friendship is more fully developed in *Desperately Seeking Susan* than in *Smithereens*. In addition, the former film's emphasis on circular and destructive fantasy life becomes transformed in the latter, with its visual economy based on a series of female "looks," into a world of fantasy that facilitates feminist enlightenment.

That *Desperately Seeking Susan* was both commercially successful and highly praised within feminist film theory is promising for women filmmakers who endeavor to blend feminist discourses and alternative cinematic directions with popular, mainstream interests. The film is one of the most prominent examples of a female-addressed and feminist-addressed movie to have reached a wide audience. In regard to feminist intent (to the extent that it is ascertainable) Seidelman claims:

> The film's attention to female points of view was, without a doubt, intentional. It was deliberate on my part and also on the part of the writer. I was drawn to the idea of a love story. Though not a sexual love story, it's a

In *Desperately Seeking Susan* (1986), Roberta's plight as a
confused and insecure housewife drives the plot. (Orion
Pictures)

romance between two women, in which one woman becomes infatuated
with this other woman and sees that as a reflection of herself in some way,
of who she wants to be. The film posed an identity question. (author's interview, 14 July 1998)

Like *Desperately Seeking Susan*, *She-Devil* features two female protagonists, but this film positions their relationship in terms of hostility and
competition. Roseanne Barr plays the role of a frumpy, middle-class
housewife who loses her husband's affections to the pink and fluffy ro-
mance-novel writer Mary Fisher (Streep). Roseanne's character, Ruth, is
aligned with her more general persona, what Kathleen Rowe has referred
to as an "unruly woman" because of her refusal to apologize for her

excessive weight and her outspoken anger about women's traditional role in the home. This she-devil transforms her anxieties about her appearance and her age—and what they mean to her femininity—into an infernal domestic rage, which she releases onto her husband and the male population at large. The film refrains, for the most part, from allowing Ruth's battle to dwindle into a catfight; although there are many instances in which Ruth voyeuristically watches her husband with Mary, she winds up targeting him, not the "other woman."

She-Devil works by virtue of its "woman as avenger" theme. Ruth mobilizes a number of oppressed groups—the working class, the elderly, other disenfranchised women. Beginning at the nursing home where she is employed, she then branches out to more elaborate actions. Her point of view, and that of her comrades, is represented with sympathy through subjective camera work, editing, and an extensive voice over; however, the film also boasts a campy sense of humor that encourages its characters and the audience not to take themselves too seriously.

Roseanne plays the sympathetic antagonist to Meryl Streep's excessively feminine "other woman" in *She-Devil* (1989). (Orion Pictures)

Although *She-Devil* did not perform well at the box office, it needs to be seen as an important precursor to the commercially successful *The First Wives Club* (1996), which centralizes many of the same themes but emerged at a time when the cultural climate seemed slightly more prepared for female anger and housewifely revenge. (*Thelma and Louise* [1991] and a number of other female-avenger films had been released in between.) In my opinion, *She-Devil* has held up quite well, and it would reward a second (or a first) viewing at this point. Seidelman agrees, commenting that she has "talked to people who did not like the film when it first came out and have watched it recently on video and 'got' it." She also points out the differences between the two films, noting that *The First Wives Club* seemed more "palatable" to mainstream audiences than *She-Devil*. For Seidelman, "*She-Devil* was extreme to make a point. The film was not simply exaggerated for the sake of humor; the goal was to provide a feminist fable. People were more ready for it in 1996" (author's interview).

In addition to its focus on dual heroines and its themes of feminist identity transformation, *She-Devil* connects with Seidelman's earlier films because it addresses female fantasy. Mary Fisher's status as a romance writer foregrounds the issue of fantasy's function for women. Her celebrity, and the cult following she has developed, point to the value that romantic conventions hold for disenchanted middle-class women—that is, for people like Ruth. Mary's femininity is depicted through codes of excess, including the many shades of pink that decorate her mansion and the layers of cushiony pillows that constantly surround her. This attention to excess finds its most obvious outlet in Streep's own performance, which functions as a mocking send-up of traditional femininity; she may be serious business to her readers, but to her spectators she can hardly be taken in earnest. Significantly, Mary undergoes a transformation after being forced to assume Ruth's responsibilities of housewife and mother. This experience causes her novels to become more attentive to mundane details and domestic life; unfortunately for her, but perhaps reflexively for Seidelman and Hollywood women directors in general, this shift proves to be financially disastrous.

In Seidelman's experimental short, *The Dutchmaster*, Mira Sorvino plays Theresa, a young woman who realizes that her impending marriage offers her no prospects for fulfillment. Like so many other women in Seidelman's films, Theresa deals with her dissatisfaction with the conventional roles available to her by embarking on a journey to escape the social structures that confine her. As she prepares for her wedding, she becomes increasingly preoccupied with a seventeenth-century Dutch painting that features a young couple, a merchant, and a housekeeper. The painting comes alive and, slowly, Theresa begins to enter further and further into the world it represents. At one point she becomes enraptured by sexual desire as she watches the merchant undress and bathe. At another, she gazes at the young couple through a peephole as they make love in their bedroom. And later, she enters their room and hovers over them with curiosity as they engage in a sexual interlude.

Theresa stages her own fantastical narrative, one she continually replays and re-organizes. She orients this narrative around axes of vision. For example, in one scene she activates the fantasy by shining her flashlight into the eyes of the man she lusts after (the male counterpart of the couple). He comes alive and winks an invitation for her to step into his world. The focus on the peephole also calls attention to the importance of her vision—her voyeuristic interest in the couple mirrors her obsession with the painting itself, which she stares at for hours at a time. In this way, barriers are established not simply between Theresa and a world of sexuality away from her fiancé, but also between Theresa and visual representation. She must transgress the boundaries of the painting in order to overcome the limitations society has placed on her sexuality. In other words, the concerns over female looking relations, identification, and desire that were explored in *Desperately Seeking Susan* re-surface in *The Dutchmaster*.

The short film's ending adds complicated layers to these themes. When Theresa fails to show up on her wedding day, her fiancé reassures the audience (in direct address) that "she will be found." He states, "We have an all-points bulletin out for her coast to coast." The next scene is guided by a track into Theresa's room, which houses a poster version of the Dutch painting. Another track moves us into the world of the painting and winds around until we reach the bedroom. The woman (from the picture) lies on her bed, caressing her body and extending her arm across the empty space as though inviting someone to join her. A cut reveals the peephole with Theresa's eye blinking from behind it as she watches the woman. A fade to black occurs, thus leaving as the last image Theresa's singular, blinking eye.

This conclusion relates to Seidelman's previous work on a number of levels. Most obviously, Theresa's escape from the institution of heterosexual marriage represents a victory, a feminist triumph of identity over patriarchal conformity. On another level, like *Smithereens, Desperately Seeking Susan*, and *She-Devil*, this film privileges female looking relations, ending with the visual exchange between Theresa and the woman of her fantasy. And like *Desperately Seeking Susan, The Dutchmaster* leaves the question of female homoerotic desire open. Does the woman in the painting elicit identification or sexual attraction from Theresa? And if Theresa finds the woman attractive, was her preoccupation with the man merely a ruse? If the Madonna/Rosanna Arquette film is any indication,

61

such questions are not easily laid to rest. For Seidelman has developed a reputation for highlighting the ambiguities between female identification and lesbian desire.[20]

The Dutchmaster relies on certain counter-cinema techniques in addition to its relatively radical approach to female subject/object relations. Multiple voice-overs by various characters and direct address to the camera help to move the story along. Theresa's two friends, played by Aida Turturro and Sharon Angelo, narrate most of the story as they attempt to explain the bride's disappearance. Theresa's "real world," her job as a dental hygienist and the Friday-night happy hours her friends describe, seems completely incongruous with the fantasy world of the museum and its seventeenth-century picture. As she tells Theresa's story, Seidelman plays with narrative and the numerous ways in which a narrative can be presented.

Many of the techniques of *The Dutchmaster* can be found in the situation comedy *Sex in the City*, which premiered on HBO in the summer of 1998. Although Darren Star (*Beverly Hills 90210, Melrose Place*) created and executive produced the program, Seidelman directed the series pilot as well as the fifth episode. It is difficult to attribute all, or much, of the series' innovations to Seidelman; however, *Sex in the City* does share many similarities with her previous work. Central concepts of the program include attention to female fantasy, engagement with feminist debates about sexuality, and concerns over how women's stories are constructed.

The protagonist, Carrie Bradshaw (Sarah Jessica Parker), obsesses over heterosexual relationships and gender politics as part of her job as a Manhattan sexual advice columnist. She has three female friends who participate in constant debates with her about the differences between men and women. For example, in the pilot episode, the women bat around the question of whether women can have casual sex (i.e., like men). They debate whether or not the femme fatale protagonist in the 1996 film *The Last Seduction* displayed behavior that was callous toward men or heroic for women. In the fifth episode, "The Power of Female Sex," Carrie is stunned when the incredible "connection" she made with a Parisian model ends in the morning with a wad of hundred-dollar bills on the nightstand. As she and her friends eat a room-service breakfast that they have billed to his room, they mull over the relationship between money and female sexuality. One friend (played by Kim Cattrell) exclaims, "What are you getting so uptight about? I mean, money is power. Sex is power. Therefore, money for sex is simply an exchange of power." Another friend (played by Cynthia Nixon) retorts, "Don't listen to the dime-store Camille Paglia."

These kinds of discussions point to the ways in which feminist discourses, especially "popular" feminism, have been appropriated into the commercial mainstream. References to the femme fatale iconography or the Paglia rhetoric demand no explanation—they are made part of the vernacular in a program such as this. *Sex in the City* blends feminist ponderings, discourses of women's advice columns, situation-comedy humor, and music video style. Its focus on upper-middle class, urban, white women certainly invites criticism, and rightly so. But an open question remains, one that seems difficult to settle: Does the series represent a popularization of feminism and a commodification of women's bodies or a rare and inspired feminist tract in a sea of relatively disinterested and homogenous cable programming? It is my contention that Seidelman's presence, as determined by her 1980s films, aids in bringing out the progressive elements of the program. Sarah Jessica Parker's character, and the feminist implications of her role as a self-proclaimed "sexual anthropologist," become primary in ways that are quite common to Seidelman's work.

A number of visual and aural measures ensure that Carrie's inner thoughts take center stage. Her voice-over recurs throughout the show, as do moments of direct address. Many characters provide this address, creating the effect of a fragmented collage; however, Carrie's interpretations seem to take precedence. She is continually framed in close-up, and she is often seen in shots in which she appears against a flat backdrop of crowds or city landscapes. The lighting also produces this effect, highlighting her three-dimensionality against two-dimensional backgrounds.

These devices help privilege her subjectivity, and, when seen within the context of the show's focus on female sexuality, they contribute to a feminist perspective on sexual power. For example, in the opening credit sequence, which appears at the beginning of each episode, a passing bus splashes Carrie. In slow motion, she pauses to look at the bus. On its side is a life-size advertisement with her image that reads, "Carrie Bradshaw knows good sex.'" The asterisk at the end of the sentence references the statement at the bottom of the poster: "and she isn't afraid to tell." This proclamation of Carrie's sexual knowledge and her courageous "voice" become underscored with a reverse shot that pulls back to reveal that the real-life Carrie wears a white leotard and pink tutu against the backdrop of a crowd wearing brown and grey business attire. The contrast between Carrie and her fellow city dwellers places her in a primary position within the frame, a position that has significant implications regarding her power as an "expert" on relations between men and women.

The run-in between Carrie and her bus-billboard image also echoes Seidelman's early work because of its focus on female representation.

Not only does Carrie have a momentary opportunity to analyze her own image, but she is almost done in by that image. In a single moment she confronts her identity as commodified femininity, with a slippage between self and image that recalls *Desperately Seeking Susan, She-Devil,* and *The Dutchmaster.* In fact, how different is this encounter from those in *Smithereens* when Wren repeatedly comes upon her own "punk star" fliers? The world of fantasy that facilitates these moments of subject/object inquiries also governs *Sex in the City.* The pilot opens, for example, with the words "Once upon a time," unraveling on a computer screen as Carrie launches one of her columns. The fairy-tale quality of the series furnishes the numerous opportunities it needs to digress into complex questions about women's power and heterosexual relations.

The possibilities in cable television, especially those stations aimed at "niche" audiences, offer promise for women directors such as Seidelman. The director views *Sex in the City* as an opportunity to explore the feminist concerns she has been interested in since the beginning of her career—only now she can do so on a repeated basis with slightly more room for play and experimentation (because of television's seriality). Seidelman explains, "I really relate to the subject matter even though it is not 'my' series, per se. The writer-producer Darren Star came to me because he felt that my sensibility would work well." Seidelman goes on to say, "Cable is an excellent alternative to film especially when commercial film seems so geared toward teenage boys. If you're interested in character and the minutiae of everyday life, television is becoming an option as promising as the one- to eight-million-dollar independent film market" (author's interview). The particular format of *Sex in the City,* and many other thirty-minute programs produced by major cable stations, provides a comfortable fit for directors who got their start in counter cinema. As Seidelman puts it, "This is a live-action sitcom, on location in the streets of New York City. So it's like filming a short film every episode" (author's interview).

While it would be naive to claim that all of Seidelman's work in the 1980s and 1990s shows evidence of her control, a flipside argument denying the relevance of "Seidelman as author" seems equally problematic. Her film and television material orient themselves around a cluster of themes and visual motifs that suggest that the director is, indeed, engaged in a perpetual activity of feminist "revision." Perhaps Seidelman herself best sums up the most critical thread that links her projects together. "I would say that the female leads in all the movies could be from the same family, even if their social position is different or their ethnic background is different, they're sort of sisters under the skin" (Robinson 6).

1

MARTHA
COOLIDGE

MARTHA COOLIDGE'S MOVE FROM feminist documentaries to commercial narrative attests to the futility of trying to uphold a strict division between alternative and mainstream filmmaking. Her career trajectory has included several exits from the studio world as well as a stint in television production. Furthermore, her films *Valley Girl* and *Rambling Rose* straddle any supposed line between independent and commercial. Although Coolidge has built a lengthy filmography, *Old-Fashioned Woman* (1974), *Not a Pretty Picture* (1976), and *Valley Girl* (1983) will be the focus of discussion regarding her independent work. *Rambling Rose* (1991), which was produced by the "mini-major" company Carolco, could be considered somewhere in between independent and commercial, in that Carolco specializes in big-budget films but made an exception for the smaller, "narrowcast" *Rambling Rose*. *Angie* (1994) represents a more commercial venture as it was financed by Hollywood Pictures and Caravan Pictures, in affiliation with Disney Studios.[1]

Old-Fashioned Woman and *Not a Pretty Picture*, which will be discussed in detail later, convey central themes of women's experiences and feminist politics. As Coolidge made the transition from women's counter cinema to mainstream film, she became more associated with the genre of melodrama. This is not surprising since melodrama is presumed to be the Hollywood genre best suited to the articulation of women's problems and desires. Sue Aspinall and Robert Murphy suggest that of all the classical genres, melodrama raises the possibility of female desire and point of view more than any other (1983). Concurring, Linda Williams points

65

out that this genre attempts to articulate a specific experience of gender rather than express a universal one (1990). Because of this, the contradictions of lived experience that emerge out of social constructions of femininity are more likely to surface here (152).

Melodrama's association with femininity means that it has also represented one of the few "appropriate" avenues for mainstream women filmmakers. Historically, women directors have been less likely to direct "universal" genres such as the Western, the musical, or the buddy film, as they find themselves pigeon-holed into women's films.[2] Not only is their exclusion a problem in the realm of production, but, as Janet Staiger notes, so-called women's pictures are rarely canonized due to an evaluative bias toward male genres and auteurs (1985: 16). Therefore, women's work, such as the more melodramatic films of Coolidge, finds itself degraded, more likely to go unwatched and less likely to win industry awards.[3] This is especially true within the political and economic context during which Coolidge's more commercial work has been distributed. With the rise of the conservative New Right (and its heavy emphasis on economic success), and with the Hollywood trend toward blockbusters in the 1980s and 1990s, women's genres hold a very precarious position. They may succeed because of their status as a differentiated product; however, they continue to represent risky "niche" pictures because of their failure to attract young male audiences.

Coolidge, however, views the position of the "woman's film" with optimism. She posits that "there is a huge female audience out there now" (author's interview, 20 Nov. 1997). The strategy she advocates involves making a film with feminist and female themes that will also attract men. With an attentive eye on the marketplace, Coolidge declares, "When you have overtly feminist themes or an overconcentration on female issues, then the men say they won't go. That kind of film isn't as successful as a movie that is driven by women wanting to go to it but that doesn't turn men off." Coolidge's comments suggest that she generally (and depending on the film) targets an audience composed of both women and men, and therefore she must balance the content and address of her films so that they accommodate several kinds of gendered viewing experiences.

Although melodrama has been pejoratively linked with femininity, its roots in "emotion" and "excess" provide the genre with potential avenues toward politicization. Jesus Martin-Barbero remarks that melodrama has always served as a political stage for emotions. Dating back to its theater days in the 1700s, melodrama has offered a space of projection for the affective nature of the masses' political situation (1993: 112). This observation facilitates an understanding of the connection between Coolidge's early political documentary and her more recent Hollywood films.

The struggles of the female protagonists in *Rambling Rose* and *Angie* are indeed presented through a political lens, conveying feminist messages about women's sexuality and female friendship.

Moreover, it has been suggested that the "woman's film" has a tradition of ending with artificial closures or forced solutions that convey the difficulty of resolving the contradictions in women's lived experience (Byars 1994: 104). *Angie* differs from many of the 1950s "woman's films" that preceded it, as in Douglas Sirk's cycle of melodramas, because it lacks an ending that is highly exaggerated and ultimately unmotivated. However, Coolidge's film refuses the possibilities of a simplistic resolution—the protagonist is presented with an either/or choice and she decides to choose neither. Though not exactly "forced," *Angie*'s conclusion calls attention to itself by virtue of its atypicality—the protagonist's rare decision to go it alone is one for which the audience has not been very well prepared by plot and theme. A film such as *Angie* suggests that melodrama, though often a marginalized genre, provides a mainstream outlet for self-identified feminist directors such as Coolidge who have expressed overt interests in exploring women's experiences of femininity.[4]

A number of similarities and continuities exist throughout Coolidge's body of work. Most specifically, in the five films under consideration, I will highlight her attention to distinctions between reality and fantasy, her deployment of maternal melodrama, and her focus on female friendships. Also of interest is her emphasis on women's connections to previous generations of women and their various origin stories.

COOLIDGE'S PATH INTO FILMMAKING

Coming from a New England, middle-class background, Coolidge entered the Rhode Island School of Design (RISD) to concentrate on print-making, but she became more interested in filmmaking after she directed an animated short. Leaving RISD early, she was accepted at New York University film school; she was told in an entrance interview, however, that because of her gender she should not set her sights on directing. So Coolidge went to Canada for several years where she gained production experience in a booming film industry and eventually returned to New York to attend classes at Columbia University and NYU. While there, she made three independent shorts, including *Old-Fashioned Woman*, an exploration of her "Yankee" grandmother's experiences in which the director herself appears.

Coolidge then directed *Not a Pretty Picture*, which depicts her own experience of a high school rape. This film, which cost less than $100,000, was funded by the American Film Institute, friends, family, and even crew members (1976a: 88). Once she completed *Not a Pretty*

Picture in 1976, and having earned an American Film Institute (AFI) internship, she left New York to try to succeed in Hollywood. Coolidge told *The Boston Globe*, "I always felt that I was not avant-garde. I make accessible movies, so I should go to a community where that's valued instead of not-necessarily-respected" (Sherman 1992: B8).[5] So began her transition from the New York avant-garde to the Los Angeles studio community, a journey that would continue to prove to be indirect and tumultuous.

Coolidge, however, remained strongly tied to her independent roots. She helped form the Association of Independent Film and Videomakers in the mid-1970s. The Association, which soon attracted thousands of members, eventually led to the birth of the Independent Feature Project. Interestingly, around this time, Coolidge wrote two articles for *American Film* with the purpose of sharing information with other independent filmmakers. In the first article, Coolidge explains the double bind of independent filmmaking caused by the fact that distributors need to see a proven audience for the film before they sign on, and yet without a distributor such a thing cannot be demonstrated. She also laughs at her own female "fantasy" of having a distributor magically rescue her like a knight in shining armor (Apr. 1976a: 88).

What is most striking about this article is Coolidge's orientation toward information-sharing and collective activity (89); she even includes addresses for all relevant festivals and showcase opportunities. In a similar vein, she later complains about the lack of solidarity among independents in the 1970s, revealing, "We were all competing for the same grants, everyone made the same mistakes and we didn't learn from each other" (Sherman B5). Coolidge's identification with feminism and her politicization of independent filmmaking in the 1970s are also evident in contemporary public accounts of her: she voices her dissatisfaction with her long and arduous path into Hollywood (which she attributes to her gender) and is outspoken about male privilege and sexual harassment of women within the industry (Cole and Dale 1993: 43).[6]

As Coolidge was vying for commercial jobs in the 1970s, she searched out a distributor for *Not a Pretty Picture*. The film was screened at a "Woman Emerging" series conducted by Los Angeles's Insight Exchange, at the AFI theater in Washington, D.C., the Pacific Film Archive, and later at the Whitney Museum (1976a: 89; 1976b: 68). Eventually Francis Ford Coppola hired her on the basis of that film to direct at his production company, Zoetrope. When that company dissipated, Coolidge left Los Angeles for Canada, where she became involved in a disappointing project called *City Girl* (1983). It was an offer to direct *Valley Girl* (1983) by writer/producers Wayne Crawford and Andrew

Lane—who wanted a "woman's point of view"—that brought Coolidge back to Los Angeles.

An independent film, *Valley Girl* has often been cited as Coolidge's "big break" that earned her major studio deals. With this film, Coolidge made a reputation for herself as an economically efficient, talented professional; at the same time, she found ways of inserting her feminist values into a project over which she had only conditional control. Coolidge directed *Valley Girl* on a budget of $350,000, and the film grossed $17 million at the box office (Quart 1988: 76). During shooting, she employed a number of strategies to control expenditures, including rehearsals with the actors at nights and on weekends, taking personal time to see locations in advance, carefully planning all of her shots, and, a trick she learned from studying the studio era, minimizing her number of takes (Coolidge 1988: 16). Coolidge follows in a long tradition of women who have proven themselves to studio executives with their thriftiness and financial savvy.[7]

Coolidge's success with *Valley Girl* marked her as a director of "teen flicks," and soon afterward she directed *Real Genius* (1985) and *Plain Clothes* (1988), both of which feature compelling portrayals of masculinity. But it was Coolidge's struggle to make *Rambling Rose* that took her back to the independent realm and revived her career; it suggested to Hollywood producers that Coolidge's skills were more diverse than her male adolescent films would suggest.

Rambling Rose, which was written by Calder Willingham (*One Eyed Jacks* [1961], *The Graduate* [1967]), has a significant history in and of itself. After being circulated through the studios for twenty years, the screenplay was re-discovered by Coolidge who, upon deciding she "had to make" the film, gave it to Laura Dern to read. Dern's boyfriend at the time, Renny Harlin (director of *Die Hard II* [1990]; *Long Kiss Goodnight* [1996]), offered to produce it through Carolco, the mini-major with which he was affiliated. Harlin soon convinced Mario Kasser, a Carolco executive who had produced *Rambo* (1985) and *Total Recall* (1990), of its worth. In effect, Coolidge's determination was aided by an informal network of interested parties and the willingness of Harlin and Dern to reduce their salaries. Carolco, which had traditionally specialized in action films, "knew that [Coolidge] had a vision and that it wouldn't cost them a lot of money" (author's interview). Coolidge says she benefited from the company's "long tradition of giving autonomy to its action film directors."

Rambling Rose's critical success and its long run in festivals and "art house" theaters launched a virtual second career for Coolidge, who has gone on to direct *Lost in Yonkers* (1993), *Angie* (1994), *Three Wishes* (1995), and *Out to Sea* (1997). Her constant movement between alternative and mainstream modes of filmmaking suggests not only the fluidity of these supposedly polar categories, but also the struggle that women face in trying to distribute their cinematic work. Her early articles on independent distribution and her later concerted efforts to fund *Rambling Rose* through a mini-major suggest that the problem of distributing films by women—a marginalized group—remains crucial to the problems of female-authored representation, whether in counter cinema or Hollywood. Commenting on the barriers posed by gender bias, Coolidge bitterly remarked in 1985, "I spent twenty years getting to where I am, which is at the beginning of my career" (Birns 4).

OLD-FASHIONED WOMAN

In the early 1970s, Martha Coolidge joined the ranks of a number of feminists who learned to make films by working on documentary productions. During that time period, the coincidence of the women's movement with the Direct Cinema Movement and cinema verité's growing popularity facilitated an explosion of women documentarians (Citron 1988: 50). Women's interest in this film form stemmed from its didactic slant as well as its accessibility to politicized audiences who might have little film literacy. Eventually feminist filmmakers and theorists problematized women's heavy reliance on documentary, an issue I will return to. But for several years this form fit the feminist agenda of gathering women's "positive images," whereby a search for role models and an attempt to undo historical erasures were made possible.

Old-Fashioned Woman (1974), one of Coolidge's first films, utilizes a realist documentary style—with many "talking head" shots, old photographs, close-ups of hands and intricate features, and details of Coolidge's grandmother's house—as she interviews this elderly, upper-middle-class New England woman. Many of Coolidge's questions involve her grandmother Mabel's perspective on the choices and life goals of middle-class women from her generation. In the film, Coolidge openly admits that these inquiries offer her, a woman in her mid-twenties, a way to fashion her own future. Mabel's outlook clearly reflects an upper-middle-class bias, with its emphasis on achieving happiness and mobility, yet her vivacious, intelligent comments on her own history suggest the complex stakes at issue for even highly privileged women.

Coolidge attempts to see her grandmother through new, adult eyes and to recover information about previous generations of women and their familial ties. One touching scene, filmed in a handheld long shot, features Mabel and Coolidge pulling Mabel's wedding dress out of its old trunk in a tiny attic. They are in a bedroom when Coolidge holds the dress up to her grandmother and begins probing her memories. In-

70

serts of close-ups display engagement and wedding photos. Then we re-turn to Coolidge and Mabel in a close-up that shows them handling the dress, fingering its lace, and discussing the dressmakers' process. When Mabel reminds her how long ago the wedding took place, superiorly indicating the length and stamina of her marriage, Coolidge awkwardly laughs at her and looks self-consciously into the camera. The scene is a humorous "pregnant moment" because Coolidge seems slightly embar-rassed by and simultaneous endeared to her grandmother in a way that marks this as a highly ambivalent inter-generational relationship.

The film also offers Coolidge and Mabel a space to confront their grief over the death of Coolidge's father (Mabel's son). As a young teen-ager, Coolidge was transported to Mabel's house while her father slowly died of cancer at the age of forty. Coolidge remembers being afraid, feeling insecure in this large, unfamiliar house and not knowing what the future would hold. As Coolidge rifles through her father's baby album, pausing to fondle his baby hair, Mabel expresses how difficult it is to lose a son. The film represents, in part, a strategic effort for Coolidge, as well as Mabel, to come to terms with their difficult past in a way that strength-ens their familial bond.

As *Old-Fashioned Woman* continues, Coolidge extracts Mabel's strong support of planned pregnancy, pro-choice politics, delayed mar-riage, and women's suffrage. The documentary moves from a personal portrait to a political inquiry with compelling implications for inter-gen-erational coalescence around an agenda for women's rights. At the same time, Coolidge makes a point of bringing up information about the long line of women artists in their family and, specifically, her grandmother's photography: Mabel received her first camera at the age of ten and en-joyed the benefit of her own dark room built by her father. In fact, Coo-lidge's images take on new meaning once we realize that she is filming photographs taken by her grandmother—a "double image" of women's representations of their lived experience. Coolidge's status as a filmmaker is reinforced by her grandmother's status as a photographer. The issue of women's relation to their representation, and their access to it, will re-surface twenty years later in *Angie*, in which the female protagonist's growth and development are measured by her changing relation to picto-rial images of women.

NOT A PRETTY PICTURE

The making of *Not a Pretty Picture* occurred at the historical moment in feminism when the term "rape" was beginning to undergo definition and illumination. Each of the actors, as well as Coolidge herself, were coming to terms with a social experience that had barely gained recognition, much less comprehension. This film, like *Old-Fashioned Woman*, represents an attempt to resolve Coolidge's past and begin to articulate her identification with what it means to be a woman. Carolyn G. Heilbrun has suggested that women's writing of autobiography is inevitably about anger, specifically the degree to which women can express their anger (1988: 12). Heilbrun dates a revolution in autobiography to 1973 where she begins to track women's angry voices with the publication of May Sarton's feminist memoir. *Not a Pretty Picture*, with its autobiographical implications, is clearly informed by Coolidge's movement (which occurred only a few years after 1973) toward an acceptance of the anger she feels about her victimization and a conscious attempt to reclaim agency by telling her own story.

Not a Pretty Picture (1976) is a semi-autobiographical film depicting Coolidge's own rape through the use of documentary, dramatizations, and fictional narrative.[8] Its experimental format places it squarely in the middle of a debate about Hollywood narrative film and documentary. In the 1970s, feminists criticized classical Hollywood films for their glossy realism and praised women's documentaries for more realistically representing women's lived experience. A debate ensued, however, when critics such as Noel King suggested that realist documentaries are no more progressive than Hollywood films because they rely on conventions of continuous time/space relations (and hence cater to certain ideological norms) and are predicated on the idea that there is an "immediate" reality "out there" that can be captured in an unbiased way. E. Ann Kaplan describes the links, whether causal or not, between poststructuralism's alteration of film theory and 1970s feminist documentarians' problematization of the notion that art could imitate life and recognition of the ways in which "reality" is always constructed, or at least mediated (1983: 132).

Coolidge's oscillation between documentary and fiction in *Not a Pretty Picture* suggests that she was interrogating some of the assumptions present in her earlier documentaries. The introductory titles of the film read: "This film is based on incidents in the director's life. The actress who plays Martha was also raped when she was in high school. Names and places have been changed." The film's autobiographical nature, coupled with the reality of the actress's experience (she can't be thought of as "performing" in the traditional sense), results in a constant tension between fact and fiction. As the title *Not a Pretty Picture* suggests, Coolidge calls into question whether the "pictures" she presents are real or fiction—as Coolidge's experiences blend with those of her character and the actress playing her, the notion of unmediated experience is altogether de-privileged. This experimentation indicates the problems involved in representing rape, whether in women's documentaries (which

72

claim to record women's "authentic" experience) or in Hollywood (which tends to approach rape through male fantasy).

While Coolidge constantly interrupts the "realism" of her staged episodes with footage of rehearsal with the actors, she also allows herself to appear in the documentary portions of the film, reminding the spectator of her role as narrator. Hollywood director John Huston has written about the conventional auteur in Hollywood (especially during the studio era) who remained invisible, hiding "his" own brush strokes from the audience (1980).[9] In *Not a Pretty Picture*, Coolidge refuses to suture herself out of the film, conveying an oppositional move against this tradition of continuity. The frequent interruption caused by shifts from narrative episodes to rehearsals to conversations among actors—and Coolidge's repeated appearance in the film—reflects the 1960s and 1970s oppositional context in which the film was made. Influenced by theories of the avant-garde, these conventions might distance the viewer from an acritical, passive role by reminding her that film, even documentary, is an artificial construction.

The aesthetic style of this film also creates a modernist effect. Coolidge, working with her two cinematographers (Don Lenzer and Fred Murphy), most often relies on handheld camerawork or a stationary zoom into a close-up on an actor's face instead of smooth, unjolting takes. The lighting is awkward, often casting shadows over the faces and bodies of performers, even in the fictional segments. And jump cuts dominate the editing style (conducted by Coolidge and one other editor, Suzanne Pettit), in which transitions between shots do not depend on continuity aesthetics. Even in the initial scene, the shadow of a boom microphone dances on Coolidge's shirt when she appears on camera.

The film opens with Michele, the actress who plays Martha, in a tight close-up (shot from over Coolidge's shoulder) discussing her own rape and her previous naivete about personal safety. Michele questions why she is taking this role now and suggests that she does not feel that she is "acting" when she plays the part of a rape victim. She explains that her goals are to teach others about her experience, to gain further self-understanding, and to learn more about the long-term consequences of her rape. These goals echo Coolidge's, who early in the film "teaches" Jim Carrington (who plays the rapist) about women's relation to rape and concludes the film by contemplating the consequences of being raped, even twelve years after it occurred.

In this initial scene, Michele and Coolidge concur that they both feel somewhat responsible for their own rapes, which affords Coolidge the opportunity to further state her purpose: she hopes to counteract the information passed along to her by her mother who told her "there's no such thing as rape" (in other words, women allow themselves to be

73

raped). Coolidge insists, "I really want to confront that." While the audience probably does not yet realize it, this female conversation about male violence and feminist possibilities takes place in the location where the rape sequence will be filmed. Long before the rape sequence, this apartment location has already become a powerful site for investigating women's relation to powerlessness and resistance.

In the next scene, which launches the actual "narrative," Curly (Jim Carrington) and his friend West Virginia watch Martha from a distance as she sings a folk song. This song is actually performed by Coolidge—yet another slippage between director, character, and actress. The men whisper to each other and then shake hands, the rape plot obviously set in motion. Next, a cut takes us back to the apartment: Coolidge interviews Jim (Curly) about his perceptions of this film. Jim is confused by the notion that certain women he has known have expressed rape fantasies. His confession leads Coolidge to "instruct" him about the difference between fantasy and real rape, suggesting that his confusion supports the blaming of women for their own victimization. The didactic function of this film becomes quite clear. At the same time, though, one cannot be sure that Coolidge and Jim have not staged this interaction in order to interrogate rape definitions. In other words, the difference between fantasy and reality is discussed in a context that may or may not be truly spontaneous and "real."

The characters who will dominate the rest of the film are developed in a "narrative" car scene. A couple, Cindy and Brian, sit in the back seat with West Virginia while Curly and Martha sit up front.[10] The camera slowly pans left from Cindy and Brian, who are kissing, toward Martha who reveals an uncomfortable reaction. The camera then pans back right, passing over the couple to show us Curly at the wheel. The space articulated by the camera offers up a series of teenage romantic relations, including an overly-involved couple, a couple who barely know each other, and a "fifth wheel." This scene also illuminates a kind of "rapist" ideology in that Curly dominates the dialogue with outbursts of male privilege, racist epithets, sexist jokes, and self-centeredness. In contrast, Martha is revealed to be hyper-responsible and somewhat uptight—she collects mountains of pennies because she wants to be prepared for any unexpected emergency.

Once the characters have been established and the narrative set into motion (the group is taking a detour to Brian's brother's apartment in order to drink and loosen up), the camera cuts to a rehearsal scene of the events that occur in this apartment. Coolidge is shown providing directions to the actors, outlining the blocking, suggesting improvisational techniques and guiding the rehearsal. In this way, as previously mentioned, her role in constructing this film, and exploring her own experience, is made quite present. Refusing to "hide the brushstrokes," Coolidge reveals herself to the extent that she is the "stager" of these various sequences. Also, in this scene, she asks Michele to tell a story of how her rapist got her into an apartment much like this one, hoping that the actors will draw on this particular experience in their improvisation. Yet again, the impact of personal experience on this process of storytelling is made clear.

The film is strategically crafted so that the "rape sequence" occurs exactly halfway through the film, rather than at the climax. Its timing allows a great deal of the film to be spent on the aftermath of the rape. Also, only rehearsals of the rape sequence are shown. The avoidance of traditional narrative continuity blocks almost any possibility for voyeuristic pleasure in Martha's rape, encouraging the viewer instead to ask larger questions about how rape is represented, perhaps legitimated, in our culture. What emerges is a statement, on the part of both Coolidge and Michele, about the importance of representing rape through dual lenses, one that attends to personal experience and one that acknowledges the difficulty of portraying such experience on film.

The plot, the loose map that guides the improvisation, entails Curly luring Martha out of the living room, where the other characters are, into an isolated bedroom. This room, because the building is so dilapidated, is accessible through a large hole in the wall. The sexual imagery of this gaping hole is made even more symbolic by a "Keep Out" sign posted above. Once the two characters are in the bedroom, Curly is supposed to attack Martha and rape her.

Two rehearsals of the rape sequence are shown back to back. In the first, Curly takes his time in trying to seduce Martha, eventually becoming extremely forceful. After shooting a prolonged dramatic struggle, the camera swiftly pans to Coolidge for a reaction shot in which she stares intensely, emotionally engrossed. Then Coolidge halts the action. Jim expresses fear at his over-involvement, telling Michele that he really did want to strike her. Baffled that he could feel so aggressive toward this person who, it turns out, he has known for four years and loves dearly, he tries to understand the power mechanism at work. In a truly eerie moment, Jim asks Michele to remove her earrings, fearing he might actually rip them out. Throughout Jim's revelation, Coolidge supports him and talks him through his feelings in a way that produces greater self-knowledge for all three of them.[11] As the handheld camera continues to grasp the reactions of all three people, Michele explains that, as the portrayer of the victim, she felt no fear of Jim.

In the second rehearsal sequence, Jim decides to physically struggle with Michele until she truly feels in touch with her own experience (taking method acting to an extreme). After a short tousle, Michele (as Martha) pauses, stares up at the wall and completely changes her reaction to one of total vulnerability. Without a doubt, Michele is now "Martha" and the scene becomes more difficult to watch. Eventually, the camera pans to Coolidge who stares in horror, her hand over her mouth in a gesture that strangely echoes Martha's earlier reaction. Soon after that, Coolidge stops the action, so shaken that she cannot speak. As Michele recovers from the emotional trauma of this experience, Jim wipes her tears out of her eyes and then endearingly calls out, "Make-up Woman," yet another reminder of the performativity deployed in this film. As an emotional beat that provides closure for this sequence, a shot over Jim's shoulder shows the two of them hug, conveying Michele in close-up. A freeze of the frame dramatizes the emotion even further.

The remainder of the film focusses on the aftermath of the rape from Martha's perspective, including the ways in which most of her female friends turn on her, her fear of being pregnant, and her thoughts about abortion. As Martha kneels on the bathroom floor, she asks herself, "Is this what it means to be a woman?" As she goes through these terrifying experiences, the film also makes room for a healing process facilitated by her best friend Annie (played by Martha's actual best friend from high school, Anne Mundstuk). They enjoy the "girlfriend" comfort of staying up late after "lights out" and giggling. Coolidge clearly offers their reclamation of friendship as an answer to Martha's traumatic experience. I would argue that the representation of female friendship in *Not a Pretty Picture* is a vital link in the chain that unifies Coolidge's work, from *Old-Fashioned Woman* to *Valley Girl*, *Rambling Rose*, and *Angie*.

Mundstuk (Annie) and Coolidge even discuss the importance of their long-time friendship on camera. In an interesting reference to an event we have seen fictionalized, Mundstuk recalls how she used exhibitionism as a tool—a strategy of resistance—to ward off men, such as one of their high school teachers, and confesses that she still does so. Another confession occurs when Mundstuk reveals that she has always been infatuated with Coolidge. Mundstuk suggests a sexual attraction to her, but this seed is never developed. While any number of reasons might have dictated this choice, I am left wondering whether Coolidge cut this short because, as a self-identified heterosexual, she felt uncomfortable with this revelation. (Still, Coolidge chose to keep this footage in the film.) At any rate, issues of sexual identity, and their relation to heterosexual power structures, are left dangling, never addressed by Coolidge herself.

Not a Pretty Picture ends with Coolidge confronting the long-term consequences of her rape with several of the actresses from her film. Their clothing and the setting suggest that this occurs on the same day of the shooting of the rape sequence. In a conversation coded heavily as a consciousness-raising group, Coolidge describes her fear of men, her inability to commit to a relationship, and her apprehension about presenting her vulnerabilities. In her final sentences, she begins to stumble and, to her own consternation, starts to cry. The close-up on her becomes a freeze frame and the credits roll. Coolidge's decision to include this segment suggests that she was working against the director's mystique as awe-inspiring and in control. She inscribes an alternative aesthetic here that records the director's vulnerabilities and refuses a "male" stake in omnipotence. Clearly, *Not a Pretty Picture* resists the technique of "hiding the brushstrokes" for the sake of cinematic realism by allowing the director's emotions to interrupt the flow of the narrative.

One of Coolidge's greatest talents, according to press coverage and public accounts, is her ability to work well with actors. Having been very involved in the theater in the early 1970s, she is said to have a solid sense of what actors need from a director. When Robert Duvall told her his close-up reaction to Diane Ladd's triumphant speech in *Rambling Rose* would be a "first take phenomenon," she moved in on him during the first take. The result was so satisfactory that she did not even print a safety take (Horton: 20). Coolidge explains that most of her directorial decisions are "based on what the actors have to do" (Cole and Dale: 45). Coolidge's directive—her particular emphasis on the actors and theatrical choices—suggests the need for breadth in critical criteria regarding "what makes a good film." Too much focus on visuals and formal stylistics obviously deflects critics from directors who centralize other aspects of film production. The structure Coolidge fashions in *Not a Pretty Picture* foregrounds her interaction with the actors and could be interpreted as a signal about how to read her films. The centralization of actor interaction *becomes* her directorial style, and it represents a criterion for comparing and evaluating her later films.

Most important, though, is the film's status as a women's narrative, specifically autobiography, which Heilbrun links to anger. To tell a story about a woman (in the context of contemporary middle-class America) is to give voice to her subconscious or conscious dissatisfaction with patriarchal constraints, in whatever form they take. Coolidge's decision to play with the conventions of autobiography—blurring the boundaries between fiction and reality through her use of actors as well as narrative structure, camerawork, editing, and even music—suggests that she was actively engaged with the theoretical arguments of 1970s women's counter cinema. She simultaneously experimented with film form and female experiences. This attention to women's experiences included an emphasis on affect and melos. The melodramatic component of Coolidge's documentaries foreshadows her interests in the "woman's film," specifically *Rambling Rose* and *Angie* but also *Valley Girl*.

CHAPTER 1
VALLEY GIRL

Coolidge's *Valley Girl*, an independently produced film that established her as a mainstream director, helped to inaugurate the Los Angeles "valley girl" culture into a national phenomenon. The film occurred at a cultural moment when California suburban middle-class language and fashion ("like, fer sure, you know") was becoming popularized, as well as satirized, as a mainstream fad. This low-budget take on the story of *Romeo and Juliet* probably gained its momentum, eventually becoming a cult hit, because its characters are not the stick figure caricatures that might have been expected; they're three-dimensional protagonists who elicit the spectator's care and compassion.

Although producer-writers Crawford and Lane brought Coolidge in after completing the screenplay (and had certain stipulations regarding nudity), they gave Coolidge a great deal of latitude in re-shaping the picture. She recalls this film and *Rambling Rose* as the two over which she had the most control and autonomy. Coolidge explains: "*Valley Girl* was one of those unique situations where [the producers] left me alone. They were worried that I would not deliver the sex and the nudity because I was a woman. But they also wanted and needed input. The story was from a valley girl's perspective" (author's interview). Specifying how she brought a "woman's point of view" to the film, Coolidge enumerates: "What I brought to many of the movies I've made, *Real Genius*, *Rambling Rose*, and, in particular, *Valley Girl*, is the fact that I was a woman. I would not settle for cliché female characterizations. We hired actresses who were more interesting. We pursued relationships which were deeper. And we took the material which was, for *Valley Girl*, simple, and we deepened it."

With the characterization of Julie, the protagonist in *Valley Girl*, obvious attention is paid to her as a budding young woman, with emphasis placed on the peer pressure she faces as well as on her emerging sexual desire. Julie (Deborah Foreman) first sees Randy (Nicholas Cage) on the beach, with a point-of-view shot offering Julie's first impression of him. In a shot/reverse shot, Randy looks at Julie who tries to seduce him with a smile. She is an active agent in the pursuit of romance and sexual knowledge, and her desire drives the narrative. Through visual and narrative structures, Julie is positioned as a "feminine subject of desire" as often, if not more often, as she represents a "feminine object of desire" (Stacey 1989: 122). Much like that of Roberta in Susan Seidelman's *Desperately Seeking Susan*, the representation of Julie's subjectivity at crucial narrative moments helps to encourage spectator identification with her and to establish female looking relations as an underlying structure of the film (Stacey 126–27).

A second series of glances, like the first one at the beach, occurs the next time Julie and Randy meet, this time at a party. A shot of Julie actively trying to get Randy's attention follows a shot of him from her point of view. According to Coolidge, these initial scenes between Julie and Randy were some of the most important places where she "deepened" the material. Coolidge states: "I helped to structure the love story in a more sound way. The sort of 'two-bit' conflict scenes where Julie and Randy fall in love and break up—the key moments—did not really have focus" (author's interview).

Julie's point of view is also privileged in the scenes with her former boyfriend, Tommy (Michael Bowen). Tommy has just made up with her and asks for a bite of her hamburger. The camera cuts to a side shot of him so as to offer Julie in close-up experiencing disgust at the arrogant chomps he takes from her food. In all three of these scenes, the character blocking, exchange of glances, and camerawork call attention to Julie's reactions, stressing the centrality of budding female desire.

I would suggest that stitched within these formal methods Coolidge's presence as a director encourages identification with the female characters. In fact, several scenes point to an ideological negotiation made by Coolidge. She was offered *Valley Girl* with the producers' condition that she include four scenes of female nudity, but she was given free reign in how she handled them (Corliss 1986: 82–83). One of those occurs when Julie's ex-boyfriend Tommy cajoles her friend Loryn (Elizabeth Daily) into "making out" with him at a party. After the two characters have undressed, Tommy takes the background as Loryn faces the camera. The camera angles slightly over the bed in one stationary shot. Loryn asks him if they are "now going together," to which he clearly signals that he has just exploited her for his own pleasure. The shot composition offers her reaction of pain and insecurity. According to Michelle Citron, Loryn's clear command of the camera offers her "emotional point of view," and her "nudity becomes an indictment of Tommy's sexist manipulations" (1988: 60).

In another nude scene, a teenager convinces his girlfriend to "make out" in the bathroom at this same party. Randy happens to be hiding out here, and so the scene is filtered through his point of view. He watches from a distance as the man takes the blouse off the woman and she gets angry, deciding to leave. As they go, Randy mumbles, "Creep." His visual and verbal narration provides a critique of the teenager's aggressive actions. Yet, Randy, our male protagonist, is not immune from judgment. Having been rejected by Julie, Randy gets drunk in a bar and winds up in the arms of an old flame. As he begins to undress her, they are blocked in the same positions as the first pair at the party. He has now become the "creep."

79

The "axis of vision" is concentrated on the perspective of
teenage girls in Coolidge's *Valley Girl* (1983). (Atlantic
Releasing Company)

Each of these scenes imply that Coolidge framed women's bodies in
an attempt to subvert the scene's purpose of female objectification—in
effect, she created a new purpose. The scenography, blocking, and camerawork chosen by Coolidge helped her avoid compromising her vision
of the film—that vision incorporating a critique of male bravado with the
centralization of adolescent female subjectivities. Regarding the producers' requirement of female nudity, Coolidge remarks, "In fact, I delivered
what they asked for. But, when they looked at the movie, they had so
much more than they had ever dreamed" (author's interview).

If the film dramatizes the female protagonist's active romantic desire, it also depicts her growing awareness of the social conditions that
govern her life. Julie begins to resist the expectations placed on her by
valley culture. She looks out at Randy through vertical blinds after he
has been thrown out of the party. From outside the house, the blinds are
shown slowly closing until she is no longer visible, intimating that she is
caged inside. Julie's girlfriends turn on her because she has chosen an

inappropriate match. At a pajama party, Julie scrutinizes herself in the mirror, reflecting upon her uncertain identity, as her friends castigate her. They continue to insult her as she is framed from a high angle. She looks less powerful than them, but she is realizing their immaturity and confronting her own isolation. *Valley Girl* is quite clearly a coming-of-age film for Julie as she navigates her passage through various stages of self-empowerment. Her journey toward a raised consciousness is also marked by melodramatic affect, particularly in the moments when her friends no longer understand her.

Valley Girl re-writes the *Romeo and Juliet* scenario, transforming the conflicts of two rival families into a competition between Julie's friends (which involves the conformity to valley girl norms) and heterosexual love and romance (Randy). (Of course, choosing her friends would still involve heterosexual romance with the bully Tommy.) Julie's decision to shed her friends and pursue Randy also means that she accepts her parents' hippie ideology, which privileges non-authoritarian and non-superficial values. While this could be interpreted as a conservative resolution (in which Julie accepts her parents' social rules and is directed into a heterosexual relationship), it has feminist implications. Her consciousness now raised, Julie comprehends the dangers of ideological conformity.

RAMBLING ROSE

After several Hollywood films and television productions in the 1980s, Coolidge revitalized her career with the critical success of the low-budget *Rambling Rose*. A blend of domestic comedy and melodrama, this film is set in 1930s Georgia and tells the story of a troubled woman who comes to help care for the Hillyer family. (The production designer actually studied Coolidge's grandmother's house in *Old-Fashioned Woman* to prepare for the construction of the Hillyer house [Horton 1991: 17].) The son Buddy's nostalgia for the Old South accounts for the evocation of the past in the film. However, alternative points of view— such as the Mother's perspective on Southern ideology as oppressively reliant on tradition, racism, and sexism—soon send any single narrational focus into question.

The story is framed by an older version of Buddy (John Heard) returning home to hear news of Rose's death. He candidly remembers the quirky, offbeat family in which he grew up. Buddy especially recalls his respect for his now also deceased mother (Diane Ladd) and his sexual attraction to Rose (Laura Dern), the woman who came to care for him and his sisters. Coolidge did not want to understate the father-son theme of the film, but she wanted to frame it in feminist terms (author's interview). Whereas *Rambling Rose* could have been the story of an over-sexed woman told through the objectifying eyes of an adolescent male, Coolidge shapes it into a subtle treatise on female sexuality and women's relationships that presents a complex number of moral standpoints.

The opening credits appear over the image of a single yellow rose. As the camera very gradually zooms closer, spectators are presumably encouraged to interpret the rose's significance in their own way. This introductory visual image harkens back (whether self-consciously or not) to Hollis Frampton's experimental film *Lemon* (1969), in which a lemon is filmed from various angles for eight minutes conveying the point that the process of interpretation is integral to film viewing. The initial "rose" metaphor establishes a cinematic theme as various characters judge Rose in ways that reflect more on their own world views than on her. For example, thirteen-year-old Buddy (Lukas Haas), setting out on a quest to acquire as much sexual knowledge about her as possible, views her as a sex object. He is described as having a "mean streak," which accounts for his fascination with women's victimization and abuse. Daddy (Robert Duvall) sees a sexually predatory naivete in Rose's clothing, in her interactions with men, and in her relation to her own body. He attempts to contain her. Daddy expresses the notion several times that it is the responsibility of women to control their sexuality, although eventually his attitudes will be changed.

In contrast, Mother resists Daddy's tendency to judge Rose at all, suggesting that she only needs love and nurturing. While these various stances illuminate character motivation and development, they also underscore gender ideologies, in that the men see Rose negatively while Mother views her positively. Through its narrational style, the film does not conceal its own partiality to Mother's viewpoint. She takes on the heaviest "moral" voice in *Rambling Rose*, articulating philosophical wisdom and lessons in humanity at every turn. Mother is also earning a Ph.D. from Columbia University, which lends more authority to her knowledge, portraying her as an early feminist who refuses to be confined to stereotypical Southern roles of docile femininity. Her internal understanding of Rose's needs and motivation proves to be correct. At one point, she tells Daddy that despite Rose's sexual mishaps, it is love, not sex, that Rose really desires. Near the film's conclusion, Rose indeed authenticates this speculation by telling Buddy to remember that women care much more about love than sex. Mother's dedication to Rose even causes her to threaten Daddy's life if he attempts to force Rose out of the house.

While Buddy's narration initiates the film, Rose's point of view takes over shortly after she arrives and that point of view is shared by other characters as well. We are told of Rose's entry into the household by the grown-up Buddy in a voice-over, leading us back to 1935. Then Rose's arrival is shown through younger Buddy's point-of-view. However, as the family gathers and Daddy walks into the living room, the camera zooms into a close-up of Rose for a reaction shot. She is clearly taken aback by her attraction to Daddy. The scene *becomes* Rose's and from that point on shifts continuously from Rose's to Buddy's to Mother's to Daddy's points of view. In one scene, for example, Rose serves food to Daddy who "gratefully" slaps her on the behind. She runs away blushing, which he attributes to her "time of the month." But because the camera has privileged her point of view, the audience is encouraged to understand her emotional reaction as shame at being attracted to him. In other words, the slap has not offended her; it has fed her confusion and desire.

Rose's emotional vulnerability and her confusion about sexual desire continue to be framed through her point of view. She experiences sexual rejection from Daddy after attempting to seduce him. Then, she slips into Buddy's room worried that she is mentally imbalanced. In an often-cited sequence, Buddy explores Rose's body, eventually giving her an orgasm, while she worries over her own "nature." The camera cuts back and forth from close-ups of Rose to a medium two shot of Rose and Buddy. The camera positioning, in addition to the dialogue, work to display Rose and Buddy's competing narrative agendas and individual distraction in a way that discourages any indictment of them. In other words, the narration creates a space for them to each confront their sexual desires without judgment. As Rose becomes more aroused sexually, the camera tracks forward from a two shot to a close-up of her, facilitating her command of the camera as she reaches orgasm. Of course, Rose leaves Buddy's room even more afraid that she is going insane—a link she makes to her sexuality and which is compatible with the historical (and sexist) association between women's sexuality and hysteria. This acknowledgment provides an important punctuation mark for the scene, as it suggests that Rose has internalized the ideological linkage and offers little promise of escaping it.

Rose, in her constant questioning of herself, gains increasing support from Mother. In an early outdoors scene between the two women, Rose kneels down at Mother's left side and asks about Mother's own past as an orphan. In an exchange of only a few words, the women clearly begin to form a mother-daughter bond as they share their history as orphans. Mother extends her hand to Rose and they momentarily hold hands to close the scene. The ambiguity surrounding Rose's "origin story"— where did she come from, how did she end up an orphan, has her past made her morally impure?—becomes the film's governing question, and it begins to centralize her relationship with Mother and her search for a familial tie.

It is Mother's ultimate defense of Rose—when doctors want to de-sexualize her by performing a hysterectomy—that most legitimizes her position in the film. Rose has an ovarian cyst, stemming from teenage STDs, that requires an operation. Mother and Daddy sit in the darkly lit doctor's office as the doctor (who himself has been taking advantage of Rose) tries to coax Daddy into supporting a hysterectomy "for Rose's own good." Here, the power relations that govern both Rose's and Mother's lives become clear as Mother's only chance of imposing her will is to convince her unenlightened husband not to consent. Mother turns her supposedly powerless position into one of agency and control with an incredible speech to the two men: "Are you human beings or are you male monsters? Is there no limit to which you'd go to keep your illusions about yourselves? You'd go so far as to mutilate a helpless girl who has no means of defending herself?" She succeeds in convincing Daddy, saving Rose, and enacting one of the most memorable feminist speeches in recent film history.

Mother's salvation of Rose suggests that all along it has not been the lack of a man's companionship but the desire for a mother's love that has driven Rose to "ramble." The ambiguity surrounding her origins—which contributed to the sexualization and condemnation of her—are clarified by the film's conclusion. The doctor's description of Rose's health assumes that she had been a promiscuous teenager, because of her STDs, and that she had lied about being poor (due to the fact that her teeth suggest a high protein diet). However, Rose's final conversation with Buddy (in the forest setting where he will ultimately mourn her death) reveals that she had lived off of rabbits bred by her happy family until her mother died, her father started harassing her, and she ran away to the city. The loss of her mother, then, set off a downward spiral that could only be reversed with the substitution of Mother. Rose even associates the two women, telling Buddy that her mother was a saint like his.

The function of the mother in this film lends itself to a psychoanalytic reading, such as that posed by Freudian feminist Nancy Chodorow. *Rambling Rose* has certain similarities to 1950s maternal melodramas, which, as Jackie Byars has argued, are best understood within the context of Chodorow's arguments. Chodorow contends that girls, who are first attached to their mother in the pre-Oedipal phase, must transfer their love object from their mother to a male in order to "successfully" achieve heterosexual object relations (Byars 1994: 103). Yet, because of their early female bond, women will continue to search for and maintain female friendships out of a desire to recover and repeat that relation. Given this

84

theory, Rose's attachment to Mother and her eventual growth, facilitated by Mother's care, into a "healthy" woman who becomes happily married (albeit four times) suggests that Rose is driven by a sense of maternal loss.

The maternal theme in *Rambling Rose* is, of course, enhanced by the fact that Rose and Mother are played by actual mother and daughter, further encouraging a reading of the centrality of their relationship. An interesting extra-textual conflict actually shores up this reading. As previously mentioned, Coolidge, Dern, and Harlin (the film's producer and Dern's boyfriend) each took a reduction in salary in order for this film to be made. Just before the deal was signed, Dern and Harlin split up amicably. Then at the last minute, Ladd decided to demand more money. In a move that echoes the mother-daughter solidarity in the film, Dern chose to stand by her mother and insist on Ladd's pay raise even though it might have risked her own role (Richardson 1994: 25).[12]

In terms of the film's mother-daughter discourse, the final sequence in which Buddy cries over Rose's death oddly implies that Rose has returned to this "original" maternal bond. This sequence between Buddy and Daddy significantly takes place outside, in a natural setting inhabited by "the creative force behind the universe" (Mother's words). Daddy assures Buddy that "Rose lives," insinuating that she has transcended death in part because she has always been close to "nature." Then, Daddy comments, "She's at rest with Mother." The eternal pairing of Mother and Rose results in a sense of closure, offering a somewhat feminist message about the power of women's creativity and spiritual togetherness.

This closure also reflects on the relationship between Daddy and Buddy as they attempt to make sense of their collective past and come together in their grief. Coolidge says she valued the "father-son theme" of the film and did not want to undercut that relationship by myopically focusing on the female characters: "The two female characters are unbelievably unique because they were beautifully written and very deeply realized by myself and the actresses. But the male characters are just as beautifully unique and just as well-performed" (author's interview). Proudly, she remarks, "*Rambling Rose*, by the way, tested [in previews] better with men than with women." The film serves as an instructive illustration of Coolidge's interest in addressing both male and female audiences and balancing out feminist representations of femininity with those of masculinity.

By ending with the "immortalization" of Mother and Rose, the film could be accused of elevating these women as idealized figures that, operating at the level of metaphor, do not do other "real" women any good. Perhaps it could also be criticized for continuing certain stereotypes about women as closer to nature than men (who are instead associated with rationality) and for universalizing motherhood. However, the meticulous treatment of Rose's story—where she is seen as a three-dimensional human being rather than as a sex object—and its efforts to uphold Mother's feminist beliefs refute any easy pronouncements about *Rambling Rose*. Coolidge's strategies instead invite complex, nuanced responses to its representations. Especially given *Old Fashioned Woman*, in which Coolidge explores her own familial ties, and *Not a Pretty Picture*, in which Coolidge spends a great deal of feminist energy fighting myths about women's sexuality, *Rambling Rose* offers an example of a low-budget, "small" film that tries to appeal to a broad audience through its balance between character-driven motivations, gendered identifications, and feminist philosophies. The film also marks a shift toward melodrama at which the earlier counter cinema only hinted. Perhaps, as Coolidge moved into more narrative ways of depicting women's lives, she discovered melodrama to be a strategic tool for conveying the intricate subtleties of women's relations to each other and the ideologies that govern their lives.

ANGIE

Coolidge's 1994 film, *Angie*, is more squarely in the tradition of melodrama, with ties to the maternal melodrama of the classical era. Backed by Hollywood Pictures in conjunction with Caravan Pictures (a Disney company) and based on a novel by Aura Wing, the film has a complicated production history. Screenwriter Todd Graff (*Used People*, 1993) originally wrote the part for Madonna, who then handpicked director Jonathan Kaplan (*The Accused*, 1988; *Bad Girls*, 1994) to direct. The film was at Twentieth Century-Fox, but went into turnaround when studio head Joe Roth exited. Fox gave the producer permission to shop it around and the project wound up back with Roth, who was then heading up Caravan Pictures (Abramowitz 1994: 59). After several problems with Madonna, the film was offered to Geena Davis, who nixed Kaplan in favor of Coolidge. (Davis would have known Coolidge not only because of the director's high visibility within the industry but also through Renny Harlin [producer of *Rambling Rose*] who was by then married to Davis.)

Chronicling a young woman's decision to have a baby without marrying its father, *Angie* has been hailed as Coolidge's "most feminist film to date" by Gwendolyn Audrey Foster (in her *Women Film Directors Bio-Critical Dictionary*), who compliments the film for refusing to punish its female protagonist for her choices (1995: 91). Geena Davis says she brought her feminist perspective to the role as well. (In *Premiere* maga-

Director Martha Coolidge on the set of *Angie* (1993).
(Hollywood Pictures)

zine's promotional coverage of *Angie*, Callie Khouri, screenwriter of *Thelma and Louise*, comments on Davis's "feminist spirit" [Abramowitz: 1994: 57].) Yet, just as the film interrogates maternal ideology, its ending also perpetuates a problematic romanticization of motherhood. This contradiction suggests that, due to studio forces and multiple expectations, Coolidge had minimal control over the final product, or at the very least, more of a stake in creating a film with a multitude of social logics.

Coolidge describes the difference between independent and mainstream production, remarking: "The more money, the more people above you, the more pressure, and the more the director becomes squeezed between the frying pan and the fire" (Cole and Dale 54). This pressure, I think, results in the proliferation of desires and ideologies expressed in the film, which derive from both individual and institutional sources. Hence, *Angie* offers a prime example of how cinematic competing logics (of economics, industry standards, and genre) operate to produce contradictory and incompatible ideologies.

A recognition of these internal multiple logics is conveyed through several devices early in the film. The opening credits begin with a twilight landscape of New York City. Subways whirl by in fast motion producing blurry lights to the tune of "I'll Take You There." As the credits appear, white stencil letters spell out the title (i.e., of the screen credit) and neon pink cursive writing spells the name of the person credited; for example, "Directed By" appears in white stencil while "Martha Coolidge" takes the form of pink neon cursive. In another instance, the title "Brooklyn, NY 1972" appears in white letters above the smaller pink cursive specification "Bensonhurst." These juxtapositions hint at a dialogue of divergent "realities" that run alongside each other in the text. Soon after this, Angie describes a current fault line in her identity, namely that between her neighborhood home life in Bensonhurst and her glamorous job as a career woman in the city. Again, two identities parallel each other, implying a tension between reality and fantasy. (Later, Angie leaves a movie theater where the marquee advertises "Cliffhanger" in large letters and in smaller letters underneath "What's Love Got to Do with It?" Here two versions of fantasy compete, one being the mainstream blockbuster featuring a white male action star—perhaps not coincidentally directed by Harlin—and the other a narrowcast picture plotting the biography of the African American rock singer. Perhaps Coolidge provides her own critique of the studio presence within her film, offering a political message about the privilege of the blockbuster.)[13]

Angie's cinematography is similar to that of *Rambling Rose* in that it emphasizes the subjectivity of its female protagonist, and the film devotes a great deal of screen time to female points of view. This should not be surprising given that the films were shot by the same director of photography (Johnny E. Jenson).[14] The film begins with a slow pan of Angie as a young girl painting baby dolls' faces with her best friend, Tina. While with Tina's numerous sisters, Angie pulls out an old picture of her mother and explains in voice-over that her mother ran away many years ago. Upon spotting the picture, the sisters offer various reasons for her mother's abandonment, none of them positive. But Angie prefers to

Angie (Geena Davis) and Tina (Aida Turturro) walk down their
old neighborhood street, on the brink of experiencing their
former childhood selves at play. (Hollywood Pictures)

think of her mother as a "free spirit." Angie and Tina are left alone to
discuss their ideal future, which consists of marrying twin boys and living
happily ever after as best friends.

Then, a spine-tingling device allows past and present to meet briefly.
A fast-motion blurry pan takes us to Angie and Tina (Aida Turturro) as
adult women walking to work on that very same street. The techno song
"Release Me" begins as the image of the adult Angie and Tina resumes
normal speed. The older pair recognize their younger selves and both
sets of characters stare contemplatively at each other. A close-up of the
adult Angie, which coincides with the song's words "release me," sends
her along her way. This powerful scene raises a number of questions
about Angie's character: Can she achieve her future goals without the
loving support of a mother? Is she a "free spirit" like her mother, and, if
so, how does that enhance or impede the fulfillment of her dreams? In
other words, can she "release herself" from the past? And, furthermore,
will Tina's friendship sustain her in this journey?

This scene establishes a visual economy of female looking relations wherein the past and present selves engage with varying degrees of fantasy, desire, anticipation, and anxiety. Angie's fixation on her mother's photo also activates these tensions: every time she looks at the photo she confronts her maternal fantasies as well as her self-image. As long as Angie's mother embodies her primary object of desire, her desire to reclaim their relationship and to better understand her own identity is based on this visual economy of women's looks.

The rest of the movie deals with Angie as an adult woman and her realization that she is pregnant. Her boyfriend abruptly warns her that this means they will finally settle down and strive toward "normalcy"—a family, a house, a lifestyle toward which Angie has always felt ambivalence. We also come to learn that Angie has a complicated relationship with her own family, especially her "irritating" stepmother. When her father brings over her mother's old wedding dress, offering it to his daughter for the ceremony, Angie fingers it longingly, feeling a sudden connection to her lost mother; the scene recalls Coolidge's own exploration of her grandmother's wedding dress in *Old-Fashioned Woman*. However, once Angie realizes that her father misrepresented its origins, and that it is her stepmother's dress, she entirely rejects it. In fact, she begins to doubt the longevity of her relationship with her boyfriend and eventually breaks it off. However, she continues to feel the pains of restlessness she attributes to her mother's "free spiritedness," and she worries about her ability to be a parent.

One device that characterizes Angie's changing relationship with her ideals and goals involves her connection to artistic representations of women. Surveying a book vendor's inventory with her boyfriend, Vinnie (James Gandolfini), Angie complains that they never go to museums. Turning the pages of an art book, she spots the Degas painting, "Absinthe Drinkers," in which a woman sits glumly alone next to a man who has left some distance between them. While Angie seems drawn to this image, her boyfriend interprets the woman's sullen look in terms of her "need to get laid." Later, Angie sees the original of this portrait in a museum and tries to make meaning out of it. Her impending love interest, Noel (Stephen Rea), attempts to seduce her by offering his own interpretation of the misunderstood woman's loneliness and isolation.

Similar to the image of the rose in *Rambling Rose*, this one becomes a tableau on which characters project their own interests: Angie's own interpretation is yet to be determined. Her reading of this woman's state of mind will depend on her own ability to find happiness apart from the men in her life. The visual economy characterized by Angie's looks at the Degas mirrors her fixation on her mother's photograph, reactivating a series of women looking at women (in representation). This film harkens back to *Old-Fashioned Woman*, with a "double lens" effect whereby female representation is used to examine art in terms of its ability to get at women's lived experience.

In *Angie*, until the protagonist can find a way to match the photograph with some sense of her mother's lived experience, she will not be able to overcome her own restlessness. So, after giving birth to her son who undergoes a series of medical complications, Angie runs away to find her mother. All the while Angie is fearful that she is replaying her own mother's mistakes. She embarks on a bus ride where she is joined, and then abandoned, by her friend Tina (who chastises her for not seeing the overriding importance of her own son). Angie then tracks down her mother in Texas. (Curiously, the status of Angie and Tina's friendship is left unresolved, although Angie's stepmother implicitly replaces Tina.)

Although she had imagined a woman who escaped to a better, more adventurous life, Angie discovers that her mother has been slowly deteriorating from schizophrenia. Once she realizes that her mother had no choice but to leave her, and that her father has actually been sending news of Angie to her mother all these years, she kneels at her mother's side. The composition of the frame clearly reflects the scene in *Rambling Rose* where Rose sits to the left of Mother and holds her hand. Kneeling there, Angie comes to terms with her mother's reality. And, just before she leaves, her mother accidentally (?) burns the old picture of them together, erasing any lingering fantasies Angie might have had about a nostalgic connection. Having resolved to be the mother her mom never could, she returns to Bensonhurst to nurse her son back to health.

Judging from revisions to the screenplay, the few changes to the original adaptation that Coolidge made involved slightly decreasing the idealization of Angie's mother while also limiting the demonization of her.[15] One dream sequence was cut from the second act, after Angie meets Noel in the museum. Angie dreams that she is a little girl watching a ballerina dance on stage. Once she realizes that the ballerina is her mother, little Angie leaps on stage. Her mother says "I'll never leave you again" and then promises Angie that Tina can come live with them as one happy family. This dream perpetuates the "fantasy version" of Angie's mother as a free spirit who has the potential to fulfill Angie's desire for a mother (quite different from the mother Angie finds at the end of her journey).

In another scene, a line of dialogue was deleted that implies the mother was not merely ill-equipped to care for her daughter but was actually a fatal threat to Angie. Toward the end of the screenplay, Angie's father tells her that he withheld the truth about her mother's whereabouts because the mother had tried to kill Angie in the snow (by exposing her to hypothermia). With this information, the mother goes from a mentally ill woman who likes to dance in the snow to a villainess who had no regard for her daughter's life. Coolidge's dual reductions in the idealization and demonization of Angie's mother suggest that she was attempting to escape the traditional "good girl/bad girl" trope and to add dimension to the mother's character by deflating both her fantastical attributes and her delinquent ones.

This film has obvious thematic links to *Rambling Rose*, in which a daughter's search for familial ties, an uncertainty about her origins, and her eventual reunion with her "mother" (whether literal or symbolic) govern the narrative structure. It also interestingly activates a similar psychoanalytic discourse in its depiction of mothers and daughters. While Angie refuses marriage and does not follow through on her romance with Noel (and both these endings would connote the conventional heterosexual coupling of Hollywood cinema), she does return to her son in a way that suggests that he has now replaced any other love-objects. In Chodorow's explication of women's development, she explains that, whereas men tend to relate in dyads (first mother-son, then wife-husband), women lean toward triads (first mother-father-daughter, then husband-child-wife) (Byars 103). *Angie* maintains a conflicted relation to the melodrama genre, a relation I assume Coolidge had a hand in forging; the film proposes to revise a conventional melodramatic ending while still heightening certain social tensions and mother-daughter conflicts.

Two triads are actually at work in *Angie*. First we have the formation of the Angie's mother-Angie-Angie's baby triad that implies Angie cannot come to terms with her maternal identity until she resolves her past. Chodorow's formulation would suggest that Angie's recovery of her mother enables her to then reproduce motherhood. Second we have a triad involving Angie's stepmother who, unbeknownst to Angie, has lost a child of her own. The stepmother continually evokes an ideology of motherhood in which "the baby comes first, no matter what." She is highly critical of Angie's lack of direction and ambivalence toward her son. Once Angie has resolved the "original" triad involving her mother, she enters into a new one, stepmother-Angie-Angie's baby. Here, the stepmother represents a mother substitute and Angie can resume her maternal role without the same degree of ambivalence. This film, then, provides contradictory readings: on the one hand, it perpetuates "the reproduction of motherhood" through which maternity is idealized and the stepmother's voice becomes the moral loudspeaker of the film. On the other hand, Angie never "successfully" completes the Oedipal process that would pair her into a heterosexual relation. The paradox, then, occurs because Angie has accepted the Oedipal ideology, entering into the contract of the reproduction of mothering, yet she resists the norma-

92

tive triad (wife-husband-child). Angie has created a new clause: the new mother-daughter bond between her and her stepmother offers an alternative relation based on female friendship and familial ties. The film's ideological contradictions—which I would argue (based on her earlier work) Coolidge opens up and accepts—necessitate a tension-based, multi-vocal model of Classical Hollywood Cinema.

As previously mentioned, the melodrama genre leaves plenty of room for these tensions. *Angie* is certainly in debt to many women's films that came before it. In tracing the roots of the women's film back to domestic fiction, E. Ann Kaplan has noted two approaches to melodrama (1987). The first approach embraces the cult of true womanhood and favors a sentimental rendering of the mother along the lines of Harriet Beecher Stowe's *Uncle Tom's Cabin*. The second, with its roots in the fiction of the Brontë sisters, seems more related to *Angie*'s maternal discourse. In this kind of melodrama, women are viewed as vessels, whose central value lies in their ability to raise their children (usually sons) well (128–29). Kaplan argues that this strand of the woman's film—as seen in *The Blot* (1921), *Now, Voyager* (1942), and *Stella Dallas* (1925, 1937)— generally features heroines who are autonomous, who have class aspirations, and who are confronted with raising children out of wedlock. She posits that these films almost always question the place of the mother. Kaplan calls for more films in this category, into which *Angie* certainly falls, because they express the contradictions of women's lived experience and shift conventional mother-daughter paradigms.

I find the comparison of *Angie* to *Stella Dallas* very productive because the two protagonists attempt to embody *both* the "Madonna" and the "whore" stereotypes, which have historically governed women's lives into an either/or dichotomy (Williams 1990: 151). Similar to the divorced Stella, who attempts to be a "good mother" and date men at the same time (claiming her right to be an individual), Angie decides to be an unwed mother and pursue sexual relationships. Both characters face a downfall because of their choices, although Angie is allowed to recover. Angie most obviously defies social norms when she sexily dances in a Santa Claus costume during her ninth month of pregnancy, a scene that culminates in her performing a striptease. In commercial films, women are rarely seen as pregnant and sexy—and in male drag no less. Though the film does perhaps "punish" Angie for her indiscretion by forcing her to contend with her son's physical defect (in keeping with conventions of the "woman's picture"), the independence she gains at the film's conclusion might be seen as a step forward.

In other words, Coolidge has found a way to critique Hollywood from within by deploying a genre that refuses to provide easy answers for women. (That is to say, Coolidge and the genre—marked by its feminist possibilities—converge to participate in the critique.) Angie's realizations certainly seem to overcome her restlessness and insecurity by the film's conclusion, but her identity as mother (and daughter) is still left wide open. Linda Williams asserts that the woman's film—like women's magazines, fiction, and soap operas—carves out a space where women can speak to each other, demanding a "female reading competence" that is discursively organized around maternal experience (143). Williams explains, "This competence derives from the different way women take on their identities under patriarchy and is a direct result of the social fact of female mothering." *Angie* rewards such "competence," combining notions of female identity with those of maternal fantasy in a way that envisions women stronger and more resistant than when the film began.

Promoted as a "woman's film" that would appeal to certain "female reading competencies," *Angie* was also marketed in terms of its female director who claimed to identify with those competencies.[16] In the ten-page press release circulated by Caravan Pictures, Coolidge is said to have closely connected with the screenplay because of its themes of birth and motherhood. The emphasis on identification, which takes on rather essentialist implications, is supported even further by the fact that Coolidge's son, when a baby, had to undergo surgery for a cleft much like Angie's baby in the film. Coolidge also asserts her empathic associations with Angie's quest to resolve her motherlessness because the director went through a similar process after her father died when she was a child. In the press release, Coolidge declares: "I can understand Angie's idealization of her missing mother—in a sense this was a fantasy trip for me. . . ." The marketing strategies deployed by Caravan capitalize on Coolidge's "female" experiences to elevate her as a knowledgeable authority about the cinematic story she is charged with telling. They lean on an auteurist framework by positioning Coolidge in terms of her need to exorcise certain "demons" from her past through a personal and artistic quest.

THREE WISHES

Coolidge's 1995 film *Three Wishes,* which did not do well at the box office, offers a female protagonist much like *Angie.* A mother of two who has lost her husband in the Korean War, she chooses to be a single mother after confronting two very different male love interests. Here we have emerged from the binary logic of, for instance, *Valley Girl,* where Julie's only dilemma involves which man she should choose. However, despite the differences, there are ideological links to *Valley Girl.* Just as Julie fought off the constraints of social conformity in high school,

Jeanne (Mary Elizabeth Monstrantonio) of *Three Wishes* battles the cultural norms of 1950s suburbia.

The film begins with Jeanne's son, Tom, as an adult who seems unable to take pleasure in life with his wife and children. When Tom nearly misses hitting a hitchhiker with his car, he enters into a flashback about a period of his childhood in which he thought his father had been killed in the Korean War. During this prolonged flashback, Jeanne grieves over the loss of her husband as she attempts to raise her two sons, Tom (Joseph Mazello) and Gunny (Seth Hunt) according to the standards of their suburban community. The setting of the sleepy 1950s neighborhood is forcefully conjured through a background of *Ozzie and Harriet* television programs, Lassie comic books, bowleramas, and tootsie pops. The consequences of this setting for Jeanne are made known as her friends tell her that she should not wear shorts let alone contemplate opening up her own business. She takes in a transient, Jack (Patrick Swayze), after she accidentally injures him with her car. Jack seems to have mystical powers, as does his dog, and the duo begin to rejuvenate the family's sense of life and independence.

Jack teaches Tom, who feels like an outcast, especially when it comes to sports, how to play baseball, and he helps the boy set his sights beyond his own narrow-minded community. Jack and his dog also watch over little Gunny as he fights stomach cancer. They open up a magical world to Gunny that seems to help him journey through his illness and provides him with the power to heal. In addition, Jack convinces Jeanne not to marry for the sake of convenience or for the security of her sons (she considers marrying a banker who wants to restore her family by playing the role of condescending patriarch). Jack helps Jeanne see herself as an "explorer" before he moves on to the next small town. The fact that Jeanne and Jack do not wind up together in a "happy ending," and that Jeanne opts to live alone rather than marry the banker, suggests that this female protagonist can see beyond the two choices that seem available to her (both of which involve romance and marriage). For this reason, her choices are presented in more complex terms than those presented to *Valley Girl*'s Julie; they more closely mirror those of the protagonist in *Angie*.

By the end of the story it is disclosed that Jack is most likely a ghost (as indicated by a gravestone that dates his death during World War II) who has granted one wish to each member of the family. It is also revealed that Jeanne's husband did not die after all—he returns to the family after being released from a prisoner-of-war camp. (Jeanne's eventual coupling with her husband does not necessarily undercut the courage of her earlier decision to remain a single mother.) When the film flashes forward to Tom as an adult, he realizes that the wish granted to him by

Jack involved "finding happiness in whatever you got," which spurs him to better appreciate his family.

Perhaps the most interesting aspect of *Three Wishes* is its engagement with the politics of its particular cultural moment. Actually, Coolidge and her cohorts framed this film in political terms through an innovative marketing strategy. Coolidge (along with the producers and screenwriter) took out a full page advertisement in *The Washington Post* to publicize the film during its fall 1995 release. With a headline that reads "An Open Invitation to President Bill Clinton and Senator Robert Dole," the ad boasts that *Three Wishes* will meet both of their criteria for a "family values" film. It proposes that if the two of them screen the film together, Rysher Entertainment will donate $100,000 to the Make-a-Wish Foundation, with even more money to be given if Mrs. Clinton and Chelsea attend.

According to Coolidge, the marketing strategy was conceptualized when the filmmakers realized the film was getting very little attention, in part because it was being distributed by Savoy Pictures, which was going bankrupt at the time. Coolidge remarks: "We had a movie we loved. We all understood that Clinton was begging for more family-type pictures, *begging*, but we were being ignored. Go to the source, we decided" (author's interview). The maneuver did not actually bring the two presidential candidates together but it did provide some short-term publicity for the film. Coolidge remembers: "The response was immediate from Dole. He said he'd do it. Clinton's response was more guarded, but then he had more to lose. It got us some attention. It probably boosted ticket sales, but there's not much you can do when the company is going under" (author's interview).

Coolidge's participation in this endeavor is marked by a politicization of the "Violence in Hollywood" debate and a desire to foster governmental coalescence. While the ad might be considered mere marketing skill, it also suggests that she continues the thread of politicization she initiated in her 1970s experimental work. At the same time, as a mainstream film, *Three Wishes* participates in the phenomenon of national film publicity, which has yet to be fully incorporated into independent distribution.

While Coolidge introduced *Three Wishes* into the discourse of family values through its publicity, she surprisingly (although not so for those who know her work) reverses family values rhetoric within the film. The son, once grown up, realizes the value of his family, learning how to be content with what he has. I would argue that this lesson, in the rhetoric of family values, ordinarily involves not a man but a woman. The ideology goes that if women would only resign themselves to their domestic role, our country's so-called moral bankruptcy would be rectified. In

Coolidge's film, though, the father realizes his family's worth, joining his wife and two daughters as they dance at a cemetery. While this ending might be viewed as a conventional reconstitution of the nuclear family, it is important, I think, that Tom reaches that conclusion in the spirit of non-conformity and spiritual adventure.

It is not just Coolidge's decision to politicize *Three Wishes* in the press that points to her status as a "progressive auteur." Feminist discourse, in fact, surrounds her in almost every public account of her work. *The Boston Globe* ran an interview with her under the headline "An Independent Woman" (Sherman 1992). Coolidge has spoken out about gender inequality and sexual harassment in *Time, The Los Angeles Times, The New York Times, Premiere,* and *Ms.* Her outspokenness has not threatened her relative visibility in Hollywood—she is on the board of directors of the American Film Institute and has served on numerous committees for the Directors Guild of America. While Coolidge has not achieved "star" standing as a director, she *has* become positioned as a model feminist director. Her status in Hollywood demands a new set of criteria through which we define "auteur"—one that recognize ideological choices, political investments, and social context.

Most important, for the purposes of this book, the corpus of Coolidge's work provides fertile ground for interrogating any facile distinctions that might be made between counter cinema and Hollywood. Through the great variety in her films, I have traced certain continuities from her early and later work that serve as evidence that feminist theory gains a great deal from breaking down distinctions between marginal and mainstream films. Coolidge's career has moved her inside and outside Hollywood, starting with her experimental work, including her independent *Valley Girl,* her studio-produced *Real Genius,* the independent (mini-major) *Rambling Rose,* and the mainstream films *Lost in Yonkers, Angie,* and *Three Wishes.* This career path suggests that Coolidge is never wholly outside nor inside Hollywood.

As more evidence of this, having directed her last three films through studio affiliations, Coolidge continues her advocacy of independent work. When she won the Best Director award for *Rambling Rose* from the Independent Feature Project, an association she helped form, she claimed she was much more honored than if she had won an Academy Award (Sherman 1992: B8). Coolidge is also currently on the Board of Directors of the newly founded Independent Film Channel. Though the development of this cable station presents a new host of problems and questions regarding the commercialization of independent film (and television, for that matter), Coolidge's involvement facilitates a feminist agenda in the station's mission of targeting television audiences with alternative fare.

97

2

KATHRYN
BIGELOW

THE EARLY WORKS OF Kathryn Bigelow, *The Loveless* (1982) and *Near Dark* (1987), are particularly significant as the inaugurators of the oppositional ideologies that re-surface in her later films, such as *Blue Steel* (1990) and *Point Break* (1991). *The Loveless* and *Near Dark* were low-budget films that garnered "cult" audiences. *Blue Steel* straddles the independent/mainstream divide because it was financed and distributed independently; however, it appeared in a high number of theaters with box office rankings in the top five. In contrast, *Point Break* is a high-budget studio-affiliated film with solid returns.

Bigelow, who has taken up the traditionally "male" genre of the action film, has been criticized for lacking any new insight into gender politics. Feminist critic Ally Acker contends that Bigelow "adopt[s] the patriarchal values of fun-through-bloodshed and a relishing of violence" creating "nothing more than male clones" (67). Similarly, more mainstream male critics have echoed David Denby's remark: "I can't see that much has been gained now that a woman is free to make the same rotten movie as a man" (76–77). These simplistic generalizations do not allow for the nuances in Bigelow's work, nor do they step out of essentialist notions about what is possible in the "male category" of action films. I propose that Bigelow's films rely on a complex relationship between genre and gender, often blending genres or reversing generic expectations, and that they are best understood in the context of her independent origins.

Tom Schatz has argued that genres serve as cultural problem-solving tools, and that different genres solve problems in various ways. Genre films "celebrate our collective sensibilities, providing an array of ideological strategies for negotiating social conflicts" (1981: 29). More specifically regarding the kinship between genre and gender, Linda Williams calls for theory "that would take as its point of departure—rather than as an unexamined assumption—questions of gender construction as well as gender address in relation to basic sexual fantasies" (42). She refers to Rick Altman's discussion of generic excess, particularly the notion that every dominant formula also contains a second voice or competing logic that reveals the ideological assumptions embedded in that formula.

Whereas Martha Coolidge has spent a great portion of her career exploring social conflicts through the generic tensions of the "woman's picture," Bigelow mobilizes supposedly "male genres" like the Western, the cop film, the film noir, and the buddy film. Bigelow's later films do not necessarily break out of dominant conventions, but they do revise them by asking new questions—offering a competing ideological voice that challenges assumptions about gender and sexuality. In an industry that generally prefers a "good director-for-hire" (who is well versed in self-effacing camerawork and formulaic conventions), especially from its women, Bigelow plays one role against the other: she performs the "good director-for-hire" part, being someone who "knows" genre and produces marketable product; but she also engages in a heavy narrational style (which is one criterion by which an auteur is judged) and she capitalizes on genre tensions by revealing their ideological excesses.

One way in which she re-works genre is by challenging the static formulations of nature posed by conventional genres. Her films testify to the futility of assuming a "natural" gender or sexuality, opting instead to explore the performativity and inconstancy of supposedly natural roles. Bigelow's authorial enterprise is motivated by the goal of probing gender and genre in a way that deconstructs both terms. Therefore, she brings into relief the constructedness of gender in a way that frames her own status as "woman director" in terms of performance (rather than innate femininity).

Rick Altman's "tension-based," dialogical approach to mainstream film, which suggests that we hone in on the ideological resistances to a film's dominant logic, provides fruitful avenues for studying Bigelow's films. A thread runs through her work that continually questions the generic place of her female characters. At the same time that the dominant gender logic is questioned, a space is created in which the female characters find ways to articulate their downplayed subjectivities. However, even as she manipulates narrative logic to attend to her female characters, Bigelow questions rigid conceptions of gender by thematically

100

emphasizing the instability and "deconstructability" of the male/female binary opposition.

Bigelow's Entry into Film

Bigelow's origins in film date back to her involvement in the avant-garde art scene of the late 1970s and early 1980s. Having studied at the San Francisco Art Institute and the Whitney Museum, she entered Columbia University's MFA program to gain more theoretical expertise.[1] In fact, Bigelow is one of the few women in mainstream film today who has an academic background in film theory. (A good number of women directors have attended film school, however few have chosen to de-emphasize production in favor of a film studies track. Also, many women with a film school background, such as Allison Anders, work primarily in independent film.) This is not to say that Bigelow is a better filmmaker than her counterparts because of her theoretical background, it is simply to propose that the high degree of reflexivity in her films may be a result of this training.

Bigelow cites Andrew Sarris and Peter Wollen as her most influential advisors; this suggests that she is not only schooled in auteurist theories but probably also has a stake in presenting herself as an auteur. A *Film Comment* article on Bigelow labels her the "dark daughter of Hawks and Hitchcock," suggesting that she is being received as an auteur in some circles (Mills 51). John Powers remarks that her colleagues "speak of her with reverential awe usually reserved for Kubrick or Scorsese" (Oct. 1995: 196).

In the early 1980s, Bigelow participated in Lizzie Borden's *Born in Flames* (1983), a feminist utopian film in which radical feminists and lesbians attempt to take over the United States. (She assisted in production and played Kathy Larson, one of the "academic," socialist feminists.) In fact, strands of *Born in Flames* emerge in Bigelow's subsequent films, such as the rape-revenge theme in *Blue Steel*, which echoes the group of women in *Born in Flames* who travel on bicycles and blow their whistles to stop male sexual assault of women on the street. And one could argue that the science fiction elements of *Born in Flames* are recalled in Bigelow's *Strange Days* (1995) in an effort to come to terms with racial tensions and political negotiations. Borden's name also appears in the credits of Bigelow's *The Loveless*.

Despite Bigelow's association with the self-identified feminist Borden, her connections to feminism, as represented in public discourse, have always been ambiguous. She seems quite conscious of feminist politics and willing to engage with feminism, but she remains ambivalent about labeling her films in terms of gender or politics. For example, in her promotion of *Blue Steel*, Bigelow remarked: "I subscribe to feminism emotionally and I sympathize with the struggles for equality. But I think there's a point where the ideology is dogmatic. So I'm not saying that *Blue Steel* is a feminist tract, per se. But there's a political conscience behind it" (Peary 93–94).

One of Bigelow's most noted collaborations has occurred since her release of *Blue Steel*—her association with producer-director James Cameron (*Aliens* [1987], *Terminator* [1984], *Terminator 2: Judgment Day* [1991]), who produced *Point Break* and wrote and produced *Strange Days*. That Bigelow was married to him raises the uneasy issue for feminists about how to approach the work of women who seek production opportunities and financial success by making use of their male connections. Certainly many contemporary women have achieved their start in partnerships with men—for example, Elaine May's collaboration with Mike Nichols in the 1970s, or Joan Micklin Silver, who found independent financing for *Hester Street* (1975) through her businessman husband after studios turned her down. These director/producer partnerships have antecedents in the writing teams of Betty Comden/Adolph Green, Ruth Gordon/Garson Kanin, and Frances Goodrich/Albert Hackett.[2] Rather than attempt to gloss over these relationships, which are inevitable in a male-dominated industry, by positing a binary opposition in which a female author either exists alone or not at all, we need to acknowledge this kind of partnership as a valuable and fruitful avenue for women's access into mainstream film and as a pragmatic necessity. We also need to critically circumvent the long history of the ideology of "sexual favors" ("sleeping one's way to the top," "casting couch," etc.), through which women's hard work and professional authority are undermined by sexual innuendo.[3]

I received correspondence from Bigelow on this particular issue after I sent her my original manuscript. I had initially written the sentence, "Married to Cameron at one time, Bigelow's ability to push her projects through certainly relied somewhat on him," thinking that Cameron's role as producer granted him greater professional power than she on whatever project they worked on. Bigelow responded that *she* had suggested to Largo Entertainment that they bring in Cameron as executive producer on *Point Break*, not the other way around. Elaborating, she wrote:

> For some reason, it would appear that whenever analysts (whether they be journalists or academics) study the career of men and women in the entertainment business, they assume that any collaborative effort between a man and a woman, somehow is more beneficial to the woman rather than the man. (Personal correspondence, 4 Mar. 1996)

While, again, I had been thinking in terms of the hierarchical power structure of the Hollywood mode of production, I realized how my assumptions about gendered power relations did inherently grant Cameron more authority in their collaboration. The specificity of Bigelow's situation—that she suggested Cameron for the position of executive producer and not vice versa—reveals the need for feminist film theorists to continue interrogating the nature of male/female collaborations within mainstream production.

As for Cameron, he has developed a reputation as one of the few commercially successful male directors who pointedly collaborates with and mentors women. In addition to his multiple projects with Bigelow, he co-produced and co-wrote *The Terminator* (1984) with Gale Ann Hurd, whom he met through Roger Corman. In his own production office, three of the four executive positions are held by women, including that of president. (Most top producers have one, or rarely two, women in executive positions; so these figures are slightly above the norm. See the 1996 and 1997 volumes of *The Hollywood Creative Directory* for comparisons.) In an interview I conducted with his Director of Development, Stacy Maes, she commented on Cameron's uniqueness in the industry in that he offers a great deal of opportunities for women (author's interview, 16 Feb. 1996).

Bigelow's personal and professional relationship with Cameron obviously complicates any easy assumptions about authorship; because they share similar visual and narrative styles, with an emphasis on special effects and physical violence, the notion of a single author becomes problematized. Cameron's status as producer (on *Point Break*) as well as co-writer (on *Strange Days*) makes disentangling their individual contributions difficult. Indeed, because collaboration is often such a fuzzy generation of shared ideas, it seems not only impossible but undesirable to detect what might have been Bigelow's lone, raw ingredients from the final product.

Another facet of Bigelow's identity as an auteur, in addition to her often quoted association with Cameron, involves the media construction of her star persona. Often depicted as a glamorous woman who could have succeeded just as easily in front of the camera, Bigelow is discussed in terms of her appearance in nearly every press account I have read. Whether it be to describe her as "strikingly attractive" or "tall" and "willowy," popular press and academic journals alike tend to categorize her with regard to her body (Travers 47; Hamburg 85). A good example of this appears in a 1995 *Vogue* article titled "The Director Wore Black" in which John Powers recalls an earlier meeting with Bigelow: "Tall and dark, swathed in black leather and endowed with an icy, daunting beauty, she looked like the world's highest-priced dominatrix" (Powers 194). Mentioning Bigelow's height and her model-like beauty works to further the construction of her "star" status.

Rolling Stone's Peter Travers recounts that when he was exiting a screening of *Blue Steel*, he "overheard one male viewer telling another male viewer that a woman had directed the film. The listener seemed unfazed, except to ask, 'What does she look like?' " (Travers 47). Whether or not this reportage is true, it is certainly not impossible to believe. Such an overwhelming focus on "what she looks like" undoubtedly directs attention away from what she looks *at*. Ironically, however, these very press accounts also increase her circulation as a star and serve to enhance her reputation as a notable director, possibly even as an auteur.[4]

Bigelow's first film, an experimental short called *Set-Up* (1978), depicts a fight between two men in an alley accompanied by the dialogue of two theorists as they interpret the violence. Since then, she has deployed images of violence, which illuminate symbolic issues of power, in cinematic contexts that tend to affect audiences immediately and emotionally. Bigelow has been outspoken about the contention that women can direct action films as well as any man, balking at the industry's tendency

Director Kathryn Bigelow arranges a shot for *Blue Steel* (1990). (Vestron Pictures)

to pigeonhole women into making "relationship pictures" (Mills 1989: 59, also see Peary, 1990, and Powers, 1995). What is not generally known, and what is further obscured by the tendency to isolate Bigelow as an exception, is that she is preceded by several women who have worked with violent images. These include screenwriters such as Betty Burbridge, Marguerite Roberts, and Leigh Brackett, as well as the early director Grace Cunard.[5] Cunard appeared as an action heroine in thirteen silent serials from 1910 to 1928, the most successful of which was *The Broken Coin* (1915) (Rainey 29). Eventually she formed a partnership with Francis Ford (brother of John Ford), in which she wrote action screenplays and performed. But Cunard also directed, first for Universal and later for independent companies.[6] These antecedents to Bigelow, although not necessarily directors, remind us that Bigelow is not the first woman to tackle "male" genres, even though contemporary reviews often label her as a true aberration.[7]

THE LOVELESS

Bigelow's first independent feature, *The Loveless*, co-written and co-directed by Monty Montgomery, follows biker Vance (a young Willem Defoe) in a day in the life of a 1950s biker gang. With its focus on the macho posing and male flirtation of this group of bikers who boast a spectacular array of black leather, chains, knives, and, of course, motorcycles, the film becomes somewhat of a spoof on Kenneth Anger's films combined with several psychological elements of the film noir. The film is most obviously a response to Laslo Benedek's renowned motorcycle film *The Wild One* (1954) starring Marlon Brando. In a BBC2 interview, Bigelow explained:

> *The Loveless* was a psychological bikers' film. We wanted to suspend the conventional kind of plotting where everything spirals into problem solving after problem solving, and create a meditation on an arena, on an iconography, using the bikers as an iconography of power. (Bigelow 313)

This decisive resistance to cause and effect is accompanied by the use of a generally stationary, single camera and long duration of takes, often filmed in long shot. Clearly grounded in the avant-garde style discussed in the introduction, *The Loveless*'s camerawork results in a strong sense of local culture (the bikers stop for a day in a small Southern town to repair one of their motorcycles), a lingering on minute detail, and a plot driven by geography. Each of the characters are strategically positioned and re-positioned in relation to one another and to her or his environment. (In fact, this orientation toward geography and spatial relations established through camerawork recurs in Bigelow's work.) At the

105

same time, connecting the scenes is an almost non-stop soundtrack, featuring Little Richard, the Diamonds, and Brenda Lee, as well as a number of 1950s-sounding tunes powerfully performed by Robert Gordon (who plays Davis in the film).

However, if *The Loveless* is a meditation on power, and I believe that it is, the biker genre is only a backdrop against which the disempowerment of women, and one woman in particular, Telena (Marin Kanter), is painfully illuminated. One of the narrative's early sequences, in which Vance unsympathetically takes advantage of a woman stuck on the side of the road with a flat tire, is ultimately critiqued by the end through the entirely sympathetic portrayal of Telena's oppressive circumstances. But despite its male conversion theme, this film is less an attempt to document Vance's "transformation" into an understanding character than an experiment with the limits of its internal knowledge about women's experience within the parameters of the biker genre in which that knowledge is expressed.

This film could similarly be read as a revised Western, wherein, although the biker rides into town at the film's beginning and rides off into the sunset after the final shootout, the character of Telena keeps interrupting his narrative with her own story. A role such as Telena's recurs in Bigelow's films. Her character articulates the problem of generic conventions for women, but only after continually carving out a site in which the figure of the woman can speak. The alternative logic represented by Telena's problematic status works to resist the marginal positions typically held out to women by the biker and Western genres.

In the early sequence with the stranded woman (who remains nameless), Vance takes all of her money and, framed in shadowy close-up, imposes on her a long kiss and fondles her breasts. Then he laughs and walks off, leaving her to go on her way. Although we see her nervous distress, the camera's attention remains focused on him. However, Vance only selectively takes advantage of women. For soon after this scene, he looks disgustedly at his friend, Davis (Robert Gordon), when Davis asks a diner waitress, "Are you on the menu?" while surveying her behind. Though the waitress ignores Davis, she immediately offers herself up to Vance and he refuses.

Telena is clearly marked as the female protagonist as she drives her red convertible up to the garage where Vance and the other bikers are temporarily holed out. In fact, the song by Gordon that introduced Vance, "Relentless," also accompanies her entrance. In her flirtations with Vance in front of her car, one of her first lines consists of "Got any cigarettes," to which he quips, "Yeah, but I'd feel like I was promotin' child abuse." Although his response suggests her young age (she looks about fifteen), it also foreshadows the eerie information we eventually learn about Telena—her father has been sexually abusing her since her mother's suicide.

While the film discloses very little about Telena, and she appears in only three sequences, her character is more fully developed than any of the others in the film, including Vance. We know the most about her and, because the film does not disclose much about even her, we want to know even more (possibly grieving that we never will). This creates a significant tension in the film, one that encourages us to become self-conscious about that which the narrative never provides. In the most extended sequence featuring Telena, in which she and Vance take an excursion in her car, he asks her how she got a facial scar. She reveals that her father cut her cheek right after her mother committed suicide. Then, intimating that her mother's actions were a cumulative result of years of abuse, she remarks, "He used to tell her, 'I'm gonna give you a smile from ear to ear.' " In a close-up angle on her face, Telena gestures her fingers across her neck and then watches for Vance's reaction. Her own feelings about her father seem beyond verbal expression. Interestingly, Bigelow/Montgomery immediately cut to the garage where Davis asks his girlfriend Debbie to stand against the wall so that he and his buddies can engage in live target practice with their knives. The unfortunate and compromised positions of both these women in relation to men are articulated side by side.

Nevertheless, both women refuse to assume the role of victim. Debbie never goes to stand against the wall; in fact, she goes outside and embarks on a seduction of the garage mechanic's son. Significantly, another male buddy readily takes her place as Davis's target, recalling the homoeroticism of Anger's biker films and destabilizing hegemonic notions of masculinity. And, later in the garage, one of Vance's friend's glances at Telena and asks, "Does it have a name?" Telena angrily retorts, "It has a voice too." She refuses to be objectified, not to mention silenced, and her isolated voice will continue to haunt Vance throughout the film. While the trope of the "tough broad" is common in biker films, this trope is not often capitalized on, as it is here, to function as a critique of the "tough" male characters and their buddy relationships. *The Loveless* is best read as multi-logical and heterogeneous, in that the masculine iconography of the motorcycles, knives, and chains are examined lovingly by the camera while there is also a commentary on the effect of that iconography on the female characters. Within this contradiction, Telena represents a "competing ideological voice" in the film, one trying to win out over—or at least be heard with—the macho power plays demonstrated by the male buddies.

The depressing nature of Telena's situation is further disclosed soon after she and Vance have sex (which is not pictured) in a hotel room.

Vance's naked body is draped around hers as sunlight streams into the dim room through venetian blinds. Vance gets up and is barely dressed when gunfire rings out and Telena's father (J. Don Ferguson) barges into the room. As her father grabs her and leaves, she squeaks out, "Daddy, he ain't done to me nothin' you ain't done a hundred times before." Her statement suggests that her mother's suicide left Telena abandoned in the face of her father's violence and control. In this context, her sexual act with Vance might be seen as a rebellion against her possessive, abusive father.

The climax of the film, which again centralizes Telena, is set up through two acts of resistance by the other female characters, the diner waitress and Debbie (Davis's girlfriend). Everyone in the community, including the bikers (but not Telena), has gathered at a late-night bar. The waitress, whose husband left her some time ago and who feels rather trapped in this small town, initiates a strip tease on the bar. As she unselfconsciously performs for the patrons, her dance is coded as a resistance—as an attempt at escape from this town. The waitress casts off the narrow minds of her neighbors, whom she knows are judging her harshly, by creating a personal and intimate relationship with the music.

Meanwhile, outside, Debbie cheats on Davis, seducing another biker and having sex with him against the building wall. As soon as the waitress's strip tease is over, she is humiliated by the men who taunt her. But her degradation triggers Vance's remembrance of Telena's voice. The camera simultaneously tracks and pans toward him, until it reaches a tight close-up in which he is brightly lit against a dark backdrop. Telena's squeaky rebuttal about her father's abuse replays in his head. Notably, this voice is the only instance of subjective sound in the film, indicating the prominence of Telena's point of view.

Next, a fight breaks out in which Telena's father (a dominating oil man who has been spouting off about the "Commie" bikers all night) grabs one of the bikers while he is going to the bathroom and drags him out into the bar for a fight. Just as Vance is about to attack the father, shots ring out and Telena's father goes down. A medium shot reveals Telena in the door frame, barely visible through thick smoke, but brightly lit. All the music and commotion eerily dies down as we realize that she has just murdered her father. Her story has once again interrupted the action, but in an ironic way: she provides the Western shootout and the culmination of this seemingly aimless narrative. Not only does the shoot out save her from further abuse by her father, but it also saves the biker her father had attacked, while the other men in the bar stand around ineffectually.

It is important that the mise-en-scène presents her as a "surprise": where we expected to see Vance take action, she steps in. In fact, the camera frames him in a way that we cannot see his hands, and we assume that he holds the gun until the insertion of the shot of Telena. This editing strategy may indeed be seen as anticipating the opening sequence in *Blue Steel*, in which the protagonist, Megan Turner, is caught off guard in a training simulation when the "female victim" shoots her. Both sequences work because of the "surprise" of the woman.

Telena goes into her father's car and the camera tracks toward her, tightly framing her as she sits holding the gun. She looks at it, cocks it, puts it in her mouth and closes her eyes. As she fires, we see Vance's flinching reaction in medium shot. He then has a quick flashback to Telena in her car, laughing. One last close-up returns us to her bloodied face—she has died just as her mother did, by shooting herself in the head.

The few articles on Bigelow that mention *The Loveless* recount it as Vance's story. Two *American Film* articles and one *Interview* description reference it as a story about a gang of bikers and the film in which Willem Defoe makes his debut (Powers 1988: 49; Mills 1989: 59; Hamburg 84). However, *The Loveless* seems less about Vance or any transformation he may experience (he will certainly continue on his aimless journey) than about the tragic position of Telena and her limited forms of resistance. The centrality of her story acts as a subtle critique of Vance and his friends as they interrelate through superficial symbols of power and laugh at their one-upmanship of each other. It is Telena's story that adds the film's psychological "noir" component mentioned earlier; the thematic mystery is located in the examination of the ways in which Telena is prevented from representing her own experience. Telena's voice in *The Loveless* is the first of several that appear in Bigelow's subsequent films; it is a critical voice that questions the equity of gender politics and implicitly examines women's roles in the genre films that have traditionally been available to them. The slightly parodic portrayal of the biker gang also foreshadows the macho posturing of the surfers in the later *Point Break*.

NEAR DARK

Bigelow's second independent feature film, *Near Dark* (1987) (cowritten by Eric Red), quickly developed a youth cult following; because it is now part of the film collection at the Museum of Modern Art, it can be seen as straddling the distinction between high and low culture. This early work was only distributed to two cities, and it grossed $484,000 in its first week. According to *Variety*, it ranked number eleven at one time and averaged $4,360 per screen. (*Variety* employed different survey strategies than in later years, so comparisons are difficult to infer) (14 Oct. 1987.)

Near Dark, I will argue, employs the female character Mae to articulate alternative notions of "woman's" place in conventional genres. The film features Caleb, a farm boy growing into adulthood, who becomes kidnapped by a band of vampires and falls in love with the sexy vamp named Mae. He oscillates between his attraction to the unknown world she represents and the safe refuge promised by his return home. After finally conquering Mae's vampire family, he brings her back to his farm to join his family.

Near Dark provides a meeting place for two genres. The film combines elements of the Western and the vampire film, both of which have traditionally been used to work through ambivalent feelings toward nature and civilization, and both usually tell stories in which threatening natural forces are purged for the sake of society. The shot in *Near Dark* in which the vampire family's Winnebego glides into the frame to swoop Caleb off his farm visually recalls a similar one in *Nosferatu* (1927) in which the vampire's ship enters the landscape of the ocean. Even though Caleb's cowboy hat falls off, abandoned to the deserted landscape, references to the Western continue to mingle with vampire imagery throughout the film.

The tension produced by clashing signifiers like hats and horses (the Western) and blood and fire (the vampire film) corresponds to a series of dissonances involving gender and sexuality. If, as Steve Neale suggests, "genres do not consist only of films: they consist also, and equally, of specific systems of expectation and hypothesis that spectators bring with them to the cinema," then *Near Dark* represents an attempt to confound those expectations and revise generic categories (160).

Bigelow's genre blending results in an interesting tension between nature, femininity, and the home. In the vampire genre, nature yields a threatening side, as represented by the sexually ambiguous, animalistic vampire. Whether the vampire is male or female, s/he connotes a cultural threat: unstable femininity or, often, homosexuality. Meanwhile, the Western genre depends on the simultaneous promise of the frontier and its threat. Women traditionally represent both the threat of femininity (in association with the savage wilderness) and the threat of domestication. In this sense, men of the Western are both afraid of nature and intimidated by civilization—the genre provides a space for those fears to be worked out (Schatz 1988: 45–80).

In the odd formula of *Near Dark*, the sun, which allows for the development of Caleb's farm, becomes fatal once he is bitten by Mae. And, like the typical Western hero, who generally expresses uncertainty about nature, Caleb, after Mae's bite, experiences *multiple* ambivalences. Interestingly, Mae represents the threat of both nature and civilization (or domestication) at various places in the film. This is a result of a compli-

110

cated grafting of generic positions enabled by the intersection of the two formulas.

Most important, it is Mae who stands out. Through brighter lighting and make-up, she appears out of place in the film's generally dark and shadowy mise-en-scène—even more out of place than her vampire cohorts. She also prefigures Bigelow's tomboyish heroines, such as Megan in *Blue Steel* and *Point Break*'s Tyler. Mae is no sexually ambiguous male of the traditional vampire genre, nor is she a re-hash of the predatory female vamp. Although she eventually becomes the "civilizer" of the farm (by replacing Caleb's missing mother), she complexly represents both the threat of the animalistic vampire and the untamed nature of the Western. As the former, she is the dangerous vampire *and* the female victim, both of whom must be drained of their threatening repressed sexuality, i.e., sacrificed for the community. In other words, she complicates the place of the woman in the vampire film, refusing to embody Ellen, say, from *Nosferatu* (or Mina in Tod Browning's *Dracula* who follows in 1931). However, at the same time, she resists completely embodying the idealized, exalted woman of the Western, like Jane Ellen in *The Westerners* (1940), for whom civilization is restored at the end.[8]

While Mae does not have to uphold tradition by giving her life in order to stamp out the vampire's threat, her dangerous blood does get sucked out of her by film's conclusion, and by a rancher's veterinarian equipment (more animal imagery) no less. Nevertheless, the most significant aspect of this film, I think, involves Mae's ability to state her position within this convoluted and confused generic formula. In a sexualized exchange between Caleb and Mae, where his sucking of her blood intercuts with the bobbing of an oil rig, he nearly sucks too much from her. Her life in a delicate balance, she is forced to stop him, insisting that he will kill her if he takes too much. Unlike *Nosferatu*'s Ellen or Jane Ellen of *The Westerners*, Mae has the power to stop Caleb, to articulate his contribution to her demise. This scene illuminates the generic woman's position within both the vampire film and the Western—her life is put on the line to restore order in the former and, because of her alignment with civilization, to render nature's threat less powerful in the latter. Her character also functions to question the notion of nature altogether. Because any easy relation to nature is called into question, *Near Dark* suggests that "natural" categories, such as an inherent or essentialist "male" or "female," are unproductive.

To go further with this notion that Mae voices an alternative logic, we should look at the character of Sarah (Marcie Leeds), Caleb's young sister. Sarah ironically becomes captured by the same vampire who "turned" Mae, a young boy (Homer) who has of course been alive for many decades. Sarah realizes her situation early, however, and refuses to

111

Bigelow with Jenny Wright, who plays the conflicted vampire,
Mae. (De Laurentiis Entertainment Group)

become bitten, "like Mae" she says. Instead, she runs out of the hotel,
allowing the fatal sun into the room. Sarah's stubborn actions enable
Caleb's escape and, indeed, facilitate the family's return to the farm. Rebellious Sarah becomes the reason that Mae decides to allow the death
of her vampire family and to be transfused with cowboy blood, presumably to take on the role of mother who has been missing so far from this
picture. The potential for Sarah to grow into a woman unlike the generic
Western heroine—someone who echoes Mae's stubbornness and resis-

tance but with even more of a sense of vengeance—is enhanced by Mae's decision to join the farm.

In other words, *Near Dark* deploys a process of cultural problem-solving that questions women's places in genre pictures by refusing to offer the typical tropes. Although its finale restores order and recuperates femininity, my focus remains on the "genre problems" it has raised. Not only does the film bring into relief the typical woman's position (as sacrificial victim in vampire films and as tamed and elevated figure in the Western), it also searches out a new place for her—as heroic agent, as authoritative conveyor of sexual knowledge, as articulator of ideological constraints. In fact, whereas traditional genre films try to solve the problem of "woman," *Near Dark* (and, in turn, *Blue Steel*) attempts to solve women's problems.[9] Therefore, generic formulas are not only being revised but exploited to solve "new" ideological problems, ones not ordinarily addressed in conventional genres.

BLUE STEEL

Bigelow makes a similar authorial mark on *Blue Steel* (1990) (which, like *Near Dark*, was co-written by Eric Red) in three ways: combining two genres, challenging generic expectations, and centralizing the role of the female character. On an economic level, *Blue Steel* bridges counter cinema and Hollywood because it was produced independently by Ed Pressman and Oliver Stone, it was distributed by Vestron, and yet it made it onto 1,307 screens. It ranked number five at the box office, bringing in $2,895,744 in its first week. Aesthetically, too, *Blue Steel* is in between mainstream and counter cinema primarily because of the reversals Bigelow performs with the film noir and cop-psychothriller genres. One major reversal in the latter is her decision to place a woman in the typically male role of police officer. She also alludes to several Alfred Hitchcock films, namely those in which a woman investigates the riddle of sexual difference.

Cora Kaplan points out that with Jamie Lee Curtis's Megan Turner at the center of her narrative, Bigelow "mocks and mimes" the genre as she goes along (68).[10] (Also remember that Jamie Lee Curtis functions intertextually, not only because she played the "Final Girl" in John Carpenter's *Halloween* [1978], but also because of her mother Janet Leigh's famous role as a female victim—her death in *Psycho* [1960] is investigated by a Turner-like figure.) This is not to say that the position of "woman" functions on an essentialist level, inherently posing a "female difference." Rather, Megan's role as a cop calls definitions of "essential" femininity into question. Moreover, *Blue Steel* centralizes its alternative logic through a series of reversals and a recontextualization of the phallic status of the gun.

The first five sequences of the film represent a series of reversals in which Bigelow toys with the gender expectations embedded in the genre. In the film's first sequence, which establishes a tension between smooth tracking and unsteady hand-held shots (which continues through the film), Megan makes the mistake of letting her guard down during a training exercise, a simulation of a domestic violence call. In an unexpected turn, the female "victim" pulls a gun on Megan, suggesting already that gender reversals will make the difference here. The training officer tells Megan she needs to have eyes in the back of her head, which hints at the impossible position she's in within this simulation—not to mention within the parameters of the cop and film noir genres. As Mary Ann Doane has pointed out, film noir involves a crisis of vision, whereby the female character holds "the other side of knowledge," an epistemological status that disarms her and enables the drive of the narrative, which is always on some level a quest to decode femininity (102–3). In other words, Megan's position of knowledge, as well as her ability to see her way through this particular genre, is hindered by her gender—she "knows" what it is to be a female victim in a scenario such as this and, hence, blindly identifies with the woman who winds up turning on her.

Linda Mizejewski compares this opening sequence with the similar "rehearsal" sequence in *Silence of the Lambs* (1991) in which Clarice Star-ling (Jodie Foster) is accidentally "shot" from behind, mirroring the image of Megan's lack of vision (in the back of her head) (20). Mizejewski suggests these two sequences point to "rehearsals in genre," functioning as enactments where women test their own position of knowledge within the narrative. She lends further support to the interpretation of *Blue Steel* as a film that investigates the current possibilities and limitations for women's self-knowledge within so-called male genres.

Another notable attribute in the film's opening sequence involves the initial camerawork, where we at first see Megan's point of view through a hand-held camera. Megan then steps into the frame, from the left angle, and we are left with the filmmaker's, presumably Bigelow's, point of view. The original conflation of Megan and "Bigelow's" vision functions as obvious encouragement to consider the "woman behind the camera" in *Blue Steel*. Certainly many journalists have received the film in this way, likening Megan's pointing of the gun with Bigelow's aiming of the camera (Brown 62; Peary 93–94; Sharkey 7, 26). I am not suggesting that we should automatically agree with this connection between Megan and Bigelow, as two women in men's worlds; however, the metaphor should be acknowledged and considered (whereas the reviews I have read propose it unproblematically) as a possible reading of the film.

Jamie Lee Curtis's Megan Turner investigates her own
problematic position in *Blue Steel* (1990). (Vestron Pictures)

Moving on to the smokey blue opening credits, Bigelow offers a
second reversal: via close-up tracking over a Smith and Wesson, she re-
contextualizes the iconography of the gun by coding it as female. Rather
than impart the point of view of the bullets going into the chamber from
the outside in, she presents the insertion "from within" the chamber,
perhaps suggesting a point of view that is gendered female. Exaggerating
the fetishism of this phallic symbol—a fetishism common to the cop
genre—the film defamiliarizes conventional connotations of the gun,
asking us to examine the relation between the whole and the parts (i.e.,
the theory of phallic power and the practice, or how that theory breaks
down into everyday life). Also, during this caress of the gun, Bigelow
frames the spinning of the chamber as though it were a movie reel linking
the phallic discourses of weapons to those of the cinema (Mizejewski
15–16).

The third reversal occurs when, in the next sequence, the camera
tilts up a supposedly male body donning a police uniform. Once the camera reaches the upper torso of this figure, it reveals a lace bodice, yet
again confounding the expectation of a male body in this "male suit."

Bigelow toys with this scene as a drag performance, which foreshadows a later drag in which Megan steals an oversized police uniform from a male officer in order to do away with Eugene, the doppelganger figure who has become obsessed with Megan because of her weapon-wielding status. Following this early sequence, Megan graduates from the police academy with her best friend, Traci, at her side. While the other graduates pose for photographs with their wives and families, Megan is pictured with Traci, a fourth unexpected reversal of family where female homosocial bonds replace the nuclear unit.

In their pose, Megan jokingly points a gun at Traci's head, unwittingly providing the image we will later see when Eugene kills Traci while holding Megan around the neck. Until Traci's death, however, her enduring support for Megan provides a counterpoint to the typical homosocial male arrangements in the cop genre. Mizejewski contends that the female investigator in the cop genre "threatens to disrupt established power relations, calling into question not just her own heterosexuality, but that of the entire homosocial male milieu that she has infiltrated" (6). Through Megan and Traci's bond, which threatens to further disrupt those power relations, Bigelow lays bare and questions conventional constructions of gender and heterosexuality—constructions on which the genre is built but at the same time effaces.

A fifth reversal occurs as Megan returns home from her graduation. Wearing her new uniform as she walks down the street, Megan catches the eyes of two women who turn and smile at her. This gesture operates simultaneously as an acknowledgment of surprise at seeing a woman in (typically male) police attire as well as the possible expression of female desire (and hence a reversal of the "male gaze"). In any case, that the women take notice of Megan suggests that—because of her androgynous, boyish appearance—she transgresses conventional body politics governed by the binary opposition masculinity and femininity. Gender transgression is also implied by her last name, "Turner" (remember that her eventual male love interest is aptly named "Mann").

Toward the end of *Blue Steel*, Megan confronts Eugene as he searches for his gun, offering him a chance to grab at her own weapon, a move that would incriminate him. In a medium close-up of Megan's torso, she unzips her jacket to reveal her gun resting against one of her breasts. The mise-en-scène actually literalizes an equation where Megan's "phallus" depends not on male sexual imagery, but on a female breast.

Megan's dare—a symbolic challenge for Eugene to grasp her "phallus"—triggers flashbacks of Eugene's original vision of Megan when he witnessed her killing a supermarket robber. If he grabs her gun, he would in turn be admitting his dependence on his image of her as the symbolic carrier of the phallus. For his identity is now fed by his desire to mirror that image—to inhabit Megan's body because she represents the investment of the gun with lethal power, again power tied to female sexuality. Eugene's desire, which positions him as an outlaw (i.e., serial killer), is catalyzed by Megan's own status as an outlaw in the realm of body politics. Megan cannot "be" a woman's body in a male role; her gender trouble literally drives Eugene to violence.

At the same time, it is important to acknowledge Eugene's problematic portrayal as "ethnic other"—he is coded as "dark," "swarthy," perhaps Jewish. As his hysteria grows, he becomes more animalistic, so that by the time we reach the above sequence, he literally digs through the ground in search of his gun. His characterization implies the necessity of throwing a male body into crisis in order to attempt to investigate "woman" as body outlaw. Eugene's class status as a Wall Street stock trader also complicates Megan's struggle as a street cop who comes from working class roots. Somehow, Megan's desire to transcend her class designation also sets into motion Eugene's and her "gender trouble."

Although Bigelow may stay within the boundaries of the cop/psychothriller genre—where the gun is fetishized and women present a sexual threat—she reverses its terms by exploring what happens when the governing symbolic imagery changes due to a female presence that oscillates between femininity, masculinity, and androgyny. (Megan takes up various positions throughout the film.) At the same time, Bigelow underscores Megan's own illegitimate relationship to power, where she lacks credibility in the police department and struggles to punish not only the symbolic father, e.g., the police and lawyers who restrict her mobility, but also her own father who has abused her mother for years (a familial abuse that echoes *The Loveless*). Bigelow refuses to suggest that a mere substitution of a woman in a man's role—and one who is masculinized at that—ultimately reverses male power structures. Rather, she privileges the slippage between gender codes and modes of power, entertaining the possibility of disrupting those structures.

As suggested above, Bigelow also revises generic conventions by featuring the strength of female bonds, through Megan's friendship with Traci, perhaps as an answer to the central presence of male homosocial bonds in the cop genre. (Cop films traditionally centralize male partners whose buddy relationships displace any homosexual feelings by highlighting homosocial relations. A film such as *Lethal Weapon* relies on both the buddy relation between Danny Glover and Mel Gibson as well as the stable ties of Glover's nuclear family. Megan and Traci offer a counterpoint to both of these conventions by emphasizing female friendship, which is relatively unexplored territory in the cop film.)[11]

117

POINT BREAK

Bigelow's *Point Break*, distributed by Twentieth Century-Fox, is certainly more commercial than her previous three features. The film grossed $8,514,616 in its first week, appearing on 1,615 screens and ranking number eight at the box office. (Interestingly, Cameron's *T2* took first place, at that time in its second week of release.) With spectacular visual effects that include long surfing and skydiving scenes, Bigelow often experiments with the Steadicam in this film, creating fast-paced sequences with surprisingly minimal editing. (In this way, *Point Break* oddly harkens back to *The Loveless* with its unbroken shots and long takes.) While differences certainly exist between Bigelow's first studio film and her previous work, she continues to adapt generic conventions with *Point Break*, exploiting ideological contradictions in the interaction between Johnny (Keanu Reeves) and Bodhi (Patrick Swayze). Johnny's initial stint as an FBI agent, on the side of law and order, leads him into a friendship with the bank robber he is chasing—a spiritual surfer who justifies his crimes by indicting an overall patriarchal and callous system that produces mindless drones.

Predictably, Johnny finds himself drawn closer and closer to Bodhi and the lawless, more "natural," world he represents. The film's tension between civilized order and nature calls gender ideologies into question by positing two versions of the male action hero: Are gender categories innate? Are they performed? How does gender performativity destabilize other related power structures? Also typical of the cop/suspense genre, the narrative's epistemological drive is governed by the question of Johnny's similarity to Bodhi. How far from law and order can Johnny get? How should he confront the Bodhi within himself? However, if *Point Break* is at least partly a cop film, it is also very much a male buddy film, where Johnny and Bodhi's attraction to each other borders on male homosocial desire—a kinship driven by a longing to get outside the law.

The homoerotic overtones in Johnny and Bodhi's relationship, which usually occur implicitly in the action and buddy genres, are addressed rather overtly by the film. Alexander Doty notes the pleasure of the "space of sexual instability" created by classical Hollywood texts that focus on woman-woman or man-man relations (8). Indeed, *Point Break* feeds on the sexualized pleasure of the male bonding between Johnny and Bodhi, or, at the very least, it destabilizes masculinity by positing varied relations to male norms. Yvonne Tasker cites that Bigelow has referred to the film as a "wet western," noting that "rather than being centered on any tradition of detection or investigation, the film is usually given over to the spectacle of the male body engaged in physical feats such as surfing and skydiving" (163). For example, the way in which

118

Bigelow appears to be at home with the male stars of *Point Break* (1991). (Largo)

Johnny finally makes the connection that Bodhi is his sought-after criminal involves, as Tasker puts it, "a surfer's ass" (163). Toward the beginning of the film we see a security videotape of one of the bank robberies, where one of the robbers masked as "Lyndon B. Johnson" pulls down his pants and "moons" the camera (the words "Thank You" are etched on his behind). Johnny responds to the tape with an innuendo: "Good moves." Later, as Johnny watches Bodhi's gang surf the waves, one of them pulls down his bathing suit, "mooning" him, and he experiences a moment of recognition. He realizes the bank robbers have been right in front of him all along.

The fact that Johnny's identification occurs vis-à-vis this bodily spectacle suggests that the physical eroticism involved in "male bonding" represents the underlying drive of the narrative. Tasker argues against any simplistic interpretations of their relationship as typical "machoism," insisting that the film "draws out the implications of Utah and Bodhi's flirtation with death which is intimately bound up with their flirtation with each other. . . ." (164). (Their death wish, which is also common to the crime and buddy genres, is romanticized almost to the point of spoof.)

In fact, Patrick Swayze reveals that he "wanted to play it like a love story between two men" ("Swayze" 70). Swayze's decision to emphasize the homoeroticism in *Point Break* is shaped intertextually by his star persona as well. Because of his popular performance in *Dirty Dancing* (1987), Doty places him in the category of "a gay beefcake musical history . . . [which] provided the impetus for many gays to be more vocal about their 'low brow' sexual pleasure in supposedly high-cultural male bodies" (11). Given this history, Swayze's portrayal of Bodhi is more easily seen in terms of its bodily spectacle, which challenges conventions of masculinity, and homoeroticism (suggested by the growing attraction between Bodhi and Johnny), which exposes the implicit seams of the buddy film. His later performance as a drag queen in *To Wong Foo* (1995) may also contribute to a retroactive reading of the homoerotic overtones between Bodhi and Johnny.

At the intersection of gender and genre, the alternative logic I see in this film highlights the way in which the male buddy system relies on a problematic power structure that defines masculinity along a terrain of superficial symbols and facades. Underpinning Johnny and Bodhi's growing relationship is their tacit agreement on a certain critique of systematic power. Bodhi's articulation of this critique occurs once the two of them have "the same goal"—saving Tyler, a woman they both love whom Bodhi has put in jeopardy in order to manipulate Johnny. Tyler's character, yet another masculinized heroine in the tradition of Telena, Mae, and Megan, unfortunately has little screen time in this film, becoming a pawn between the two men. She functions as an object of exchange between them, for they seem more attracted to each other than to her. However, Tyler is remarkably self-conscious about her situation in relation to the two men, at one point leaving a campfire scene because "there's too much testosterone around here."

Once the two men have this agreed-upon goal of saving Tyler, which involves robbing a bank together, an act that will clearly get Johnny fired from the FBI, Bodhi explains: "It's basic dog psychology. . . . Project strength to avoid confrontation." In other words, wear the facade of the phallus in order to make peace. This statement is ironized by Bodhi's signature disguise for robbing banks, a Ronald Reagan mask. Gavin Smith has made the point that *Point Break* provides a satirical critique of the Reagan years with its visual imagery of Reagan (Bodhi's disguise) spraying fire out of a petroleum pump and ransacking the houses of a quiet suburban neighborhood. In response to Smith, Bigelow laughingly replied, "That's what's so fabulous about the medium. It enables you to work on so many different levels. If you were simply to do a critique of the last decade, it'd be so didactic it'd be painful. Satire is such a potent tool" (Smith 49).

The film also operates as satire because in acknowledging, perhaps winking at, the 1980s Reaganite ideology of hypermasculinity and what Susan Jeffords characterizes as male fantasy films, Johnny and Bodhi's own status as male buddies becomes implicated within the world of the film (1994). That is, the over-the-top romanticism and easy familiarity with the conflicts of these characters forces a distancing wedge between the 1980s formula films and this reflexive take off. The test of which character is the better man, the masculine ideal, is decided by the one who projects the most strength as they self-consciously posture their own symbolic power. Ultimately, Johnny will win because he has better learned the lesson that masculinity is performed.

Their most marked difference appears when they are supposed to have "the same goal," the final bank robbery. Bodhi has emptied the bullets out of Johnny's gun and neglected to give him a presidential mask. Johnny's power, then, depends on how well he can "project strength to avoid confrontation." How well will he live up to the patriarchal ideal that they both profess to despise? After the robbery, one of the film's most surprising twists occurs when Bodhi parachutes out of a plane, leaving Johnny with his gun but no chute. Unexpectedly, Johnny grabs the gun and jumps out of the plane after Bodhi, eventually grabbing onto him in mid-air. Having established that power is more posture than "truth"—and that guns, though they are real weapons that can kill, serve as the surficial symbol on which power lies—Bodhi forces Johnny into a major conflict by refusing to pull his chute. Hence, Johnny must drop his gun to save their lives or hold on pointlessly to a weapon that suddenly serves him little purpose in the face of death. As the two men cling to each other, Johnny must contemplate which choice—pulling the chute or pulling the trigger—holds more meaning and the best opportunity for survival. (Bodhi cares more about meaning while Johnny is more invested in survival.) Johnny is forced by these circumstances to temporarily drop the "phallus."

A second major twist occurs in the final sequence and suggests their simultaneous rejection of the masculine ideal that rests on external symbols of power. Johnny has tracked Bodhi down and is backed up by an FBI squadron ready to take him in. He signals his presence by throwing the Reagan mask into the ocean at Bodhi's feet, the facade of their male dance with power now down. However, surprisingly, Johnny releases Bodhi, letting him surf his last wave—knowing, though, he will die in the process. In a final gesture, Johnny throws his badge into the ocean, presumably to see it join with Bodhi's mask. Both law/order and nature have been refuted out of hand—Johnny now subscribes to a new directive based on performativity, which may hold options other than a symbolic power governed by gestures and masks or "natural" definitions of strength and identity.

My argument here is not to elevate *Point Break* as a progressive film but rather to suggest that, yet again, Bigelow addresses discourses of power, specifically gender politics, by exploiting generic tensions. She re-writes the ideological tensions of sameness and difference, and law and nature, by implicitly critiquing the very values of the Reagan era that fostered the success of the action genre. For all of my work to defend *Point Break* as a reflexive and politically intriguing film, it can of course be read "straight" as a genre film geared toward male adolescents. My point is that several logics run through the film, some mainstream and some alternative, each contradicting the other and undermining a monolithic reading.

I would argue that Bigelow's constant re-writing of generic convention and her shifting iconography of symbolic imagery signal her own authorial enterprise as a woman working within commercial cinema. Taking *The Loveless* as her point of departure enables us to specifically locate a trajectory where genre-blending, narrative twists, and cultural problem-solving formulate a critique of dominant representation from within. The alternative "voice" represented by Telena in *The Loveless* (which questions its own fragile position while also demanding to speak) continues to grow—in *Near Dark*, *Blue Steel*, and *Point Break*—into resistant logic that questions easy or natural definitions of gender and power. If I had to sum up that logic, it would be Bigelow's insistence on the irresoluteness of gender oppositions.

STRANGE DAYS

I would like to briefly mention Bigelow's 1995 *Strange Days*, although this film does not engage in generic tensions as obviously as other Bigelow films. *Strange Days* does raise similar issues of gender and power by positing a future noir world where a technological device called a wire trip circulates like a narcotic throughout a seedy underground culture. The male protagonist (Ralph Fiennes) deals out these virtual reality experiences (sexual follies, store robberies), which can be played back by his customers through the brain. He is launched into a mystery when a prostitute friend of his is brutally raped and murdered while her attacker wears a wire trip—and forces her to wear one too. Set in a world of social chaos where racial tensions have reached a threatening intensity, *Strange Days* becomes an odyssey into male voyeurism. Clearly influenced by postmodernism, it breaks down the supposed line between subject and object, spectator and spectacle. It also presents a rare inter-racial romance between the characters of Lenny (Fiennes) and Mace (Angela Bassett). According to co-writer/producer Cameron, his greatest contributions involved the technologies and setting of the film, while director Bigelow introduced the subplot of racism, which involves the police brutality and murder of an outspoken African American rapper, Jeriko One (1996: i–ii).

Through several wire-trip rape sequences, *Strange Days* explores the possibilities of male identification and empathy with female victims. Lenny undergoes a transformation—a coming to terms with female victimization and racial conflict—by being able to "experience" these realities first-hand. He also confronts something of a Lacanian "mirror phase" moment toward the end of the film when he turns to a mirror after seeing a simulated rape of his former girlfriend through the rapist's eyes. Lenny looks at himself in the mirror and beholds the rapist reflected back at him, because he still wears the superconducter. Is the rapist what he was (i.e., an ideal ego) or who he wants to be (i.e., an ego ideal)? Would he "know" the difference?

However, despite Lenny's transformation and the compelling issues of voyeurism and looking relations raised by *Strange Days*, it also seems governed by Lenny's male narcissism with numerous reaction shots that emphasize his "pain" rather than that of the victims. In this scenario, Lenny battles the threat of the female subject-position by territorializing it. As I have argued thus far, both logics—one that centralizes male subjectivity and re-secures masculine identity, and one that critiques the very male fantasy it features—probably exist alongside one another, articulating contradiction and creating internal pressure.[12]

By rewinding and fast-forwarding through Bigelow's films—and thereby refusing to adhere to the counter-cinema/Hollywood divide—we can begin to locate her complication of genre conventions and her re-casting of the politics of gender and sexuality. While there is no need to label Bigelow's films "feminist" per se, they certainly move within a "feminist orbit" and engage political issues. Her films encourage spectators to ask questions about gender, genre, and power.

3

LIZZIE
BORDEN

LIZZIE BORDEN'S INDEPENDENT FILMS, *Born in Flames* (1983) and *Working Girls* (1986), which have been aimed at female audiences, centralize feminist debates by creating fantasy spaces in which women's relationships to one another can be examined. *Born in Flames* depicts the coalescence of diverse women into a feminist revolution; *Working Girls* interrogates both male and female fantasies about prostitution by focusing on a day in the life of a middle-class working girl. Her commercial film, *Love Crimes* (1991), shares a similar fascination with female fantasy in that the protagonist begins to explore her own sexual desires after she becomes drawn into an investigation of a voyeur who exploits women. All three films represent a commitment to working through various forms of women's fantasies, although they approach the narrativization of those fantasies in very different ways.

The term "fantasy" carries several connotations, including the classification of certain (typically demeaned) genres and spectatorial modes. But "fantasy" has also achieved a certain currency in feminist theory in reference to a subjective process whereby the film industry circulates and makes dominant public fantasies for mass consumption. Elizabeth Cowie and Teresa de Lauretis, in particular, have discussed the psychic processes of fantasy and desire as they occur in the structurings of film and in spectator responses (1984 and 1994 respectively). Cowie reminds us that "fantasy is the *mise-en-scène* of desire, the putting into a scene, a staging, of desire" (71). In other words, fantasy does not require a desired object—there is an absence or lack involved. Fantasy moves forward through a series of stagings or wishes that provide a setting for the subject. Perhaps Cowie's most valuable, and most controversial, assertion is the proposal that while sexual difference may be fixed in film spectatorship, subject positions are not; therefore, the spectator may shift his or her identification between various characters and film structures (102).

While de Lauretis shares Cowie's interest in fantasy as both a private and public process, she responds to Cowie with a certain degree of skepticism. De Lauretis worries that she affords the spectator too much agency; de Lauretis also shifts the origin of film fantasy away from the author and toward the spectator (126). She suggests that any given classical film "becomes the mise-en-scène of the spectator's desire" through the Oedipal positions figured in original fantasies (127).

The works of both Cowie and de Lauretis provide compelling terms through which to study filmic fantasy: original fantasies (as described in the psychoanalytic model) offer up positions of desire that are then utilized by spectators as they psychically respond to narrative. As Cowie explains: "What is necessary for any public forms of fantasy, for their collective consumption, is not universal objects of desire, but a setting of desire in which we can find our place(s). And these places will devolve, as in the original fantasies, on positions of desire: active or passive, feminine or masculine, mother or son, father or daughter" (87). With this understanding of fantasy, Borden's films prove quite interesting for the way in which they activate positions of desire, most specifically, women's desire to see their way out of a culturally bound system that defines their lives through sexual difference. If primal fantasies provide the child with a framework for attempting to solve the enigma of sexual difference, then Borden's films deploy fantasy in order to better understand the social and cultural riddles of women's oppression. In this context, Oedipal struggles and origin fantasies are seen as political sites. Her films, all of which I would argue represent "works in progress" (in the sense that they serve as vehicles for thinking through particular social problems), set out to better navigate women's relation to their material world.

While *Born in Flames*, at its release, incurred some resistance from female audiences for its militaristic representations of women bearing arms, Borden insists that it be read as a "what if" fantasy for women who might otherwise become disillusioned by a backlash against feminism. She contends that the film is "about reformulating desire, rekindling hope" for women who were becoming depoliticized after the launch of the second-wave feminist movement (Sussler 1983: 29). In a similar move, *Working Girls* addresses the political debates about prostitution that became incredibly heated in the middle 1980s, especially between groups such as Women against Pornography and Anti-Censorship Feminists. The film displaces sexuality in favor of a focus on the economic issues of middle-class prostitution, thereby deromanticizing very power-ful mainstream images of prostitution. *Working Girls* eventually becomes a film about the female protagonist's desire to quit her job, which is shown to provide good pay and special female friendships, but, like many women's jobs, very little respect or self-fulfillment.

Love Crimes, while a commercially backed film fraught with ideologi-cal tensions, most explicitly attends to female fantasy and sexual desire. Sean Young plays a masculinized assistant district attorney (Dana) who pursues her own masochistic fantasies through her investigation of a sex-ually exploitative photographer. Her simultaneous desires to succumb to his mastery and to arrest him are related to an early childhood trauma where she witnessed her adulterous father murder her mother. This film, in and of itself, represents an intersection between independent and com-mercial film in that after its theatrical distribution by the pre-Disney Miramax, Borden released an unrated director's cut through HBO that now appears on many video store shelves. The inclusion of six scenes changes the power configuration between Dana and the photographer, ultimately encouraging a progressive reading of Dana's agenda.

BORDEN'S BEGINNINGS

Lizzie Borden's history as a feminist filmmaker begins with her ap-propriation of the name of an accused murderess. The 1890s Lizzie Bor-den who "gave her mother forty whacks" (and her father forty-one) with an ax has become an American legend. Who was this (deviant) woman who allegedly murdered both of her parents in the family parlor? As history books convey, Lizzie was found innocent of the crimes; however, through oral tradition, the legend continues to name her as guilty. Linda Borden took a fascination to this rhyme at age eleven, and she announced to her parents that she was changing her name to Lizzie (certainly a preferable alternative to whacking them to death). Positioning herself as a resister of cultural norms, Borden says: "At the time, my name was the best rebellion I could make" (Mills 47).

After graduating from Wellesley College, Borden moved to New York City, seeking out a "bad girl image" and moving away from writing art criticism (in part for *Art Forum*) into painting (47). A retrospective of Jean-Luc Godard films inspired her to experiment with cinema, and she insisted (until recently) on remaining "unstudied," favoring a "naive" approach to film production. Borden began by financing a short film about abortion through her work as an editor for Richard Serra. She continued to support herself through editing over the five years it took to make *Born in Flames* on a budget of $40,000. That film was a collabo-rative process in which actors, many of whom were grass roots feminists,

Director Lizzie Borden on the set of *Love Crimes* (1991).
(Sovereign Pictures)

played themselves and sometimes improvised. What began as a project about white feminist responses to an oppressive government evolved into a story about women of color, lesbians, and white women of various classes mobilizing into collective action. Anne Friedberg has noted how the production of *Born in Flames* enfranchised black, Latina, and poor women in the telling of their stories; and the distribution attempted to reach audiences composed of these groups, constituencies not always targeted by experimental cinema (1984: 43).[1] This first feature helped make a name (albeit a controversial one) for Borden as a self-identified feminist interested in pushing the representational limits of women's experiences.

BORN IN FLAMES

Born in Flames establishes a kaleidoscope of women's perspectives, including a militant women's army, two underground radio stations,

128

black women (many of whom are reluctant to embrace feminism), lesbians (many of whom are women of color), middle-class white journalists, housewives, and labor unionists. However, three major points of view are represented by Adelaide (a black woman highly visible in the women's army), Isabel (a white punk rapper at Radio Regazza), and Honey (an African American DJ on Phoenix Radio). Adelaide's position is reinforced by Zella Wylie, played by Flo Kennedy in a rendition of her real life role as an outspoken civil rights attorney. Borden sets into motion a conversation between these different and stubborn perspectives, bringing various feminisms to the screen "in the worlds of living, breathing people" (Hulser 1984: 15). She attempts to cinematically map the slogan "the personal is political" in all of its contradictory meanings.

Teresa de Lauretis has celebrated *Born in Flames* for the way it uses a pervasive musical beat to evoke spectatorial identification (1988: 189–90). She finds an alternative means of identification in the film, arguing that the music provides a unifying point of contact for the various women's voices, replacing the classical approach of cinematic psychological identification. De Lauretis also posits that Borden produces a "feminist de-aesthetic" (as opposed to a feminine aesthetic) through the layering of women's articulations and a dialectical expression of feminist voices.

The strength of *Born in Flames*—its radical aesthetic quality—relies on compelling editing techniques. Borden's gritty, pseudo-documentary style presents a disjunctive collage of women's individual and collective work. For example, one montage combines images, all shot in medium close-up, that include the feeding of a bottle to a baby, the accounting of records, the wrapping of chicken parts, rolling a condom onto a penis, washing dishes, preparing surgical instruments, cutting hair, and passing out political flyers. The seemingly unrelated details link up through their rhyming juxtaposition of women's work. A later montage edits together women's various actions as they rally for gender equality. Women's work appears in its political context; the film presents their labor not haphazardly occurring within the rubric of false consciousness, but rather as deliberate, self-conscious, political action.

The layered and disjunctive style of *Born in Flames* delivers a fantasy that sees women's differences as an asset to collective efficacy rather than an obstacle. Borden and her collaborators set the stage for a fantasy of women gathering together to overcome divisions by race, class, sexual orientation, and political identification. There is, for example, the fantasy of Adelaide approaching Honey, a woman she barely knows, in a supermarket and asking her to help publicize the woman's army. Honey replies, "I'd like to say yes, but I'm working with some other women right now. And I wouldn't want to commit myself for them. So maybe we can talk some other time. Okay?" Honey does not run away from this "radical" when approached while doing her grocery shopping. No manager

comes forth to say, "No soliciting on the premises." Honey coincidentally already has feminist ties. She respects them so deeply that she would
not presume to speak for others in her constituency. This is a slice of
feminist fantasy.

In her desire to imagine feminist mobilization, Borden presents a

Considered "guerilla filmmaking," *Born in Flames* (1983) uses
pseudo-documentary fragments to tell the story of women who
come together from very different backgrounds. (First Run
Features; call 1–800–488–6652 to order *Born in Flames*.)

130

variety of women's rhetorical positions, thereby concentrating on issues of language and communication. For example, Zella Wylie expounds on the collective power of women's difference. She tells Adelaide that a hypothetical group of white businessmen would be much more frightened by five hundred mice storming their doors down than one lion. Wylie insists, "Five hundred mice can do a lot of damage and destruction." Her assertion quite clearly states the film's thematic position: a coalition of differences ultimately becomes more powerful than a small, but unified front. In another (humorous) example of managing difference, Honey fields the criticism of an African American friend who is skeptical about the women's army. The woman makes fun of the white feminists who ride on bicycles blowing whistles in order to stop sexual assault; to her, this kind of activism seems ridiculously bound in whiteness. While supportive of the army, Honey understands her friend's rhetorical stance.

In further discussion of difference and communication, the Belle Gayle talk show furnishes a forum for white middle-class discussions of rhetorical and political strategies. Gayle's program conveys sardonic humor in its portrayal of feminist and psychoanalytic rhetoric. At one point, she and the socialist feminists featured on her show (played by Kathryn Bigelow, Becky Johnston, and Pat Murphy) reduce the desires of the women's army's to "revolution envy"—a jealousy of the 1960s political movements. In a second instance of biting humor, Gayle hosts a psychoanalyst who unwittingly satirizes Oedipal theory by posing that the women's army is merely expressing its primary masochism through secondary sadist acts of violence. In other words, white academic feminists, whose viewpoint is usually privileged over other feminists', provide answers for women's mobility that are no better than anyone else's.

The power of the media, in its communication of rhetorical stances, comes to represent the centrifugal force of the film: "documentary" footage of the women's army mingles with the Belle Gayle show, news briefs, televised presidential and mayoral speeches, newspaper headlines, and FBI surveillance tapes. The insidiousness of the media creeps in as one becomes confused as to whether she is watching Adelaide Norris through the eyes of cinema verité or through the lens of FBI secret cameras. Characterizing the odd distortion of subject/object relations—the refusal to acquiesce to notions of cinematic truth—Hulser suggests, "Sometimes 'we' watch them . . . sometimes 'they' watch us" (14). The camera is deployed from a number of sites, suggesting that its power is neither absolute nor static. Hence, the language of *Born in Flames* seems to make claims about language more broadly, which is to say that it is mediated, and a rhetorical mediation at that.

Once Adelaide has been killed by the government, the socialist-feminist reporters debate how to visually represent her death, highlighting

131

the larger internal debate about women's access to and power over the images that represent their experiences. A close-up on the photograph reveals Adelaide's dead body lying on a jail cell floor. The three women reporters are off-screen, with only one of their hands shown in the frame as it lays out the photos. In their conversational voice-over, the feminists discuss whether it is okay to fetishize the image of Adelaide's body in order to mobilize women. One reporter asks, "Can't you mobilize them in other ways?" *Born in Flames* uses this supposedly real image, which is of course a fiction of the film, to catalyze a discussion about the potential function of visual images for the purpose of political movement. As a director, Borden self-critically asks, How are my images working? Doesn't their "violent" content activate valuable discussion? How might public modes of communication be appropriated by feminists?

Adelaide's murder indeed becomes a catalyst for the various constituencies of women. The socialist-feminist reporters rally together and write a newspaper story when Adelaide dies, eventually leaving their jobs after the socialist paper threatens their position within the women's army. The Phoenix and Regazza radio stations come together to build a new underground station when Regazza is destroyed, agreeing to represent Adelaide and the women's army. And significantly, the station announces that it will be moving around the dial in order to avoid any one fixed position, a symbolic move toward resolving the women's rhetorical differences. The film ends with the women's bombing of a network television tower, clearing the politically stagnant airwaves for new feminist communications by this nascent coalition. The setting for Borden's fantasy of women coming together to bridge the real and hypothetical spaces that keep us divided concludes with a context for a fresh fantasy— she sets the stage for imagining what new forms of women's collective language might look like when broadcast nationally.

Although the film frames the mobilization of the women's army in terms of fantasy, it was attacked by some feminists for celebrating violence. The point of the critique was that the militaristic discourse in *Born in Flames*, and the final "answer" of anarchic brute force, recalled precisely the "male" ideologies of violence that feminists were trying to avoid (Friedberg 1984: 40). Because the film presented such an optimistic picture of women coming together across differences, it disappointed some when it began to "spiral" into destruction. These responses deserve to be taken seriously and they point to the gravity and materiality of the film's subject matter. It seems to me that the scene in which the reporters debate the use of Adelaide's photograph suggests that Borden was grappling with the implications of violence throughout the film and attempting to present those theoretical struggles as self-consciously as possible.

I read *Born in Flames* as an attempt to fashion a new primal fantasy.

132

The social overthrow of the father, as represented in the socialist government, is a necessary part of this fantasy. But it is markedly overshadowed by the attempt to create positions for all kinds of women, not one "theoretical" daughter. If this is an Oedipal journey—and I use this term loosely to convey women's coming into knowledge about themselves and the material conditions around them—it is one in which women move away from questions of sexual difference and toward discovering and embracing the differences among them, as de Lauretis has proposed. Their desires to challenge oppressive social struggles are intertwined with their desires to discover the strength in each other.

In addition to the critiques of the use of violence in *Born in Flames*, the film has been attacked for its emphasis on fantasy. At the 1985 Society for Cinema Studies conference, some panelists suggested that Borden was "politically naive" for positing fantasy as an out for difficult questions about women's difference (Brunette 1986: 54). While Borden was congratulated for her refreshing approach to feminist politics, she was accused of ignoring the material, economic, and racial problems that keep the kind of coalescence she envisioned from actually coming about. It may indeed be problematic to confront politics with fantasy, and Borden's continual work within this realm may perpetuate this difficulty. However, she casts a unique light on fantasy each time she takes it up in a film, continuing to probe complex and controversial feminist questions—even if she admittedly lacks concrete, untroubled answers.

WORKING GIRLS

Borden's second feature maintains more than stylistic and thematic similarities to *Born in Flames*. *Working Girls* was inspired by some of the women who participated in *Born in Flames*, who coincidentally supported themselves through prostitution. In fact, as Borden discovered that more and more women she knew worked in middle-class prostitution houses (although because of their appearance or demeanor they might not be suspected of it), she decided to make a film about their experiences. Borden directed, edited, co-wrote (with Sandra Kay who plays Gina in the film), and co-produced this film on a budget of $110,000. If in *Born in Flames* Borden works through the fantasy of women coming together across racial, class, and sexual lines, here she confronts both male and female fantasies about prostitution. Because prostitutes are positioned as social outcasts, and because their film often hyper-sexualizes their world, the realities of prostitution remain elusive. *Working Girls* is committed to de-romanticizing prostitution, exposing it as the economic contract it inevitably is. In so doing, the film debunks many myths about prostitutes and deconstructs the good girl/bad girl stereotypes that keep many mid-

133

dle-class "good" women guessing about what goes on behind "closed doors."

Borden's filmic technique represents a decision to go behind these doors in order to paint her subject matter unglamourously and unerotically. She demystifies the myths and taboos that enshroud paid sex by routinizing the work of a middle-class prostitute. Women are shown inserting diaphragms, taking showers, setting out sheets and towels, and gargling with antiseptic. They enforce similar rules of hygiene with their male clients. As Ann Snitow points out, Borden concentrates on the ways prostitution is merely "sex-on-the-job and we get the details, daily schedules, and job conditions of workers" (1987: 20). Romance and pleasure are drained out of the cinematic imagery as male tricks are turned again and again; the motivation for all the women portrayed here is economic, period.

For example, Borden provides a close-up on Molly (the protagonist played by Louise Smith) positioning a Kleenex just so as she eases a used condom into her hand and wraps it up. This shot recalls the similar one in *Born in Flames* of a woman's hand rolling a condom onto a penis—both shots stress the centrality of women's work when it comes to servicing male desire. In another instance, the voice of a client is heard inquiring "Is there anyone else like me?" as a close-up of Molly's hands shows her recording her most recent payment in her tabulation booklet. This film disputes the common stereotypes that prostitutes are spurred into the profession through abused childhoods, drug addiction, or nymphomania by clearly positing middle-class prostitution as an alternative to the many lower-paying jobs open to women. Molly, because she has two degrees from Yale and is a feminist photographer, further challenges prostitution stereotypes and functions as an indication of how difficult it is for even middle-class, well-educated women to survive economically.

It's worth noting that, as might be expected, this film's consideration of women's exploitation is defined more politically and sensitively than it was in the film that emerged two years later and boasted the similar name of *Working Girl* (starring Melanie Griffith, Harrison Ford, and Sigourney Weaver). Melanie Griffith plays a hard-working secretary who combats sexism, classism, and corporate elitism in order to become a top executive—yet her struggle is configured as a personal and often comical one. Ironically, one of the most quoted lines of that film—"I've got a head for business and a bod for sin"—echoes one of Molly's lines: "I'm already renting my body; I don't want to sell my mind." The former attempts to diminish the protagonist's threat by sexualizing her; the latter demonstrates the protagonist's determination to retain her individual strengths and autonomy in a world resolved to objectify her.

The aesthetics of *Working Girls*, which are grounded in conventions of 1970s counter cinema, contribute to its deconstructive slant. While the film is not as gritty and disjunctive as *Born in Flames*, it operates as pseudo-documentary, often utilizing minimal camerawork and real time. Its simplistic lighting, reliance on medium and close-up shots, and re-strained editing create an unself-conscious style that frames women's bodies realistically. Molly's repeated dressing and undressing in front of the camera eventually becomes commonplace and asexual. At the same time, Molly's home life is barely featured, as though the film protects her love relationship as "private space." At the beginning and end of the film she lays in bed with her lesbian lover, Diane (played by Deborah Banks), who is African American. However, that is the extent to which their personal life is subjected to "the look" of the camera. In the few scenes at home, the routinization of Molly's job is foreshadowed by the morning routines that she, Diane, and Diane's young daughter perform. They practically sleepwalk through the house during their daily preparations, which include going to the bathroom, dressing, pouring juice, and reading at the breakfast table.

The minimalist aesthetics of the camera coincide with an acting style based on women's performativity. The actresses (with the exception of Smith) might be said to be overacting, often relating with a high pitched, slightly contrived tone of voice. Their performances, though, occur within the context of male desire—the "masquerade" in which they participate offers them a degree of power with their male clients. The women deploy their femininity strategically and defensively as a way of denying the supposedly phallic power of the men who enter the house (for a more complex discussion of "masquerade," see Doane 1991).[2] Lucy (played by Ellen McElduff), the exploitative madam and the one who has most perfected the art of performativity, explains, "It's the only tone of voice a man responds to."

The women clearly go into performance mode once they are with a trick, as suggested by a camera tilt down through a glass table that captures Molly sliding her stockinged foot into a pump at the sound of the doorbell. Working girls "perform" their roles, feigning pleasure for the purpose of income. The acting style in the film asks us to question the authenticity of women's pleasure when framed within the context of male desire. Borden's emphasis on what she calls "the theater of sex" suggests that while white, heterosexual, middle-class men have social power, their weakness is that they can never be sure when they are getting sex contrived or for real (Kramer 1987: 219).

In fact, Borden's characters derive power from the way that their customers remain at the mercy of their own male sex drives. According to Snitow, the women "can look down on the vulnerable flesh of the very men" who might dominate them outside of this sex-for-hire arena (21). The controlled atmosphere of the "house" allows the prostitutes to demand exact payment for finely outlined services: the male consumer seems somewhat defined by the female "producer." One particularly resonant shot occurs when Jerry, an obnoxious, joke-telling misogynist, requests oral sex from Gina. All that is shown, once she has moved below his waist, is Jerry's ripe naked belly in the foreground and a jar of Vaseline, a clock, and baby wipes in the background. Even without Gina in the shot, her subjectivity takes over, demeaning, indeed satirizing, any pleasure Jerry might experience.

The women also enjoy a degree of power because of their collective spirit, although working in this prostitution house does not afford them much time to connect with one another. Not all of the women get along, and some of them are divided along lines of race and age resulting in female competition. However, Molly, Gina, and Dawn (Amanda Goodwin) establish a model for female friendship that empowers them in the face of their condescending, profit-driven employer Lucy. In an early scene, the camera frames them extremely closely as they discuss their reasons for "working." (In keeping with the film's refusal to romanticize, the women also rambunctiously stuff their faces with food in a way that de-glamorizes them.) Here, the women are as close as they are going to get to each other: they giggle and chat, forgetting for a few minutes that they are at work. When the doorbell rings, interrupting their conversation, Dawn responds by groaning, "I don't feel like fucking." The context in which these characters perform their labor detours them from any sustained connection or opportunity for lasting friendship.

Borden's insights into common prostitution fantasies, which rely on sexualized and sexist portrayals of women, extend beyond this study of a particular prostitute's daily life by illuminating the male-female power dynamics of middle-class prostitution. Borden suggests: "It's much less about prostitution than about heterosexual codes and rituals in our culture" (Jackson 1987: 6). She agrees with advocates of legalized prostitution who argue that many women barter their bodies within the context of marriage or dating. By emphasizing the economics of prostitution and then offering it up as a metaphor for gender relationships, the film critiques cultural codes of heterosexuality. For example, in one *Working Girls* scene, the soundtrack presents Gina describing the prices and availability of the girls to a caller while the image on screen shows Molly politely fixing her client a drink. The economic underpinnings of this rehearsal of heterosexual romance—"can I get you a drink?"—are exposed. Borden would like for her viewers to notice how these relationships ultimately become "policed to a level of routine" (6). Marriage and the nuclear family are implicated by the mere existence of prostitution—

its existence implies that the former fail, on some level, at channeling sexual desire and organizing heterosexual relationships.

While this critique of heterosexuality seems more apparent in Borden's public discussions about *Working Girls* than in the film itself, the film nevertheless functions quite well as a critique of the fantasies and myths that have been built up around prostitution. An anti-erotic approach to the generally secretive practices of prostitutes re-focuses the issue onto economic concerns. Molly's decision to quit the job at the end of the film reflects more on her desire to escape the materialistic and exploitative Lucy, who represents a kind of "Everyemployer," than on the profession of prostitution itself. The primary reason for her quitting is that she has been forced to work a double shift. Whereas *Born in Flames* relies on the building of a fantasy world, this film endeavors to tear one down by inserting it into a material context.

Working Girls also provides a counterpoint to mainstream images of prostitution, which Borden describes as a highly developed body of cinematic imagery generated by male fantasy and focused on working-class prostitutes, street culture, and violence (5). The fact that this house represents a "protected space" in which the women have a certain degree of agency and a reduced risk of violence means that Molly's world is largely disassociated from the more threatening aspects of working-class prostitution. Borden's attempt to re-codify these traditional images of prostitution, in order to more adequately represent women's experiences, also exists as a re-appropriation of the fantasies surrounding prostitution.

LOVE CRIMES

Love Crimes, Borden's first commercial feature, fits squarely in the category of the woman's psychothriller. Films like this one, including *Blue Steel*, *Silence of the Lambs* (1991), *Sleeping with the Enemy* (1991), and *Copycat* (1995), portray women's investigations of their own victimization and are located within the broader socio-historical context of a political backlash against women. These thrillers centralize female protagonists as investigative heroines trying to overcome their own powerlessness through their conviction to stop some kind of male villain from preying on women.

As I mentioned in my introduction, a paradox currently exists in which, though women are gaining more power in executive and creative roles within the industry, there is a political backlash against feminism that continues to be waged with this industry's very own representations. The psychothriller/"rising heroine" films have occurred contemporaneously with this paradox, perhaps as an outlet for women to cinematically

137

explore the effects of sexism and backlash politics (albeit not in a political or economic context). Perhaps this category of film functions as an allegory for the growing numbers of women confronting male-dominated structures within the Hollywood industry.

The woman's psychothriller is one of the few genres that focus on women's subjectivities, especially women's experience as sexual objects. Unlike most in its category (with the exception of *Blue Steel*), *Love Crimes* was directed by a woman. The film was also re-written by Laurie Frank (after originally being scripted by Allan Moyle), a female screenwriter requested by Borden. Borden's presence on the film, however, does not insure a feminist viewpoint. Although she found herself in the position to direct a mainstream production, with a six-million-dollar budget and a credit as co-producer, her degree of power over the film, in terms of executive decisions, distribution and marketing measures, and technical choices ended up being rather limited. As Borden puts it, she was "dealing with everyone else's psyches . . . with their fetishes, and what they don't like" (Lucia 1993: 7). In other words, various incarnations of male fantasy informed the narrative drive, or perhaps even created multiple narrative drives. The fact that *Love Crimes* was financed by two companies—one American and one European—contributed to these tensions. Borden told me: "I was dealing with two companies that had different visions of the film and, therefore, there was lots of interference not just with me, but between each other" (author's interview, 7 Aug. 1996).[3]

I should also note that Borden never meant for the film to be classified as a women's psychothriller. It was pressure from Miramax that cumulatively shaped *Love Crimes* into a genre film. Borden explains:

> It was a movie basically constructed for a certain kind of audience that was not originally the audience that I intended the film to be for. So it changed intention mid-stream and it turned into a genre movie, where in the beginning I had no intention at all of making a genre film. (author's interview, 7 Aug. 1996)

Industry demands for a definable product, and the general commercial success of genre films, influenced the nature of the film. The thriller aspects developed once the film was in production and had as much to do with executive priorities as with Borden's own intentions.

In part, *Love Crimes* suffered from the current contradictions of New Hollywood, where distinctions between independent and mainstream were slowly collapsing. Whereas Miramax (who produced the film in conjunction with Sovereign Pictures) saw the film as a mainstream erotic thriller targeted at males between eighteen and thirty-four, Borden envisioned a small, art film aimed at women over thirty (Lucia 7). The film was most heavily publicized through the star Patrick Bergin, who plays the voyeuristic photographer, because of his similar role as an abusive husband in the lucrative *Sleeping with the Enemy* (see, for example, Drucker 1991). Ironically, Miramax's decision to distribute the film rather widely to seven hundred theaters may have doomed Borden's intentions from the start. They censored four major scenes that deal explicitly with perversity—Borden's main focus in the film—reducing the film's coherency and taking away part of its "art house" edge. *Love Crimes* arrived at and left theaters quickly, and it was later released in two versions (one of which includes the censored scenes) on home video.

Lizzie Borden once said: "Unless you really believe in narrative you can't go to Hollywood. You really have to want to tell a story" (Friedberg 1983: 45). When she finally did "go Hollywood," one might say she "went narrative with a vengeance" (although not intentionally—see note 3 to this chapter). Recall de Lauretis's claim that "feminist work in film should not be anti-narrative, and anti-Oedipal, but quite the opposite. It should be narrative and Oedipal with a vengeance" (108). Dana, the female protagonist in *Love Crimes*, works through a childhood trauma—a primal nightmare if you will—by tracking the sadistic photographer in order to experiment with the limits of her own desires.[4]

As a child, she witnessed her father commit adultery with various women. Each time, he would lock her into a closet, punishing her for watching. Flashbacks link these incidents with Dana's desire to punish the photographer, Hanover, for looking, as she was punished by her father. However, her ambivalence about her desires to play out the victim role in his sadistic stagings prevents her from seeking her revenge on him until the end of the film.[5] In Oedipal terms, Dana is attracted to Hanover to the extent that she can substitute him as a father figure and take on the role of both her father's lover and his wife (whom he ends up killing) in a fantasy scenario over which she repeatedly gains and loses control. The conclusion of *Love Crimes* leaves it rather ambiguous as to whether or not Dana has resolved these early conflicts, or her ambivalence toward Hanover.

Dana's struggle to overcome her traumatic past is accompanied by a transformation from a masculinized, male-identified district attorney to a woman comfortable with her own sexuality and her gender identity. (It is not so much that Dana becomes feminized, but that she recognizes her own value and the more general merit of women's relationships to one another.) Her investigation begins because she is gathering evidence in order to prosecute Hanover; however, she is as much identified with Hanover as she is with the police. Her relationship to patriarchy aligns her with both. As she purges her desire for Hanover, she also grows increasingly disillusioned with the "law" and is eventually fired.[6] Dana sets out to "use" Hanover to explore her own perverse desires and, in this way, the two of them are similar. Borden explains that she wanted Dana and Hanover to be seen as "a matched pair of control freaks" (Lucia 8). She saw *Love Crimes* as a film where

> a woman doesn't have to conquer the bad guy in the end, but where an exchange takes place and both characters have to give up control in order to learn how to feel. I saw it as a man who victimizes women coming to understand his own vulnerability and a woman who is able to explore the masochistic part of herself and come out better understanding her own strengths. (author's interview, 7 Aug. 1996)

In this context, Dana and Hanover operate on a level playing field; however, it is up to Dana to recognize her own degree of power.

The director's cut opens with a scene where police interrogate Dana's best friend, Maria, who is a detective on the case. The police ask Maria (Arnetia Walker) why Dana threw herself into the case, endangering herself and the investigation.[7] Because this scene, which is returned to at the film's conclusion, does not exist in the original version, the central question of each film differs. The inclusion of this frame in the director's cut sets up the governing question of Dana's motives, which is answered in terms of her own desires, fantasies, subjectivity, and exploration of power dynamics. Without this scene, the central question of the original version deals with Hanover's motives. We are trying to discover, with Dana, why Hanover abuses women by exploiting their own perverse desires. This quest, linked to the film's title of *Love Crimes*, is answered by the psychological explanation that Hanover believes he is "helping" these women probe their unexpressed sexuality—that is "loving them" by overpowering them. In essence, the original and the director's cut are two different films: the first one is Hanover's, while the second one is Dana's.

In both versions, however, women's interest in other women's victimization is quite present. Two key scenes foreground an axis of vision governed by the female desire to comprehend the reasons for male violence against women—to register the status of the female victim in a way that prevents further abuse. For instance, the first victim we see searches through Hanover's camera bag after posing nude for him and then having sex with him. She discovers a series of Polaroids of many other women posing for Hanover, some of whom appear to be frightened or out of control. In a simple shot/reverse shot sequence, the camera reveals the Polaroids one and by one and then cuts to the woman's reaction. One possible reading of this sequence might highlight the axis that is drawn between the woman and the photographs—an axis which forms a new relationship of knowledge. She suddenly understands her own experience—which before had only been confusing and unspeakable—in the context of numerous other women. She now interprets it as exploitation.

In another scene, Maria examines photographic evidence of previous victims while Dana works at a computer. Maria sits to the left of the frame holding the photos up at a distance all the way right of the frame. Dana sits in the foreground right of the frame. This shot composition establishes a dramatic axis between the two women, intimating that this scene is about women studying women. But it also aligns Dana with the Polaroids, associating her with the look of "mutual fascination" that Maria reads on the faces of the "victims."

While Maria's role is rather minimal, she was not in Moyle's original version of the screenplay at all. Borden insisted on hiring screenwriter Laurie Frank to revise *Love Crimes* and specifically to add the character of this African American woman detective. Maria's investigative status contributes to the thematic implications of Dana's own position as a female investigator, in part because both women repeatedly face the undermining of their authority. When Maria travels to Savannah to search for a missing Dana, the Savannah policeman completely misses her because he is looking for a (white) male detective. His misrecognition of her accentuates the precarious status of both Dana and Maria in that they are generally fighting male outlaws within the "man's world" of the police force and legal system.

Dana's self-curiosity leads her to Hanover's remote cabin, where he finds her snooping and locks her in a closet. Once it is daylight, Hanover pulls her out of the closet and handcuffs her to a sofa. A slow zoom to a close-up of her frightened reaction frames her as he begins to cut her clothes off. This reaction shot highlights her point of view minimizing, I think, any possible pleasure that might be derived. And, importantly, Hanover backs off as soon as she stops him, suggesting that indeed she has a degree of control over this "fantasy" scenario. The scissors appear to hold symbolic meaning more than any real threat of violence. They carve out a space between her desire and her fear, establishing certain rigid parameters of her control.

In the Miramax version of *Love Crimes*, the clothes-cutting scene is followed by a sequence where Dana is approached by Hanover while she sits in a bathtub. He throws her the gun she had brought to the cabin and then begins to photograph her. She stands up and stretches her arms out, allowing herself to be photographed. Then she enters into a sexual fantasy featuring Hanover and her together. The events that lead up to this highly stylized fantasy still suggest that Dana has staged the scenario herself. Given that she has access to her gun at any time, she probably consents to this experience.

Borden's director's cut places two scenes before the bathtub se-

Dana (Sean Young) is both victim and avenger in Lizzie
Borden's *Love Crimes* (1991). (Sovereign Pictures)

quence, scenes that made American executives nervous (Lucia 6). One of
these scenes, in which Dana and Hanover hover around a campfire,
shows Dana exploding with a speech about her own dislike of sex and
her repressed desires. In the next scene, Hanover catches her about to
attack him with a knife and then spanks her into submission. Both of
these events connoted excess perversity for producers (6–7). However, it
seems that Dana's powerful speech about her own sexual subjectivity may
have played into their insecurity as much as its "perverse" content.
While the "repressed heroine" has served as a classical Hollywood trope
since the 1940s, it might be the extent to which Dana expresses a self-
consciousness about the "riddle" she represents, and the "hysterical
mode" in which she articulates this self-understanding, that implied excess.

Interestingly, the Miramax version begins in the bathtub with Dana
sitting alone in the water, rather frightened. Borden's version, though,
starts with Hanover lovingly bathing her, suggesting yet again that Dana

has engaged in some kind of fantasy play. All of these changes lend further evidence to the notion that Borden's original vision was restrained by producers' reluctance to see the story through Dana's point of view.

The director's cut follows the bathtub scene (where Dana fantasized about having sex with Hanover) with a shot of Hanover massaging Dana's back as she lies passively on the porch. When Hanover stops massaging her because she refuses to resist him, she goes to get her gun, fires it in the air, and proceeds to take him into the police station. However, because this scene was edited out of the Miramax version, the original film goes directly from Dana's fantasy in the bathtub to her coming onto the front porch with a gun. Without the massage scene, Dana's actions seem highly unmotivated, if not absurd.

The Miramax target audience—males between the ages of eighteen to thirty-four—would almost necessarily read *Love Crimes* as an incoherent psychothriller, especially because of this sequence of events. Given the thriller genre, these spectators would probably expect Hanover to be not only a villain, but also the character with all of the power. They might not realize that Dana's fantasy guides the action and that she has a certain degree of power—she goes to the cabin in the first place, and she leaves there when she is ready.

Both versions of *Love Crimes* contain a climactic ending where Hanover enters Dana's apartment and "attacks" her with the camera. While he clicks away at her in the dark, flashes of light appear to stab at her and the shutter noise sounds like a gun. Dana's reactions suggest that she perceives his photography as rape. His visual assault sends her into flashbacks of her parents. Tinted in a light blue, her memories reveal her father murdering her mother with a gun she had turned on him when she discovered he was cheating on her. Now back in the present, Dana reaches for a glass vase and knocks out Hanover. She temporarily "replaces" her father in this origin fantasy (or as I called it earlier, a nightmare) in order to overcome her childhood trauma. The camera, however, eerily continues flashing until a final flash cuts to all white.

Characteristic of the protagonist in the women's psychothriller, Dana has resolved her own traumatic (childhood) experience by confronting other women's victimization. Ironically, she has confronted the damage of male voyeuristic desire within the context of classical cinema. But also, because of the presence of the "primal fantasies" that have haunted Dana up until now, Dana has in a sense re-written an origin story. Whereas her mother was defeated in her attempt to oust the abusive father by shooting him, Dana has empowered herself to evict Hanover, the father figure, from her fantasies. In doing so, Dana has symbolically rescued her mother. The device of the flashbacks may not have been Borden's preferred strategy for telling Dana's story, but they do contribute to a reconfiguration of the Oedipal drama that brings mother and daughter closer together in the face of adverse social conditions.

Not only does *Love Crimes* attempt to provide a space for Dana to explore her fantasy world but it offers spectatorial positions of desire in a reconfiguration of the classical Oedipal fantasy. In each of Borden's films, new primal fantasies are created—fantasies that involve women's relation to each other, to the economy, and to their own degree of social control. As previously mentioned, Borden refuses to see Oedipal origins as biological, instead situating them as social and economic narratives that women (whether protagonist or spectator) may confront and transform. Fantasy, then, as defined by Borden, can represent a site of women's agency and political development. The implications of this for the division of mainstream versus counter cinema should be fairly obvious. Commercial cinema, in its long association with (male) fantasy, need not be separated from the political agenda of women filmmakers. As the case of *Love Crimes* demonstrates, though, the relation between the two is tumultuous and highly ambivalent.

The original Miramax version concludes with an image of Dana burning a Polaroid taken when she was in Hanover's bathtub. She obviously must destroy this last piece of evidence because she expresses the very pleasure that Maria spotted in those early pictures of other women. And so, she expulses the only proof of her desire. The framing of this final image is quite powerful: Dana stares at herself in the mirror as her own representation burns. Her face only partially shows as the flames engulf her image. In effect, Dana is wedged in between these two self-images, the mirror and the photograph, as she is in the midst of carving out a new identity.

The director's cut concludes with this scene as well but, beforehand, it returns to the scene where the governing question was asked. The detectives who were questioning Maria about Dana's motives suggest that Dana was complicitous with Hanover. They ask if there is any evidence that might prove Dana to be at all guilty of becoming personally involved with him. This would of course threaten them because it implies an agenda of female sexual desire. Maria, who had discovered the photo and confronted Dana with it by holding it up to her in silence (in another interesting axis of vision between the two women), answers falsely that she has no incriminating information. Here again, the cut to Dana's burning of the photograph seems more motivated by the inclusion of this scene. Dana is forced to erase any evidence of her fantasy, an act that might also be read as self-conscious commentary in terms of the censorship that Borden endured in the making of this film.

Regardless, the inclusion of this frame (the opening and final scenes with Maria and the detectives) encourages viewers to see Dana's story less as a thriller targeted toward young men and more as a "woman's film" about desire, fantasy, and origin stories. When asked what kind of audience she had envisioned as she made *Love Crimes*, she replies: "The same as everything I do—women over thirty" (Lucia 7). As we have seen, though, a number of tensions having to do with gender politics, power, and subjectivity emerge when targeting women within the context of commercial cinema, which has traditionally been governed by male fantasy. In watching *Love Crimes*, it is often confusing as to "whose desire it is" from scene to scene. The collaborative process of mainstream film inevitably invokes multiple sites of fantasy and desire, producing contradictions that are ultimately irresolvable. In de Lauretis's celebratory remarks about *Born in Flames*, she contends that Borden inherently addresses a female, feminine, feminist spectator through the apparatus.[8] Perhaps *Love Crimes* suggests the complex difficulties, the unanswerable questions, that are raised when one assumes a female audience while working within conventional, mainstream codes. These difficulties are certainly embodied at specific points within the film's diegesis. The Savannah detective who misrecognizes Maria because he is looking for a white male officer signals the more general expectations that women confront when trying to work in a narrow-visioned, male dominated system.

While I argue that the scenes included in the director's cut lend themselves to a reading of Dana as an empowered agent, I do not mean to imply that the latter version represents a purer, less adulterated vision of Borden's. It would be too easy to make an either/or distinction between the Miramax version and the director's cut, where one only affords the producers' vision and the other only the director's. Both products are obviously informed by a number of visions, being produced within a complex web of socio-economic and historical influences. And both may be read in a multitude of ways. Borden's inclusion of "six" mere scenes—scenes that were filmed under the supervision of Miramax—by no means makes the film "hers." If anything, consideration of the director's cut highlights the many tensions involved in both films and suggests that one single vision—Borden's for example—is impossible, no matter the context in which a film is made.

Borden's own relation to the film has changed over time, suggesting that even the director's "vision" represents an unstable, contradictory site. Whereas her reaction immediately following the film's release consisted mainly of negative statements against those involved in production and distribution, Borden has now acquired the perspective that the screenplay was never quite right, especially going into production, and that a more solid knowledge of structure and form might have helped her defend herself against executives. She remarks:

> Between *Love Crimes* and now, I've really been studying film because when I jumped into *Born in Flames*, I didn't know anything. And then with *Working Girls*, it was such a narrow subject that I could write based on research and what I'd heard. . . . Unbeknownst to me, it had a three-act structure. I had no idea what a three-act structure was when I wrote that. . . . Because of the problems that happened with *Love Crimes*, I felt that I couldn't strongly enough analyze the problems with the script or solve them. I felt a complete loss of creative control where I'd come from a position in New York where I had total creative control. (author's interview, 7 Aug. 1996)

Borden's observations testify to the difficulties of changing contexts—from alternative to commercial film—in that once she entered a more mainstream arena, the experimental skills that had facilitated such celebrated work as *Born in Flames* no longer benefitted her.

I would also like to point out that Borden defines creative control not as commercial or financial power per se (high budget versus low budget), but as a number of factors, including authority over the script, preparation time, and maintaining a firm grasp on film form in order to hold out against other people's poor or ill-thought out decisions. Borden emphasizes that one major determinant of creative control is the amount of post-production time allowed the director, which is usually more limited in studio schedules. Borden comments, "With the two films that I feel are genuinely mine, *Working Girls* and *Born in Flames*, I had the ability to edit as long as I needed in order to finish the film because had I had to stop editing on either film, they would have been disasters. . . . The imposition of certain time frames, beyond any political pressures of certain groups trying to make films of their own desires, is a paramount issue" (author's interview, 3 Mar. 1997). So while issues such as "final cut" are important, the time available for the director to negotiate that cut is also critical.

Most important, Borden's attitude toward the industry has changed into one that allows her more agency in the world of commercial production. Referring to articles that appeared in *Cineaste* and *The Advocate* in which she complained about executives, she explains, "I have to put a lot of emphasis on my own lack of experience in dealing with the politics on a bigger film. Ultimately, it comes down to the script and the politics" (author's interview, 7 Aug. 1996). Borden's experience with *Love Crimes* has not soured her from taking on high-budget or studio films. In fact, she had a more souring experience directing a thirty minute short ("Let's Talk about Sex") for the low-budget *Erotique*, but she signed papers that keep her from talking about it. Such an experience serves as a reminder that so-called independent films do not necessarily insure that the director's vision remains intact.

For now, Borden is trying to take advantage of the recent market changes that have brought studios and independent companies closer together. Looking to write/direct/produce films along the lines of *The Crying Game* (1993), *The Piano* (1994), or *Leaving Las Vegas* (1995)—films that require relatively low budgets of $1–2 million but attain widespread distribution—Borden has pooled together financing from European companies for her next feature. She says, "What I'm really trying to do out here [in Los Angeles] now is to try to find a niche where I can make moderately priced movies that still address some of the issues that concern me. You know, some of the women's stuff, some political stuff. . . . I'm trying to find a place that is still independent that isn't as dependent on the kind of financing that mainstream movies are dependent on" (author's interview, 7 Aug. 1996). She plans to take advantage of the opportunities provided by major independent studios and the markets opened up by their growth.

Borden hopes to carve out a position between independent and mainstream that allows her to continue addressing the controversial issues that have been raised in each of her films up to now. In the meantime, her body of work so far will continue to elicit a wide range of responses having to do with women, politics, and fantasy.

4

DARNELL
MARTIN

WITH THE RELEASE OF the $5.5 million *I Like It Like That* in 1994, Darnell Martin was touted as the "first African American woman to direct a major studio feature" (Kroll 79). In effect, the marketing department at Columbia Pictures capitalized on the ambiguities of the terms they deployed to describe Martin's status. Euzhan Palcy, an Afro-Caribbean woman from Martinique, had directed *A Dry White Season* for Metro-Goldwyn-Meyer in 1989. Julie Dash's *Daughters of the Dust* became the first commercial feature (through Kino International) by an African American woman in 1991.[1] And Leslie Harris's independent film *Just Another Girl on the IRT* (1993) soon followed, after being picked up by Miramax. Therefore, Columbia's marketing department chose their words wisely to emphasize Martin's exclusivity, but in the process they erased previous African American accomplishments as well as previous black women's work.

Martin was outraged by this erasure, just as she also resented the studio's decision to market her film on the basis of her racial and gendered identity. Regarding the first point, Martin complains, "It's bullshit and horrible and it puts us in a subculture, subcinema" (Jackson 58). She told me, "It takes away from Julie Dash, Euzhan Palcy, Leslie Harris, and on top of which, why are they trying to sell me? They're not trying to sell all these other directors. They don't talk about Ron Howard's nationality or where he came from" (author's interview, 6 Aug. 1996). Here is a case where identity politics—the strategic assertion of one's racial, gender, class and/or sexual identity for the purpose of political coalescence—was exploited by a commercial entity looking for a gimmick. This particular "gimmick" of identity politics backfired, not only because it produced negative publicity for the film but also because the film failed to attract large numbers.

Ultimately, Martin balked at the studio's attempt to try to ride the wave of "New Black Cinema" and pitch her as the "label of the month" (author's interview). Columbia's tactics adhered to what bell hooks calls "the commodification of otherness," through which "ethnicity becomes spice, seasoning that can liven up the dull dish that is mainstream white culture" (1992: 21). Against Martin's wishes, the discourse surrounding *I Like It Like That* centered more around the identity of the filmmaker than around the film itself. Not necessarily disavowing her racial and gendered identity nor attempting to minimize their political aspects, Martin was determined to have her work viewed according to its merit and content. Martin claims, "I'm black. I'm a woman. It has little to do with me" (author's interview).

The hard work and difficult political struggles of the women who came before Martin deserve to be recognized. Many African American women have been on the "brink" of signing a deal similar to Martin's over the last decade, providing evidence to debunk the notion that no qualified women of color were trying to get a movie made until Martin's rise to success. In 1990, New Line Cinema began soliciting scripts, specifically seeking "ensemble pieces," by and about women of color. New Line paid at least one or more writers for these kinds of stories, and put several ideas into development, but none reached the production stage (Rhines 1996: 88–89). In 1992, *Sweet Nez*, written by Crystal Emory, was bought by New Line, but it languished there (89). (Jesse Algeron Rhines implies this is because the screenplay, in which an African American woman learns from the violence around her and recovers from a drug addiction, contained too "happy" of an ending.)[2] Michelle Parkerson has been trying to make the move from documentaries to feature films since 1990, as have other directors of shorts and videos, including Daresha Kyi, Ellen Sumter, and Zeinabu Irene Davis (Tate 1991: 73, 77).[3]

These African and African American women offer a counterpoint to the successful films of black male directors such as Spike Lee (*Do the Right Thing*, 1989; *Jungle Fever*, 1991; *Malcolm X*, 1992), John Singleton (*Boyz' in the Hood*, 1991; *Higher Learning*, 1994), and the Hudlin brothers (*House Party*, 1990; *Boomerang*, 1992). Just as Hollywood studios' dependence on the blockbuster paradoxically opened up space for independent films by white filmmakers, it also created more room for product by African American film school graduates and independent filmmakers (although disproportionately so). In fact, rarely have African American male filmmakers produced films in the independent sphere that have become

150

"high concept" and financially successful.[4] In general, the "New Black Cinema" should more aptly be titled the "New Black Male Cinema." The films in this cycle have alienated African American women directors like Robin Downes who says she feels intimidated by what she calls their "masculine energy" (Rhines 99). Just as African American female characters tend to be invisible or silenced in most mainstream and independent films, women of color remain relatively more absent as directors than white women or African American men.

THE "SPIKE LEE DISCOURSE," REALISM, AND AUTHENTICITY

Upon the release of Martin's film through Columbia, she was immediately contrasted with studio director Spike Lee, who has been criticized for his sexist and masculinist perspective.[5] Because Martin had worked as assistant cameraperson on *Do the Right Thing*, the comparison seemed all the more legitimate. As for Martin, she attributes her raised consciousness about the labor conditions of people of color within the Hollywood industry to Lee, but she adds: "If I was affected by anyone creatively it would be the person I was working for, [director of photography Ernest] Dickerson" (author's interview).[6]

While Martin's films have more in common with European art cinema and, perhaps, as one critic has suggested, with Douglas Sirk melodramas, I would like to consider the ways in which her work has entered into the "Spike Lee discourse" and examine the reasons why Lee's films have been problematized by feminist critics.[7] I am interested in what Martin has been asked to do (by film critics) in relation to Lee.

Lee's immense body of provocative work has been praised for bringing political issues of race and racism to a wide audience; it has also been disparaged by some African American and feminist critics for promulgating sexism and disturbing racial attitudes. Along gender lines, bell hooks attributes Lee's canonization, in part, to his "replication of mainstream patriarchal cinematic practices that explicitly represents woman (in this instance black woman) as the object of a phallocentric gaze" (126). Along class lines, Rhines argues that Lee, in his attempt to reappropriate the Hollywood system, has also appropriated dominant ideological views of that system. Rhines complains that Lee fails to explain the social problems of the black "underclass" in terms of economic structures and determinants (4). From Rhines's perspective, "Lee's depiction of the underclass does not encourage support but rather punishment of them [the underclass]" (123).

Wahneema Lubiano also criticizes Lee's films, particularly *Do the Right Thing*—the film most celebrated by white critics as well as Hollywood industry gatekeepers—for conveying the message that "hard work," instead of social and economic change, is the community's solution (271). Lubiano complains that "this film makes no critique of the conditions under which labor is drawn from some members of the community, nor are kinds of labor/work differentiated" (271). For Lubiano, the "absolute good" represented by work perpetuates conventional notions of masculinity, which revolve around ownership and property.

Lubiano is less concerned with Lee's films as such than she is with the ways in which he has been (willingly) marketed and understood; that is, she challenges the "Spike Lee discourse." She writes, "The problem with Spike Lee's sample [that is, his individual perspective], his place in the sun, is that his presence, empowered by Hollywood studio hegemony and media consensus on his importance, can function to overshadow or make difficult other kinds of politically engaged cultural work" (255). In part, this overshadowing presence is due to the auteurist convictions of mainstream Hollywood, which tend to allow only one "great genius" to emerge from the African American community. This discourse serves to marginalize, often ghettoize, African American women, forestalling perspectives that might challenge Lee's.

Lubiano also makes the important point that the Spike Lee discourse relies on essentialist notions about race and identity. Lee is often positioned as a "truth-teller" for his community, someone whose films speak of "real experience," even though he sometimes claims he dislikes that position (255). What is interesting is that while Martin finds her status as woman repeatedly essentialized—as a female counterpoint to Lee—she has also been placed squarely in this "Spike Lee discourse," which essentializes race.

I Like It Like That was distinguished by popular reviewers for being more "authentic" because of Martin's presence on the film. This tendency was heightened by the fact that the film was shot on location in the community of the Bronx where Martin spent her childhood. The production also featured many local extras. Jack Kroll of *Newsweek* commented, "*I Like It Like That* comes from the place and people where Martin grew up as a kid who didn't know where her next plate of watered-down macaroni and cheese was coming from" (17 Oct. 1994: 79). Denby of *New York* declared, "Some of the anger wore me down, but I never doubted for a second that it was *genuine*" (emphasis added) (Martin's characterization as an "angry woman" will be discussed shortly). *The Village Voice*'s J. Hoberman described the female protagonist, Lisette, as "the authentic voice of underclass desire" (18 Oct. 1994: 49).

The unexamined assumption, expressed repeatedly, that Martin's work represents a nexus of black or barrio urban authenticity and truth is embedded in a long tradition of popular film criticism, as Lubiano demonstrates; but it is also a problem in the academic circles of feminist film and literary theory. Elizabeth Abel points out that, in the wake of poststructuralist challenges to gender constructs, white feminist academics have turned to African American women writers to re-stabilize female identity by positing them as a site of authenticity and cultural authority (1993). Abel states that the "postfeminist turn to black women novelists enacts an anxious transference onto black women's speech" as a site of genuine femininity (479).

In doing so, white feminists hope to engage in a discourse of racial sameness to compensate for their fears over differences and instabilities within the category "female." In acknowledging my own position as a white academic, I try to remain aware of these kinds of desires and projections. I also avoid essentializing Martin's films by romanticizing her as an "idealized native" of the Bronx underclass or naively expecting her directorial persona to bridge the very real and difficult gaps between white women and women of color. The popular discourse of "Spike Lee," and now of "Darnell Martin," make the trap of essentialism a very easy one to fall into. But the notion of an "authentic African American experience" or a "genuine spokesperson" is very problematic because, as Lola Young explains, they imply and elevate a "singular, black perspective" that can articulate that supposed authenticity (36).

Although independent filmmaking embraces a variety of themes and styles, it is, as a whole, characterized by an underlying tension between realist and reflexive codes. Lola Young takes issue with the "positive images" approach adhered to by many African American critics and filmmakers who hope to counter negative myths and stereotypes about people of color. She likewise has a problem with African American filmmakers who have confined themselves to realist cinema without questioning how realist conventions reinforce spectatorial positions oriented toward mastery and dominance (33–37). So while white academic and popular critics typically engage tensions of essentialism regarding African American filmmaking, another sort of tension, manifested in these debates about realism and positive images, continues to take shape within African American film communities.

African American women filmmakers have found themselves working, more often than not, in documentary forms—attempting to capture their "realities" and "experiences" on film.[8] Valerie Smith's "Reconstituting the Image: The Emergent Black Woman Director" summarizes some of the work of the most prominent African American directors, such as Michelle Parkerson, Akoya Chenzira, and Alile Sharon Larkin. Smith argues that even when these women are not engaging in cinema verité per se, they rely on realism because they attempt to convey the specificity of their experiences and provide representations of their community rarely seen in mainstream cinema (1988). Similarly, Greg Tate's

153

profile of African American women directors in *The New York Times* emphasizes the important influence of documentary on these women's work (1991: 73–77). While there are obvious problems with documentary representation, especially when it is assumed to capture "real" experience, bell hooks notes the relative accessibility of documentary codes considering that most experimental film has been produced by white filmmakers for white audiences. hooks explains that counter cinema and independent films tend to connote white elitism and alienate black audiences by failing to address racial issues (127).

Martin's *I Like It Like That* is quite interesting for the way in which it draws on counter cinema and foreign "art cinema" while arguably addressing various audiences. Perhaps because of Martin's history with Sundance and her preference for Italian film, *I Like It Like That* breaks free from the grip of realist aesthetics and "positive images." Lisette, the film's protagonist, is far too flawed to serve as a traditional role model for the African American or barrio communities. Moreover, the universe she inhabits is represented through hyperbole, pseudo-fantasy, and chaos in ways that reject classical techniques of realism.

TRADITIONS IN AFRICAN AMERICAN INDEPENDENT CINEMA

Just as it is important to be aware of the pitfalls of essentialist discourse concerning African American filmmakers, it is also notable that when (white) scholars typically refer to independent cinema, they most often reference a white independent cinema. That is, African American independent cinema has a unique history, and one that is generally marginalized in both academic and popular conversations about films that counter the mainstream. The definition of "African American film," whether commercial or independent, has never been easy, most specifically because white financiers or production staff have often been involved with "black filmmaking" on some level. As Thomas Cripps suggests, films by African American filmmakers or those targeted at African American audiences are rarely made by an exclusive team of African Americans—so definitions of African American or black film must remain open. Cripps submits, "Black film must be seen as a genre, then, for what it says and how it is said, rather than for who is saying it" (9).

While African American independent cinema, in whatever ways it might be defined, has historically demonstrated a "political commitment to the liberation struggles of black and other oppressed people," it has rarely focused on gender inequities within the African American community or sought to understand how gender is racialized (Yearwood 12). Pearl Bowser has criticized Oscar Micheaux's independent "race movies" of the 1920s and 1930s for portraying women only as romantic love interests or maternal icons in service of the glorification of their male heroes (50). Bell hooks has found fault with Mario Van Peebles's modernist *Sweet, Sweetback's Badassss Song* (1971) for being less progressive than Micheaux's films, suggesting that his representations of male machismo indicated a backlash against the 1970s feminist movement (1996: 100–101).

Industry discrimination has meant that there have been very few African American or black women working in either mainstream or independent cinema, although Cheryl Dunye, Akoya Chenzira, Julie Dash, and others who have achieved career longevity should be recognized. There are even fewer who have moved from independent to Hollywood, as Darnell Martin's case demonstrates. As we will see, Martin's directorial persona is marked by a certain degree of ambiguity—a resistance to pigeon-holing in terms of racial identity or feminist politics. The fact that she refuses to embody any one fixed position—that she, in effect, refuses to articulate that "authentic" position of the Spike Lee discourse—might help explain how she negotiates the spheres of independent and studio film. With a complicated background in music video, the film school tradition, television commercials, and counter cinema, Martin brings a multi-textual and multi-layered perspective to her mainstream filmmaking.

MARTIN'S TRANSITION FROM INDEPENDENT TO MAINSTREAM FILMMAKING

Martin grew up in a Hispanic section of the Bronx and was cared for by her white mother after her African American father abandoned the family. Her childhood was financially unstable, but she recounts her mother's commitment to creative problem-solving, such as her achievement in getting Martin a high school scholarship at the Barnard School for Girls (Hoffman H28). Martin went on to receive a scholarship from Sarah Lawrence College (historically, a women's college) and then she began applying to film schools. In 1989, Martin worked as Assistant Director of Photography on *Do the Right Thing*, and it was a call on her behalf from Spike Lee that eventually aided in getting her accepted at New York University's film school—after she was rejected twice (Hoffman H28).[9] While at NYU, Martin assisted direction on Levi 501 and Nike commercials and she directed music videos for a gambit of artists, including Chi Ali, D-Nice, Ms. Melody, and Jonathon Butler ("Cinderella debut" 8).

Martin wrote, edited, and directed her independent short, *Suspect* (1991), as a student at NYU and left the program when that film began to receive critical attention. *Suspect* earned a Director's Choice Award at the 1992 Edison Black Mafia Film Festival as well as critical acclaim at

Director Darnell Martin on the set of her studio film, *I Like It Like That* (1994). (Columbia Pictures)

New York Public Theater's Young Black Cinema Showcase in 1992 (8). But perhaps most important, the short won Martin a Director's Fellowship at Sundance, which allowed her to develop future directorial projects (Hoffman H28). Martin wrote a speculation script titled *Black Out*, eventually re-titled *I Like It Like That*, which she submitted to a number of independent production companies. When New Line Cinema offered her a deal of $2 million, she turned it down in search of a larger budget and a longer shooting schedule (New Line offered her seven weeks). She also turned down Spike Lee's offer to make the film through Universal Studios, worrying that she would have to forfeit a degree of creative control. Finally, Columbia Studios responded to the industry "buzz" around Martin by offering her, after a year of negotiations, a budget of $5.5 million and a nine-week schedule (Francke, 30 Jan. 1995: 29). Columbia Executive Vice President Stephanie Allain (*Boyz in the Hood; El Mariachi*, 1994), an African American woman, contributed to the deal by both paving its way with Columbia decision-makers and offering reassurances to Martin (29).

Martin shot *I Like It Like That* primarily in her old neighborhood around Findlay and 167th Street (Stuart 23). She hired as many people of color as possible and encouraged them to join film industry unions, traditions she learned from Lee's productions (author's interview). Martin also employed numerous locals as extras, including hiring an orphan named Tomas Melly to play the major character of L'il Chino (Stuart 22). Obviously, Martin aimed to be socially responsible and politically conscious about the economics of the Hollywood film industry even as she directed a studio film. Some critics have pointed out the futility of such social responsibility. Production may temporarily aid the local economy. However, the admission fees paid by African American audiences, once that film is released, do not benefit their communities because there are fewer than one in ten black-owned theaters in the United States (see Rhines 7).[10] Even so, given Martin's constraints, she attempted to benefit the Hispanic and African American communities in the Bronx to the extent that she could.

Accounts of the production of *I Like It Like That* suggest that Martin's directorial style involved exercising a great deal of individual control. Debunking the stereotype that women directors tend to be more collaborative, and despite her communal orientation toward filmmaking, Martin declared: "Collaboration starts and stops with my actors" (Jackson, 19 Oct. 1994: 58). While Martin describes herself as a "control freak," she helped create an atmosphere relaxed enough to be conducive to practical jokes (58). These jokes later became a major aspect of film promotion.[11] (One practical joke involved false allegations of rape, which Martin refused to take lightly.)[12]

As a director, Martin has been described as "angry" by a number of critics and interviewers. In addition to David Denby's comment that *I Like It Like That* embodies an "angry" film, Kroll of *Newsweek* suggests that "Martin gets angry a lot" (79). This tag is no doubt a response to Martin's cultural "threat" as an African American woman. It also represents a response to her refusal to back down in her struggles to make a film she is proud of. About her relationship to the studio that hired her, Martin remarked: "I think Columbia is excited about my work, but maybe not about me. Sometimes I'm not easy to cop to. I don't have much of a diplomacy filter" (Kroll 80). Indeed, the fact that Columbia, and no other studio, has backed one of her films from 1994 to 1999 suggests that the studio came to feel somewhat intimidated by Martin's determination to uphold the integrity of her conception of the project.[13] I would suggest that this has less to do with Martin's individual personality than with the way mainstream culture positions her as an "angry young black woman."

The string of battles fought by Martin in order to retain creative control over *I Like It Like That* are numerous. Martin explained the primary difference between her experiences making *Suspect* and those making the latter film:

> On *Suspect*, there was complete, absolute freedom, with no stress. With *I Like It Like That*, I did exactly what I wanted. I didn't compromise. But the difference was that it was very stressful. I had to fight a lot. There were just so many arguments and so many battles. And what that does is it takes away your creative energy. (author's interview)

One of Martin's greatest struggles was with the Columbia executives' inability to "place" her film. Like the stereotyped executives in Robert Altman's *The Player* (1992), they attempted to reduce it to previous films and formulas, e.g., "this one is Rosie Perez in *Footloose* (1984)" (Stuart 22). Eventually, executives promoted the film as an "urban *Four Weddings and a Funeral* (1994)" (Francke 29). Their inability to think outside of conventional terms led producers to insist on a title change, from *Black Out* to *I Like It Like That*. According to Martin, "For them, it sounded a bit like *She's Gotta Have It*" (Stuart 22). The new title also enabled Columbia to cross-market the Black All Stars song of the same title off of their Sony Records label, with the song eventually reaching number nineteen on Billboard's Hot Dance Music charts ("Hot Dance Music" 38).

Martin faced her most concrete battle when executives decided to cut some of the "grittier" scenes (not revealed publicly by Martin) out of the film because they did not adhere to the romantic comedy genre (Kroll 80). Martin threatened to take her name off of the project, forcing executives to include the scenes after all. Their response to her threat suggests one of the rare instances in the production and marketing of this film where Martin's status as an African American woman offered her power. Columbia obviously did not want to lose their potential to market *I Like It Like That* on the basis of Martin's racial and gendered status, as well as her position as a "young newcomer." Executives were further convinced to back off of their original demand when the very scenes they planned to delete were applauded by test audiences (80).

Columbia also asked Martin to exchange her ambiguous ending, which reunites the romantic couple but leaves a certain degree of doubt about their longevity, for a more classically "happy ending" (Francke, 30 Jan. 1995: 29). In effect, Martin was being encouraged to abandon the important social message the film laboriously attempts to convey: romantic coupling is precarious, never-ending, difficult work. Again, Martin protested and eventually kept her film's conclusion in tact.

But the complaints that Martin has been most vocal about concern the marketing of both her directorial persona and the film, a process over which she had no authority once the film was completed. (Martin even created a web page detailing Columbia's unfair marketing practices.) Interestingly, Columbia participated in contradictory marketing strategies; they billed Martin as "the first African American woman" to direct a studio film in most of the promotions, but erased her gender in others. For example, an *I Like It Like That* "Coming Attraction" trailer that preceded *Blankman*, directed by Mike Binder and starring Damon Wayans, altered a *Daily News* quotation that referred to Martin's gender; she was tagged simply an "African American filmmaker." At this point, Martin felt that Columbia's marketing department was clearly exploiting and distorting her racial, ethnic, and gender identity to suit its own commercial purposes. This tactic seems ironic when one considers that *I Like It Like That* chronicles the efforts of a young black Hispanic woman to free herself from the constraints of those very aspects of her identity.

In addition to Martin's distress over being "paraded around as a novelty," it was her opinion that Columbia failed to target the correct market with its promotion (Francke 29). After *I Like It Like That* generated a stir at the Cannes and Toronto Film Festivals, it was advertised almost exclusively to upscale, very film-literate audiences (Stuart 23). While Martin had conceived of the film as being influenced by European art cinema, her goal was to design a film that sufficiently crossed-over to urban African American and Hispanic audiences, specifically young viewers (23).

Furthermore, Martin criticized the marketing department for failing to launch any full-scale publicity campaign at all. According to Martin, very few posters were placed in urban centers and no opening night premiere occurred, two strategies that can catalyze word of mouth and establish a platform (Francke 29). The film's star, a little known but very well-received actress named Lauren Vélez, was given no profile on entertainment news programs, talk shows, or in the popular press. Columbia, in fact, missed the opportunity to "manufacture" Vélez as a star, contributing furthermore to a Hollywood star system that privileges white-identified actors.[14] Martin also bemoans the poster of Vélez, as protagonist Lisette, because it painted Lisette as "some ditzy model, as if nothing is going on in her head" (Stuart 22).

Martin's press also oddly portrayed her rise to notoriety in fairy-tale terms. A quarter-page advertisement in *The New York Times* featured a long quotation from a *New York Daily News* review. In part, the ad reads:

> Columbia Pictures is proud to present the debut film of a remarkable young writer/director. The *New York Daily News* raves "Every year at the Cannes Film Festival, there is at least one Cinderella story. This year, Cinderella was an African-American filmmaker from the Bronx named Darnell Martin." ("Plunge into," 9 Oct. 1994: H22)

This review, as quoted, obviously plays on the "twist" of Martin's race by first inviting the connotation of a "white" Cinderella. The reviewer and the advertisement also work to efface the difficult labor, concrete material conditions, and complex social relations involved in bringing *I Like It Like That* to the screen. Not only does this "fairy-tale" promotion romanticize Martin and gloss over her position as an active agent in film production but it comes into direct conflict with the film's problematization of easy romance and blissful marriage, much like the "happy ending" suggested by Columbia executives. The Cinderella theme is extended by David Denby's review, in which he seems to miss the film's point entirely. Denby explains that we root for the two main characters because "they seem destined for each other, like a couple in a fairy tale" (31 Oct. 1994: 96).

SUBJECTIVITY AND ADDRESS

In exploring African American women's relation to Hollywood movies, bell hooks proposes that many women who enjoy mainstream film most likely carve out a critical space "through struggle, reading, and resistance" (126). Because African American women rarely see black characters on screen, they experience their subjectivity as an "absent presence," perhaps as maternal figures who have no children of their own or as beautiful women whose attractiveness is not recognized (119). With such an invisible on-screen history, African American women di-

rectors inevitably struggle to find legitimacy as they articulate an authorial voice.

In terms of spectatorship, hooks explains: "Even in the worst circumstances, the ability to manipulate one's gaze in the face of structures
of domination that would contain it, opens up the possibility of agency"
(116). Because African Americans have been encouraged by whites not
to "look" at whites, and they have had a history of being examined by a
medical-scientific gaze, assuming the gaze might be considered a daring
attempt at self-empowerment (Young 49). While little work has been
conducted in theorizing African American women's spectatorial experience, hooks speculates that many of her peers experience commercial
film through a radical "black female subjectivity" (131).[15]

Given these speculations, one might think that African American
women directors, having probably experienced this critical spectatorship
in the theater themselves, consciously address people of color, specifically women. This was certainly the case with Julie Dash when she made
Daughters of the Dust: she intended the film to privilege "black women
first, then the black community and white women" (Dash 66). In other
words, Dash had a very clear idea of her primary and secondary target
audiences. It is also in keeping with de Lauretis's suggestion that feminist
cinema is, in part, stitched together by the director's preconception of
her film's reception—her positing of a feminine/female/feminist spectator (1987: 132).

However, when I asked Martin to describe her approach to filmmaking, she complicated this argument. Martin asserted: "I don't think
about the audience. I just think about myself. I can't gauge what other
people with different experiences are gonna think. All I can do really is
see if this moment rings true for me. Sometimes, afterward, I might be
moved if someone comes up and says, 'I felt moved,' but I didn't make
the film for them" (author's interview). Her self-appraisal does not necessarily preclude that when she makes a movie "for herself" she also
gears it toward others "like herself," but it does suggest that the production side, not the reception side, is what motivates her.

Interestingly, Martin attributes her analytical tendencies less to her
racial or gender identity and more to her regard for film. She admitted,
"I am very critical, but I don't know if that comes from being a black
woman. I think it comes more from being a filmmaker" (author's interview). In this way, she privileges her identity as filmmaker, and film
viewer, over that of African American woman. Martin went on to say
that she is more often disturbed by a poor shot choice or a weak script
than by a stereotypical representation.

While it may seem superficially that Martin disavows her racial and
gender positioning altogether, she demonstrates that she is acutely aware

161

of them. She makes it clear that racist and sexist depictions offend her. In fact, she describes her own criteria for judging such depictions: "If you have a drug dealer and he or she is black or Puerto Rican, that in itself is not racist. What is racist is making the character *defined* by that role. This can be done by blacks; it can be done by whites" (author's interview). The simultaneous disavowal and awareness of the racial implications of her work signals the appropriateness of a Foucauldian approach to Hollywood directors. Martin's words intimate that, on certain levels, she has internalized dominant Hollywood ideologies, especially in relation to the "cult of the artist" and a "color-blind" approach to racial difference. While she has become part of the power structure in some ways, she continues to challenge dominant ideologies of race and gender through her directorial persona and her films.

Martin's approach to directing indicates a complex "subjectivity," one as tightly bound to cinematic knowledge and film literacy as to radical black or feminist consciousness. As suggested by the above comment, she goes beyond a "positive or negative images" approach in an effort to critically examine how, when, and where images are working and how they are situated within the larger narrative universe. Martin also tends to see herself in "artisinal" terms, creating film stories that satisfy her personally and placing less emphasis on the marketplace and audience. However, at the same time, *Suspect* and *I Like It Like That*, convey a complicated structuring of subject positions by posing a matrix of social and political questions about race, gender, sexual relationships, and social power.

SUSPECT

Martin's independent short, *Suspect*, runs eight minutes. Stick (Derrick Jones), the African American protagonist, is surrounded by his friends as they try to gain entrance into a club recently opened in their neighborhood by a white owner. When management is intimidated by Stick's appearance, he is denied access to the club and leaves with his friends, Ralphie (Paul Soto) and Marilyn (Tracey Vilar). Soon after, a white woman (Pam Scotto) exits the club furious at her accompanying boyfriend. Against her own better judgment, and in the heat of the moment, the woman heads toward a subway stop. Independently, a few beats later, Stick's other two friends, James (James Soto) and Lawrence (Lawrence Garcia), follow in the same direction.

The white woman becomes startled when she runs into Stick, Ralphie, and Marilyn, dropping her lighter on the street. She flees but Stick follows her in order to return her lighter. Feeling threatened by his pursuit, she draws a can of Mace and tells him to withdraw. When he tries

162

to hand the lighter to her, she sprays him in the eyes. Now his four friends are infuriated and all of them give chase to the white woman. As they repeatedly meet up with her and lose her, Ralphie and Marilyn physically taunt her. Eventually she is cornered by all five of them at a chain-linked fence. As the woman attempts to protect herself by clawing them away, Stick's friends egg him on to get revenge.

The tension builds as everyone asks him, "What are you gonna do?" Then comes a series of close-ups of Stick covering the woman's mouth, of him reaching into his pocket and pulling out the lighter, holding the lighter open as though he might ignite it, snapping it shut, and enclosing the woman's palm over it. The woman runs away as the camera shows Stick spread-eagle against the fence, a visual reference to his own entrapment within an Anglo culture that can only see him as a criminal and a threat.

This story takes place in the thick of the night and the use of darkness is carefully crafted. Light and color highlight the dense action and characters' faces against the backdrop of the night sky. The setting is composed of graffiti-strewn concrete walls, chain-linked fences, and a host of shadows. Given the small budget on which *Suspect* was produced, careful attention was applied to make the urban world of these characters seem confusing and ambiguous, but not entirely bleak. The events are accompanied by a continuous beat, made up of rap music, a synthesized beat, or sometimes, the lone sound of footsteps.

Camera set ups consist mainly of long and medium shots, with close-ups used minimally but deliberately. For example, the film opens with extremely tight close-ups of the club owner's eyes intercut with Stick's eyes as they glare at each other. The tension of their stand-off is conveyed immediately. When Stick, Ralphie, and Marilyn walk away from the club, the camera tilts down to a close-up of them stepping through a puddle. This shot is later juxtaposed with one of the white woman daintily jumping over the puddle—not only to indicate that she is walking in their direction but also to contrast her attitude with theirs. Most significantly, the shots and the editing work together to heighten dramatic tension as the film races toward its conclusion. The congested framing of multiple characters, the increasing noise of their taunts, and the rising rapidity of cutting reflects Stick's building anxiety and anger over the course of events and his limited options in dealing with them.

Suspect is effective because it plays with audience expectations and assumptions about the subject positions of various characters. By the end of the short, the white woman expects that Stick will demand her life. Instead, he demands her respect. Because Stick is a rather inexpressive, quiet character, but is surrounded by friends who advocate violence and attempt to exacerbate the conflict between him and the woman, it is dif-

163

ficult to tell where he stands until the final scene. The technical aspects of the film work to increase ambiguity about his thoughts and motivations, and, in turn, they make it impossible to predict what he is about to do at the end.

Stick's conflict with the woman is foreshadowed by the one he faces at the nightclub: In getting turned away, he shouts out, "You think you know me? You don't know who the fuck I am!" The club manager responds, "Is that supposed to be a threat?" The film eventually reveals, of course, that Stick was merely commenting on his situation as a misjudged and, consequently, "unknown" social subject. But in the eyes of the manager, Stick will only be seen as "suspect." By the time Stick finds himself literally "up against the wall," kicking the chain-linked fence in frustration, the film has demonstrated the stifling aspects of one mode of urban African American masculinity.

Suspect is unique, I think, for the way it not only posits multiple subject positions—African American "good guy," African American "tough guy," African American "tough girl," suspicious white woman, and prejudiced white man—but also for the way it critiques many of those positions at the same time. The white club owner is just as culpable as the white woman who feared Stick, and Stick is just as culpable as his friends who aggravated an already tense situation and called for violence. In this way, subject positions are presented heterogeneously (although not pluralistically) and viewed from various critical points of view. Also, the film refuses to essentialize blackness or femininity. By positing the various world views of Stick and his friends, it insists, unsurprisingly, that not all African Americans maintain the same attitudes or experiences. By featuring the white woman and Marilyn as two very different women, albeit both tough and assertive in their own right, the film's message is that not all women are the same. (At one point, Marilyn is ridiculed for not conforming to traditional femininity. Ralphie complains to her, "Why you gotta curse and shit? Why don't you act like a girl, and maybe somebody would like you.") *Suspect* operates on a plane of "difference" (as opposed to sameness) by playing on tropes, reversing expectations, and simultaneously presenting and critiquing a range of identities and belief systems.

I *LIKE IT LIKE THAT*

Martin's *I Like It Like That* has been received in a number of ways: J. Hoberman called it a "comedy of errors [that] wiggles through contrivances equally suggestive of William Shakespeare and *I Love Lucy*" (18 Oct. 1994: 49). Andrea Stuart in *Sight and Sound* labeled the film "Douglas Sirk meets *La Boheme*" (23). And in *The Village Voice*, Devon Jackson compared it to the "Coen brothers' *Blood Simple* and [Jean-Luc] Godard's *Contempt*" (18 Oct. 1994: 58). These responses suggest the reviewers' inability to pin the film down into any one category—a difficult task given that it falls "in-between" high art and low art, genre film and experimental piece, message film and formula entertainment.

The irreducibility of *I Like It Like That* is perhaps its greatest strength, and that quality better enables the film to comment on race relations, gender norms, and heterosexual romance without becoming dogmatic or didactic. Unlike Coolidge or Bigelow, who re-write or exploit generic codes, Martin attempts to work outside of genre (such as romantic comedy). Informed as much by music video and commercials as by independent or experimental cinema, *I Like It Like That* employs diverse methods to highlight themes of sexuality, desire, and sexism as well as work exploitation, marriage, romance, and familial roles.

In *I Like It Like That*, the main character, Lisette Linares (Lauren Vélez), is forced to find a job when her husband, Chino (Jon Seda), is jailed for trying to steal stereo equipment during a blackout. With three children—L'il Chino (Tomas Melly), Minnie (Desiree Casado), and Pee Wee (Isaiah Garcia)—to feed and a husband to bail out, Lisette finally decides to pawn her wedding ring for train fare to audition for a modeling job. While at the modeling agency, she talks her way into a position as assistant to a recording executive, Price (Griffin Dunne).

A black Puerto Rican woman immersed in barrio culture, Lisette begins to excel in this position because she understands the market for the musicians Price is promoting, namely the duo Tony and Ricky Mendez. Eventually, Chino gets out of jail; but the couple's marriage becomes complicated when, first, a neighbor, Magdalena (Lisa Vidal), pretends that her baby is Chino's, and when, second, it is revealed that Chino has been unfaithful. In seeking revenge, Lisette sleeps with her boss, Price, to little satisfaction. With the philosophical help of her transgendered sister, "Alexis," Lisette returns to Chino, committed to sharing child care with him but uncertain whether their relationship will work out.

Unlike *Suspect*'s use of dark/light contrasts and close-ups to reinforce its meaning, *I Like It Like That* deploys bright, colorful backdrops, multiple planes of depth, and a wide lens frame with congested blocking. With the help of cinematographer Alexander Gruszynski (*The Craft*, 1996; *Pagemaster*, 1994), Martin conveys the style of European art cinema, which she has called her greatest influence; this led one *Village Voice* critic to call her authorial signature "Neorealism with a Steadicam" (Jackson 58). The camerawork supports Lisette's point of view, showing her world to be cramped and claustrophobic through tight, narrow shots. The opening sequence moves so smoothly from the noisy, crowded street outside of Lisette's apartment into the bedroom where she and Chino make love that it accentuates the lack of boundaries between exterior and interior—leaving little guessing as to the state of mind of a character who has no space to herself, whether psychologically or physically.

While *I Like It Like That* is not necessarily a family melodrama, and it resists being categorized in terms of genre, the film's subjective camerawork and use of color operate somewhat similarly to the Douglas Sirk melodramas of the 1950s. Thomas Elsaesser quotes an interview given by Sirk in which he explained that the function of deep-focus lenses and saturated colors was to give "a harshness to the objects and a kind of enameled, hard surface to the colors. I wanted to bring out the inner violence, the energy of the characters which is all inside them and can't break through" (Elsaesser 350). The hard lighting, bright colors, and high contrast that characterize the mise-en-scène of Lisette's world point to her cluttered state of mind and the inner turmoil of being trapped in a drama over which she has little control. These elements highlight the more melodramatic aspects of Lisette's narrative trajectory and make her primary conflicts clear.

Consider, for example, the first sequence: As Lisette and Chino make love, their children try to peek into their bedroom keyhole, the neighbors shout on the street outside their window, and the elderly woman who lives below them bangs her broom against their floorboards. Meanwhile, Chino is more interested in setting a new record as he times their sex with an alarm clock than in paying attention to Lisette. A subjective shot from Lisette's point of view shows her looking upside down out of their window as she bounces back and forth—a shot syncopated to the broom banging of the woman downstairs and the thrusts of Chino's lovemaking. Finally tired of waiting this experience out, Lisette takes control by straddling Chino and screaming, "Cum, cum, cum!" Once they are through, she wades through her apartment of misbehaving children and an immature husband—no doubt on the brink of a breakdown—until finally she utters, "I hate my life" as she buries her head in her arms. Chino can only hear this one way, as evidenced by his response: "I'm your life. Do you hate me?" Lisette's narrative struggle is clear from this point on: she needs to find a way to build a life that she loves, one that extends beyond Chino. The unsettling visual style, especially Lisette's point-of-view shots, suggest her difficult starting point; and the film's jagged structure, full of detours and mishaps, suggests that she has no philosophy or vision about how to survive. But almost every dramatic beat of this film concerns her attempt to re-establish her power and autonomy.

Part of Lisette's struggle entails negotiating her sexual desires with her role as mother. Both Chino and Alexis accuse her of being asexual, out of touch with her sex drive. However, Lisette implies that they cannot see her sexual side because they only allow themselves to see her as maternal. In a culture that sees sexuality and motherhood as mutually exclusive, Lisette attempts to fashion an identity that includes both. This is made even more difficult because she does not meet conventional standards of black or Hispanic beauty. She ashamedly wears prosthetic breasts on her job interview at the modeling agency and, upon arriving, feels that she cannot measure up to the other tall, voluptuous, exotic looking models. Furthermore, Lisette's rival, Magdalena, wins Chino over with her traditional beauty and larger bank balance, fueling Lisette's insecurities.

The short-lived affair with Price becomes a lesson for her to assert her sexual desires. In comparison to her experience with Chino, which was long-lasting but insensitive, she finds that Price's lovemaking is swift but equally callous. After their first encounter, Lisette repeatedly asks him, "That's it?" as he sprays air freshener around his office. Eventually she rejects Price, and his resulting insecurity leads him to propose, "Maybe you should work for a different boss." Expressing the naive feistiness that makes her character three-dimensional, Lisette responds by asking, "Are you quitting?" Lisette's relationship with Price borders on sexual harassment, but never to the point where she loses control over their interaction. Her job in the recording industry allows the film to delve into issues of sexual harassment (and the low status of women of color in the middle-class workforce) in relation to Lisette's self image, especially her concerns over beauty standards, sexuality, and ethnic identity.

The commentary of the film connects the recording studio's exploitation of Lisette (as a woman of color) to that of men of color, artists whose talent and culture is typically controlled by white executives. Price hires Lisette because she can bring Hispanic and African American insight to his white recording agency. Presumably, she can help him sign the Mendez brothers and then market them, because she is part of their target audience. Through Lisette's interactions with the Mendez brothers, *I Like It Like That* becomes a humorous critique of the exploitative and appropriative conditions of the music industry. In addition to this critique, the film offers a site of black Hispanic female desire, because Lisette's major role involves creating an image of the Mendez brothers that meets her own romantic and sexual fantasies.

Her active desires catalyze one "music video" sequence that intertwines three story lines: Lisette dressing up Tony Mendez for his own music video, Chino being released from prison, and L'il Chino becoming part of a gang. Embedded in the codes of music video, which are part of Martin's background, the sequence bridges fantasy and reality by making it unclear whether Lisette's interactions with Tony Mendez are imagined or concrete. Tony and Chino are also doubled, through frame position-ing, wardrobe, and jewelry, further blurring the lines between what Li-sette wants and what is truly going on.

Lisette's desires to re-fashion the version of masculinity to which Chino subscribes become more clear when she is asked to extend the Mendez's appeal beyond a female audience to crossover to men as well. She develops a marketing strategy around a "cover" of the Otis Redding song "Try a Little Tenderness," proposing that the song holds appeal to both men and women because the Mendez brothers will present a soft and vulnerable image without losing face. In other words, she envisions an ideal masculinity governed not by power over women but by respect for them, a paradigm that she is trying to establish in her domestic life (as we will shortly see). In addition, Lisette suggests the brothers sing the song in both English and Spanish, adding yet another layer of cross-over, one that is racial/cultural as opposed to gender-based.

In this marketing meeting, Lisette is yet again forced to confront the sexism of the recording industry when Price recommends that "Try a Little Tenderness" be shot on the beach with a crowd of naked women. Lisette barters him down to *one* woman and insists that she not be repre-sented as a "ho." This scene helps to position Lisette's dilemma as a metaphor for Martin's, especially after Martin's complaint that Lisette's character looks too much like a "dizty model" in the promotional poster for *I Like It Like That*. It is very tempting to compare Lisette's struggle in the white male recording industry to Martin's within the white male film industry, especially considering the accounts that Martin herself gave to the press.

Given that the film challenges the exploitative nature of the music scene, how then does it position discourses of work and labor? Does it conform to the "Spike Lee discourse" of *Do the Right Thing*? Yes and no. Like Lee's films, *I Like It Like That* does pose "a job" as the answer to the problems of urban people of color. When Lisette is being mauled by a group from her neighborhood, a crane shot pulls back to show her small and isolated as she yells at them, "I got a job. What the fuck you people got?!"[16]

However, Martin's solution for Lisette is not just any job, but rather work that helps her to feel fulfilled and that stretches her identity. Ac-cording to Wahneema Lubiano, one of the problems with *Do the Right Thing* is that it does not discriminate between various types of labor: dealing drugs is no different than slinging pizza (271). *I Like It Like That* looks toward middle-class professional jobs as an avenue out of the "un-derclass."

Class is at the heart of Lisette's struggle: she is moving from a work-ing-class consciousness to a middle-class belief system that privileges "self-actualization" and identity transformation. (This is not to say that a bourgeois belief system is the answer to class struggle but to point out that this privileged system has historically been denied to many people of color.) Lisette's status as working woman also distinguishes this film from the "Spike Lee discourse" because women, especially women of color, have traditionally been hindered from pursuing employment that is personally enriching and socially valued. Gloria Gibson-Hudson illuminates the trend on the part of black women filmmakers to "frequently isolate the necessary personal skills needed to interpret and confront issues in everyday life with the hope that a heightened sense of self will lead to individual and collective empowerment" (377).[17]

Another major social concern raised by I Like It Like That relates to marriage and heterosexual romance. A number of feminist theorists have pointed out the ways in which heterosexual coupling is socialized and institutionalized at the expense of women's emotional, social, and economic needs.[18] In an interview with Lizzie Francke, Martin frames her critique of marriage in this way: "We have an amazingly labeled culture which continues prejudice and sexism whether it be around race or gender. But when you get into family, there is another dangerous set of tags—'wife,' 'husband,' 'mother.' For me the story is about Lisette and Chino finding out who they are beyond such labels" (30 Jan. 1995: 29). It would be easy to focus only on the tensions of race and gender in Martin's films, but doing so displaces her highly significant examination of the constraining aspects of marital roles and conventional definitions of the family.

"Family" is a particularly loaded construct for many African American communities because it has a history of being pathologized and blamed for the socio-economic problems confronted by urban African Americans (Young 140). Moreover, as white feminist critics have attempted to critique the oppressive nature of "family," other scholars point out that the family has been a site of empowerment for many disenfranchised African Americans (14). While Martin accentuates the negative implications of marriage and family for her female protagonist, she also brings into relief the white, middle-class biases that govern mainstream representations. One scene in I Like It Like That features Lisette struggling to close the bathroom door on Chino as he fights to keep it open. The strained tension in that door signals deeper anxieties between them—their inability to find their own identities, their unrealistic expectations of each other, their failing communication skills, and most important for Lisette, her difficulty in matching the ideal images "wife" and "mother" with her own experience. The scene ends, not with a peaceful reconciliation, but with Lisette shoving a bathroom plunger in Chino's face just when he thinks she is giving in. The film understands that this couple will make mistakes—indeed Martin's characters make many mistakes. Their duty is to learn how to live with each other's mistakes. Because this is Lisette's story, she must also learn how to demand the respect of others so that she can define "wife" and "mother" in more comfortable ways.

I Like It Like That stresses the fragility of marriage, the precariousness of the identity "married." Lisette's wedding ring undergoes numerous incarnations, depending on character point of view, and ultimately it signifies a destabilization of the very notion of marriage. Chino tells Lisette that the ring symbolizes an insurance policy, a reminder that she should trust him, perhaps even a reminder of his "ownership." To Lisette, it represents an avenue toward greater freedom—she temporarily pawns the ring for a job interview. But because Lisette wears the ring sporadically—in hock, out of hock—it becomes a symbol of the problematic aspects of marriage. Lisette's experience of married life includes lack of privacy, burdensome responsibilities, an adulterous husband, and an unstable family life. When Price notices that her wedding ring will not

In *I Like It Like That* (1994), Lauren Vélez plays Lisette, whose questioning of heterosexual romance and traditional family values takes center stage. (Columbia Pictures)

170

stay put, he asks Lisette, "Are you married or not?" His question points
to her marriage's sliding quality, its inability to offer her a stable identity
even as it promises the label "wife."

In Lisette's struggle to gain self-respect and the respect of those
around her, she comes to a conclusive definition of what she expects from
her marriage with Chino. In one of the final scenes, as Chino is on his
way to sleep in his separate bedroom, Lisette declares she has identified
his problem: "You never think about the other person." Chino responds,
"Good night other person." Lisette remarks, "It's morning." Chino cor-
rects himself, "Good morning." Chino's sought-after acknowledgment
of "the other person" and the shift from "night" to "morning" indicate
a change in their relationship. Though not a promise, this dialogue offers
a glimmer of hope that their marriage may survive.

While Columbia executives apparently desired a more romantic
ending, Martin insisted on leaving Lisette and Chino's marriage wide
open, still fragile, continually able to fail. Implicitly, she offers a critique
of the conventional happy ending, which assumes that the restored heterosexual couple is seamless, mutually fulfilled, and the point of the
whole story anyway. Martin's counter-conclusion is reinforced by transgendered Alexis's presence as a "moral center" for the film.[19] Alexis provides a great deal of humor through her inability to "fit in" to norms of
gender and sexual identity; she also maintains a keen understanding of
human relationships and social values.

Martin's scrutiny of marriage in *I Like It Like That* is additionally
supported by extra-textual accounts that she offers regarding her own
relationship. Although she married an Italian sculptor upon the release
of the film, she noted that they continue to live in separate countries.
Commenting on their non-traditional marriage, she stated, "We get together every two or three months. It's great" (Kroll 80). Martin articulates a politics of marriage that values each partner's commitment to self,
work, and the public sphere as much as to their emotional dependence
on each other.

I Like It Like That ends with a Mendez music video, "Try a Little
Tenderness," which incorporates various shots of Lisette "directing" the
video, choreographing a dance for the video with sister Alexis, slow-
dancing with Chino, and riding a Ferris wheel with her husband and
children. The video sequence ends with Lisette and family riding the
subway home at night, passing by the Ferris wheel titled "Wonder
Wheel," perhaps another reference to the circularity of marital and family relationships. Like the earlier "music video," this sequence blends
fantasy and reality, work life and domestic life, female desire and responsibility. Perhaps the escapist music and dancing of the credit sequence
gloss over the ambiguous ending that comes before it. But they also en-

code Lisette's story with an intimation of female fantasy and agency, having allowed her to instill the commercial MTV video with the knowledge she has learned, knowledge about racial identity, gender expectations, and romantic ideals.

The last major concern addressed by *I Like It Like That* involves parenting, that is, motherhood in relation to femininity and fatherhood in relation to masculinity. The characters inhabit a universe that defies white, middle-class (and conventionally feminine) mores about child-rearing. For example, Lisette and Chino show no discomfort arguing in front of their three children, often cursing and shouting, or using them to seek revenge on the other partner. Lisette indicates little embarrassment at sharing her nervous breakdown in the bathroom with L'il Chino. Nor does she seem to mind locking the children out of the bathroom while she blares Latin music and lights up a cigarette to escape family pressures. The film's goal is not to correct Chino and Lisette's parenting skills, indeed it legitimates their choices and values. However, Lisette and Chino begin to reflect, independently, on their roles within the family and on the ways in which gender norms influence those roles.

One of the ironies of *I Like It Like That* is that L'il Chino and Minnie often seem smarter than their parents, enjoying the ability to boomerang their parents' own logic back at them and force their hand. I have mentioned that the characters in the film are allowed to make mistakes, and many of their mistakes are illuminated by their children. One of the film's most visually stunning scenes occurs when Chino, at a loss in trying to reason with L'il Chino, throws the naked nine year-old out into the hallway. An extreme long shot down the hallway conveys L'il Chino's desolation and vulnerability as it emphasizes his smallness and seclusion. Lisette and Chino may never learn mistake-free parenting, but their parallel journeys into the ideal capitulations of gender, respectively, enlighten them on their obligations to their children, obligations that include redefining gender identity and reinventing "wife" and "husband."

L'il Chino (interestingly the character Martin claims to identify with the most) experiences a difficult time developing a logic about "what makes a man" (Hoffman H28). Is it stealing? Belonging to a gang? Or taking on the well-behaved role of the man of the house while his father is in jail? The link between masculinity and fatherhood is made clear when Chino, once out of jail, disciplines L'il Chino in front of neighbors and friends. A full tilt up of the camera has revealed the new shoes and clothes of L'il Chino, indicating that he has earned money through drugs and gang banging. Chino beats him up against the very wall that contains a memorial in graffiti to Chino's heroic brother, a policeman shot in the line of duty.

172

Chino then starts to beat up on another child gang member, at which point the child argues that only his own father has the right to discipline him. The child expresses a certain code of masculinity, one that dictates only fathers can determine what is "manly" and that they can only do so through physical punishment. Chino and L'il Chino struggle to achieve an alternative definition of masculinity, free of violence and authoritative ownership, an alternative paternal ideal. Chino finds a way to relate to L'il Chino by releasing himself from the unreasonable expectations that he live up to his brother's heroic image, the very image (on the wall) against which Chino has beaten his son.

Chino and L'il Chino's efforts to redefine masculinity through newly found pride and acceptance are accompanied by Alexis's battle to win parental approval for "his" decision to become a woman. Alexis's presence facilitates an ongoing examination of gender stereotypes in relation to other conflicts confronted by the characters. A conversation between Alexis and Lisette toward the conclusion of the film frames Lisette's choices in terms of their own mother who is apparently strong and independent, but alienating. More than just a choice between career and family, Lisette must make decisions about what kind of mother she wants to be, and what version of femininity she will embody. She arrives at a definition that allows her to assure her children of unconditional love, an experience Alexis never felt, but requires that they respect her needs and abilities. In other words, Lisette finds a balance between always being there for them and letting them victimize her. She also constructs an ideal of femininity and a maternal outlook that better fits her everyday experience.

In bringing social and cultural concerns to bear on what are considered to be private, familial issues, *I Like It Like That* relates to *Suspect* in rather obvious ways. Like its predecessor, the more mainstream film critiques and refuses to reify social norms by keeping its positions on gender and race mobile. Whereas *Suspect* highlights issues of masculinity and the intersection of numerous racial points of view, *I Like It Like That* focuses more on marital and family roles, but still in relation to gender and racial stereotypes. Both films address these pressing social concerns through a visual style that is character-driven, allowing affect and attitude to be conveyed through light and color.

Although Martin has expressed frustration with the marketing of *I Like It Like That*, she asserts that the film, as a product, turned out as she had hoped. Claiming that "the film is what I wanted," Martin implies that the final cut matched her preconceptions (author's interview). However, perhaps because of poor promotional strategies, *I Like It Like That* only grossed $1.2 million in its first week (Rhines 75). (The film did recoup its $5.5 million budget within eight weeks [Ouillette 33].) This is due, in part, to Columbia's failure to target African American audiences, instead marketing it to white "art cinema" audiences. This phenomenon resembles that of Lee's *She's Gotta Have It* (1986), which, after its success at the San Francisco and Cannes Film Festivals, played to ninety percent white audiences (Rhines 62). Jesse Algeron Rhines speculates that studios are continuing to entice up-and-coming directors of color to make niche films just as independent companies with African American "boutique pictures" are emerging at a solid pace (74). But until both types of companies learn the nuances of distribution for people of color, these kinds of films (both high- and low-budget) have little chance of gaining great momentum.[20]

MARTIN'S NEGOTIATIONS

To the extent that she has agency in constructing her directorial persona, Martin has refused to adhere to simplistic or reductive social definitions in interviews or promotional discourse. Her ambivalence about being labeled "the first African American woman to direct a major studio feature" implies that she does not want to be defined solely according to her racial and ethnic identity, an identity that in Hollywood represents both an aberration and a commodity. Nor does Martin deny the complexity of that identity, which is informed by her bi-racial (Irish-American and African American) origins. When *New York Times* interviewer Jan Hoffman, in trying to pin down Martin's quality of self-determination, asked the director to label herself, Martin claimed, "I don't know what the word 'vociferous' means exactly, but I think it describes me" (Hoffman H28). This statement demonstrates her ability to keep the terms by which she describes herself unfixed and constantly shifting. She, and the films she has made, insist on troubling conventional conversations about race, gender, class, and heterosexual marriage by extending and destabilizing the terms of the very conversations themselves. These qualities of elision (of self-definition and cinematic meaning) and instability point out, once again, the value of considering the multiple logics in a single cinematic work. *Suspect* is able to show the many sides of one conflict just as *I Like It Like That* presents an ambiguous ending that invites both romantic and critical readings.

At the time that I spoke with Martin she was circulating several speculation scripts, including one psychological thriller about an interracial family living in the Bronx; she was considering turning this into a novel (author's interview; Kroll 80). She voiced a recognition that novel-writing might offer her more creative control. In an attempt to understand her current position in relation to the studio versus independent dilemma, I asked her whether she was pursuing mainstream or counter-cinema venues. With the pragmatism and wit of any director who has had her experiences, she asserted that she does not have the luxury to choose. She laughingly replied, "I'm inclined to go with whoever gives me money . . . and a certain amount of freedom."

5

Tamra Davis

Tamra Davis's films participate in a trend toward more commercially oriented independent cinema. Her first independent feature film, *Guncrazy* (1993), contains a relatively straightforward narrative and boasts rather elaborately choreographed camerawork. Joining the ranks of women's counter cinema a generation later than 1970s feminist filmmakers such as Martha Coolidge, Davis is influenced as heavily by popular culture as by the avant-garde.

Having directed documentaries and short segments for television and film, Davis's foray into mainstream filmmaking occurred after she proved herself in music video. The critical success of *Guncrazy* led to her being hired to direct, among other projects, the rap comedy *CB4* (1993) and the western *Bad Girls* (1994). Like other directors in this study, Davis continues to move in and out of mainstream filmmaking. One of her most difficult and controversial experiences with a studio occurred shortly into production on *Bad Girls*, when she was replaced by Jonathan Kaplan (*The Accused*, 1988; *Unlawful Entry*, 1992). The events surrounding her termination, which will be detailed in an upcoming section, demonstrate a classic case of a studio tying a director's hands and then complaining that she is not using them.

Kaplan's replacement of Davis provides an interesting test case for the limits of authorship. How much of "Davis" exists in the final cut of *Bad Girls*? Precisely what revisions occurred when Davis exited? How much of her vision, if it was her vision, was erased? The status of *Bad Girls* suggests that the Hollywood studio mode of production, though no doubt "collaborative" in a technical sense, is often merely a case of employees working "around" each other rather than "together"; when a writer re-writes a colleague's screenplay, or a new producer insists on changes that conform to his or her idea of "what will sell," there is little sense of collective action.[1] Davis's complicated involvement with *Bad Girls* invites a consideration of how authorial signatures might, or might not, be traced within a text that is fractured and multiply owned. A film is composed of contradictory impulses and ideologies—what comes, then, when one tries to divine the origins of the contradictions?

The problems of authorship that guide this chapter are compounded by Davis's collaboration with cinematographer Lisa Rinzler (on *Guncrazy* and *Bad Girls*). In addition to her work with Davis, Rinzler has directed photography for the Hughes brothers (on *Menace II Society*, 1993, and *Dead Presidents*, 1995), Nancy Savoca (on *True Love*, 1989), and Steve Buscemi (*Trees Lounge*, 1997). Rinzler has developed a self-conscious cinematic style that includes frequent use of tension-building mobile camerawork (with a Steadicam), deeply imbued color patterns by way of sophisticated lighting techniques, and devices of slow motion to isolate dramatic beats. The minimal attention devoted to Rinzler's work points to the erasure of directors of photography as a result of the romanticization of the director. Within the neglected category of "DP," only a handful of women have been inducted into the American Society of Cinematographers, and Rinzler is not among them (at the date of this writing). That Davis and Rinzler were both fired from *Bad Girls* should come as no surprise—the "failing" vision of the film that producers wanted to quickly eradicate was a result of their deeply entwined collaboration.

Tamra Davis's films provide the ground for several lines of inquiry. First, how has her MTV background influenced her filmmaking style? How does she negotiate this influence with her feminist politics, which are evident not only in *Guncrazy* but also in a film short she directed on women rockers, *No Alternative Girls* (1994)? Davis's *CB4* illustrates an interesting tension between an MTV "aesthetic" and social commentary. Secondly, how does 1990s independent women's cinema differ from that of the 1970s? A new generation of women directors has arisen in the 1990s—including Allison Anders, Maria Maggenti, and Rose Troche—who are interested in stretching the possibilities of narrative pleasure and reaching a wider audience (Ouillette 28). In part, the differences in women's contemporary films involve a change in distribution methods, and, as we will see, Davis's films have been marketed and distributed in rather non-conventional ways that reflect changing technological innovations.

Thirdly, how does Davis's work suggest the influence of multiple collaborators and participants, namely Rinzler and, less congenially,

Kaplan? Although all films are the result of diverse efforts, and Davis's films represent a norm rather than an anomaly in this regard, her particular encounters allow a more comprehensive and elaborate interrogation of the very common phenomenon of collaboration.

Davis's Start in Music Video

Tamra Davis considers herself very much a part of "young, corporate America," having been immersed in contemporary popular culture from a young age and gotten her start in the youth-oriented, capitalist marketplace of MTV. She describes herself as a product of the "Madonna age," which assured teenage girls that it was okay, indeed empowering, to be "strong about their sexuality" (author's interview). Music video has proved to be a viable path into Hollywood for directors such as David Fincher (*Alien*[3], 1992; *Seven*, 1995; *The Game*, 1997) or Michael Bay (*The Rock*, 1996; *Con Air*, 1997) especially in relation to the action or blockbuster film. But, as the cases of Fincher and Bay suggest, that pathway is paved with male bias, which means that Davis has had to struggle to succeed in the more ghettoized genre of comedy once she began working in Hollywood.

Davis was hired by MTV after catching the attention of a recording executive with a super 8 millimeter film she made in a production course at Los Angeles City College. (Prior to her film school training, Davis apprenticed at Francis Ford Coppola's Zoetrope Studios.) Although Davis says she felt somewhat excluded from the possibilities of film direction because it was difficult for her "to visually imagine myself as a director," as a woman in a male-dominated field, she made the most of the attention she began to garner in the field of music video. Her comfort with the mass media and popular culture notwithstanding, she remains acutely aware of feminist politics—thanks, in part, to her mother's participation in the second-wave feminist movement (author's interview). Also, Davis is a white woman who maintains an astute sensitivity to multicultural issues, an interest she says MTV, with its cross-cultural leanings, has encouraged.

Music video lives out a troubled relationship to both counter cinema and feminist politics. The style and format of music video are heavily influenced by several generations of anti-authoritarian avant-garde films, yet they serve the marketing interests of the television and recording industries. MTV and stations like it are commercial on many levels; they not only sell music and television programming but also a specific network identity and an "aesthetic" immersed in the commerce of a youth culture. Thus, with the music video genre it is difficult to situate a director as an "author" in relation to such a multifaceted "text." In the first

179

place, a music video is a peculiarly porous "text," given its intertextual relation to the star personas of the performers, their other products (CDs, films, posters), and live concerts; it also relates to the state of music video culture at a particular historical moment (Goodwin 1987: 41). In the second place, music video is so commercial that many participants, including the musicians, their producers and promoters, as well as the networks, have a stake in the final product. It is important to understand the performers, producers, networks, even spectators, as well as the director as potential authors. It is also important to understand that there may be no music video author, in the way that term has been used in this book—as both an origin and an "effect" that coincides with a certain set of politics, themes, and cinematic or videographic devices.

Along structural and stylistic lines, most music videos maintain a semblance of the classical three-act structure, even if it's only a simple story "spine" to keep viewer attention. However, this spine often allows videos to diverge outside the dynamics of time and space continuity to displace standard patterns of meaning-making. A flow of disparate images is organized around the principle of discontinuity rather than the logic of linearity and cause and effect. In addition, videos may lack an "anchor"—a character or point of identification—or they may offer up several "anchors" so that viewer identifications are encouraged to continually shift (Goodwin 1987: 45). This means that music video tends to be governed by "structures of feeling" that make the form "poetic and metaphoric" through its vertical layering of visual, musical, and narrative fragments (Schwichtenberg 1989: 5). Andrew Goodwin has discussed the "synaesthesia" of music video, referring to the tempo of the music as expressed by camerawork, editing, performer movement, etc. (1993: 60). Hence, the pleasure of music video is located in "the making musical of the television image. Television is musicized" (1993: 70).

Music video's fragmented and co-optive nature associates it with the debates surrounding postmodernism. As Peter Wollen suggests, "Its [music video's] characteristic modes are those of appropriation, simulation, and replication" (1986: 168). Often referred to as the quintessential postmodern form, music video blurs the boundaries between high art and low art, the authentic and the artificial, and reality and fiction. But its postmodern, not to mention commercial, qualities also raise the question of its relation to politics. Margaret Morse points out that the youth culture supported by the music video industry is less political than that which grew into being during the social movements of the 1960s because of its commercialized and corporatized environment (1986: 308). There are two sides to the argument over the political possibilities of MTV; scholars such as David Tetzlaff posit that music video is fundamentally escapist and isolationist while Mary Ellen Brown and John Fiske contend that music video operates in a more "open" and polysemous mode than the relatively closed system of Hollywood film (1986: 87–88; 1987: 66).

In approaching Davis's work, it is important to strike a balance between the polar ends of this debate so that music video is understood as both escapist and potentially politically progressive at the same time. Dana Polan advocates this balance in his proposition that MTV may produce floating signifiers but they are still controlled and contained by historically specific ideologies (1986: 48). Polan allows for the "openness," mobility, and spectator empowerment that music video might invite through its fragmentary and rebellious structure and style; but he also bears in mind the limitations of the corporate culture in which videos are produced. Similarly, Andrew Goodwin warns against assuming that the multiple layers of music video are necessarily "Brechtian" or that its "lack of closure" offers spectators unrestricted possibilities for resistance (1993: 94–95). He argues that the ambiguity effected by multiple layers or lack of narrative closure is a convention of MTV, rather than a subversion of it, because such ambiguity draws in a mass audience (95). Goodwin urges scholars to understand that "there are two MTVs. One MTV discourse is the nihilistic, pastiching, essentially pointless playfulness that is invoked by postmodernist accounts of MTV. The other is responsible, socially consciousness, satire, and parody based, vaguely liberal—and almost invisible in academic accounts of MTV" (150). Goodwin's formulation of MTV as contradictory remains consistent with the model of films, whether independent or Hollywood, as multi-vocal and "tension-based" (as Rick Altman puts it). The contradictions of MTV mean that a music video director can only incorporate progressive ideas and images into her work to the extent that she can also keep that work amusing, open to multiple interpretations, and commercially viable.

The more narrow debate within feminist theory about what music video offers to women is equally complicated. E. Ann Kaplan, for example, celebrates the postmodern possibilities of MTV as she also criticizes it for objectifying women and offering female spectators no fixed position for feminist identification (1987: 15). Dana Polan raises the point that traditional feminist film theory's notion of "woman as fetish" needs to be replaced in conversations about music video by that of woman as "unattainable," "dispersed image" because of the mobility and destabilization involved (52). Scholars such as Lisa Lewis, Brown and Fiske, and Cathy Schwichtenberg vie for more liberating perspectives on music video. For example, Lewis acknowledges MTV's "male mode of address," which draws "on the connection between male-adolescent license and adult-male rule" (1990: 43). However, Lewis provides instances of Pat Benatar and Tina Turner re-appropriating "the street," a space typically reserved for rehearsals of male privilege and access in music video (44, 223). In essence, she argues that music video offers female vocalists a stage to visually interpret their lyrics, to articulate something akin to a omnipotent voice-over narration in classical film so that their preferred meaning finds an outlet (71).

Lewis also notes Cyndi Lauper's exploitation of the "narrative fragments" of music video in an attempt to mirror the "contradictory experiences of female adolescents" (122). In a similar move, Brown and Fiske posit that stars such as Madonna offer teenage girls a space for fantasy because music video leaves open many gaps for the spectator to fill in according to her own desires and anxieties (1987: 66). Schwichtenberg's analysis of Madonna's videos correspondingly finds that they produce a "multiplicity of female pleasure" and that MTV conjures up "a pleasurable dance of meanings that circulate around and through evocative images" (8, 5). These examinations of music video suggest that the form can be manipulated in both production and reception in order to stretch feminist imaginations or to provocatively reflect the contradictions of female experiences within the capitalist and patriarchal logics of the music and television industries. While Davis has not necessarily focused on directing female vocalists (she has directed over one hundred fifty music videos), the feminist scholarship on music video suggests that Davis's participation should in no way reflect co-optation by the commercial and masculinist world MTV supposedly represents.[2]

According to scholars of hip-hop culture, commentaries on racism and classism operate differently than that of gender politics. For example, Tricia Rose claims that the tendency for African American males to posture and gesture intimidatingly has to do with a collective "fantasy of revenge" against white privilege (114). Spaces of play such as those that have made Madonna notorious need not be opened up in their videos, she claims, because the very presence of the rappers implies a challenge to the status quo. Rose asserts that "hip-hop style *is* black urban renewal" (1994: 61). She takes issue with the critical bias that deems women rappers as progressive and male rappers as "uniformly sexist" with "imaginary clarity" (147). Robin D. G. Kelley concurs, explaining that the authoritative "I" voiced by African American hard-core hip-hoppers is steeped in African oral tradition and "enables gangsta rappers to navigate a complicated course between what social scientists call 'structure' and 'agency' " (1996: 124). These insights do not mean that misogyny in rap videos is any more valid than in other media forms; but they do imply that feminist theory has developed refined tools for searching out reflexivity, parody, and political commentary regarding gender politics. Further (different) modes of discovery need to be cultivated in order to more fully understand tensions of race and class in music video.

182

The duality of MTV, as both highly profit-oriented and potentially socially conscious, means that Davis's agency as a director lies in her ability to bolster or underscore certain facets of a star persona or a song's meaning in conjunction with a performer's preferred reading of his or her own work. She is most likely navigating ways of reinforcing specific socially relevant meanings rather than originating a socially conscious concept out of whole cloth, because her role involves collaborating with a number of industry professionals, most specifically the performers, to help them sell their music and establish a repertoire of images. In the videos examined here, Davis's work tends to find feminist expression through devices such as portraying a female performer as confident and authoritative, drawing out the political implications of a song through visual references, enhancing the parodic qualities of conventional representations of masculinity, or reversing some stereotypical elements of music video such as the objectification of women by placing men in the position of spectacle. These cases insinuate that feminist reinforcement is much more likely when feminist elements already circulate within the performers' repertoire or vocabulary. If the star's persona or reputation seems less open to feminist interpretation, a music video director's room for political commentary is more restricted.

For the sake of comparison, I will briefly examine four of Davis's videos, two of which feature female-fronted musical groups with feminist interests (MC Lyte and Veruca Salt) and two of which feature male-fronted groups with more "masculinist," arguably misogynistic, interests (Tone Loc and the D.O.C./N.W.A.). The point is not to uncomplicatedly categorize the women's videos as "progressive" and the men's videos as "conservative," nor is it to argue for a simple categorization of women's versus men's videos. Rather, because music videos are determined to such a great degree by a performer's persona and social concerns, it seems appropriate to draw an analogy between male-dominated videos and male-dominated Hollywood. With such an analogy, it becomes important to gauge the extent to which Davis has been able to infuse her music video work with feminist points of view by comparing female-dominated videos to male-dominated videos.

Davis's direction of MC Lyte's "Cha Cha Cha" (shot by Lisa Rinzler) reinforces the performer's star persona and draws out the self-celebratory mood of her lyrics. At the time of the video's release in 1989, MC Lyte had built a reputation as one of the few female hip-hoppers in a male-dominated rap industry. *Rolling Stone* painted her as a tomboy who championed social causes such as AIDS education and teenage pregnancy prevention (Smith 17). One of the major themes of her songs focused on her lack of need for male approval. Critic William Eric Perkins associates MC Lyte with the "dis" style of rap, in which women compete

183

with one another to proclaim their power in terms of verbal wordplay and vocal delivery (30).

"Cha Cha Cha" articulates this self-assuredness and jovial self-glorification through lyrics such as "I'm a road runner, leaving you in the dust / I can adjust / to the times, I might just get quicker / Is that the ticker / of your pacemaker?" Much of the video frames MC Lyte in medium shot as she directly addresses the camera. Wearing various costumes, including a black leather jacket and denim jeans, a black sport suit, or a solid white dress, she postures confidently as she raps.

The video is also constructed in a way that emphasizes the tough, urban world referred to in MC Lyte's songs. Most of the action takes place by a bridge underpass along a New York City river. Shot entirely in black and white, the video conveys rather low production value, at times appearing to be overexposed or hastily shot. The recurring bright sunlight and the glowing lightbulb used during an "interrogation" sequence contribute to the harshness of the video; its overall visual aesthetic becomes one of an assaultive glare. This aesthetic supports MC Lyte's lyrics "The light will blind your sight / But the rhythm will still guide you through the night." The interruption provided by the two representations of light mimics the occasional intrusion of higher-pitched synthesizers and percussion as well as "scratch" (the scratching of a record album). Perhaps the implication of the glare is that viewers can overcome the harshness of the video's bright lights if they put stock in the rapper and her songs, just as MC Lyte has faith that her music will shepherd her through the chaotic urban landscape she sings about.

While the main focus of "Cha Cha Cha" revolves around the great degree to which MC Lyte should be admired and celebrated, the song extends this theme by illuminating the importance of male respect for all women. The only narrative strand of the video features a man being interrogated by MC Lyte and her male "posse" after he has displayed brazen disrespect for women. As the lyrics stress that MC Lyte refuses to be taken advantage of, a series of circular pans show her wagging her finger at the offender and making her hand into a fake gun, which she aims at his head. She and her comrades physically threaten the man for contemplating "ruining her name," which briefly shapes the video into a morality play.

As previously mentioned, "Cha Cha Cha" remains relatively light-hearted—anyone who agrees to revere MC Lyte can join the party. Toward the end of the video, multiple shots show the rapper and her entourage "scratching," dancing, and lipsynching the lyrics as the party atmosphere becomes more and more the point of the song. In fact, MC Lyte's entourage is made up exclusively of men who operate as spectacle and support in much the way that women have traditionally functioned in male rap or rock videos. MC Lyte, in the terms put forward by Davis, not only demands respect from men, she expects veneration. Whether or not the presentation of these adoring men reflects a self-conscious reversal of the sexist codes of music video is uncertain, but it certainly provided a refreshing variation in its late 1980s hip-hop context.

Whereas "Cha Cha Cha" is concerned with highlighting the female artist's power and authority, the video for Veruca Salt's "All Hail Me" is interested in re-interpreting a particular narrative about male power into overtly feminist terms. The video for the white, female-fronted alternative rock band furthers the meaning of the song about a serial killer by staging it in the context of a little boy's birthday party. The brightness of the video—a function of the white walls and open windows of the house in which the party takes place, as well as the pastel colors of the children's celebratory outfits—contrasts with the stark mood of the song. The lyrics in "All Hail Me" conjure up the inevitable flippancy and irony involved in the apology of a serial killer. The chorus "So sorry, so sorry, so sorry now" conveys the untimeliness of such an apology. Each of the verses—like "So sorry Mister / But don't look now / I shot your sister / I shot her down"—re-center the violence and tragedy of the serial killer's actions, which are perpetrated, the song tells us, exclusively against women. The song's bridge goes even further in indicting male privilege and the prevailing culture of male violence: "I'm a bad man / I do what I can. I'm a bad man / I do what I can. I'm a bad man / I do what I can. All hail me."

This bridge serves as the axis upon which the video pivots, because the birthday party is constructed in a way that suggests male violence is simply an extension of cultural attitudes that make up part of everyday life even for a child. The children, particularly the birthday boy, play with guns and masks as they test their parents to see how far the "game" of violence is allowed to go. The video focuses increasing attention on the birthday boy, whose white clothing, suspenders, and oversized cardigan sweater distinguish him from the other children. In a continual oscillation that suggests there is a fine line between a charmer and an abuser, the boy goes from sweetly blowing out his pastel blue birthday cake to pounding the cake with his fists. One shot shows him cutely tapping the piñata with a stick; but in the next shot he strikes it viciously. By the end of the video the boy is throwing a large stone across the fence into a neighbor's yard and revealing a sadistic face against a desolate backdrop of barren trees. The convergence of images and lyrics implies that men will exploit male privilege and access when given the chance. They, in fact, lay the blame of a single serial killer's actions on a society that promotes misogyny by way of the subtle rites and rituals of childhood.

Three strands of action make up the narrative trajectory of "All Hail

Me." Veruca Salt performs the song at the birthday party as the children dance and sing along. This allows for a "live concert" dimension in which band members directly address the camera through off-center close-ups and two-shots. The action of the party is also centralized through small vignettes (birthday boy gets disciplined for being reckless with toy gun, children scrounge for piñata candy on the ground) that provide the video with a general narrative drive. The visual look and character blocking of these vignettes also recall the techniques of domestic home video and family snapshots, which help to reinforce the video's theme that societal conflict is rooted in the concrete gender and class dynamics of the everyday. A third strand consists of close-ups of various children as they lip-synch the words of the song. While the children's performances function to lighten the mood of the song—that is, to provide contrast to its disturbing subject matter—they also invite dual readings of the children as both innocent and jaded. If the birthday boy is cute and yet the incarnation of a "bad man," then these children are naive and yet well schooled in the violence and inequity that surrounds them.

With "All Hail Me," Davis extends the critique of male privilege suggested in the song by re-contextualizing it within the supposedly harmless atmosphere of a child's birthday party. By suggesting that the children are already assuming their positions within a gender drama that promotes violence against women, she implicates an entire culture for the wrongs of an individual. This implication is part of the Veruca Salt song but becomes overstated in the video. Also, the setting of the party enables this critique to be expressed in a way that is not too heavy-handed for music video audiences. The mood of light entertainment, the bright splashes of color, the excessive performer movement, and the spectacle of youth reflected in the children's faces contribute to the video's sense of playfulness and enhance the ambiguity of its underlying meaning. Obviously, Davis's success in the marketplace of the music video industry depends on her ability to balance escapist entertainment with social commentary.

In comparison to "All Hail Me," the video for mainstream rapper Tone Loc's "Funky Cold Medina" offers fewer opportunities for cultural critique. The video takes place mostly in a nightclub that is cast alternatingly in primary colors and black and white. Loc plays the role of the sleazy "man on the prowl" as he sits at the bar or roams the club while directly addressing the camera. The video opens on a close-up of a mug full of the "medina," a foamy, green liquid with steam rising from the top. As Loc explains, the medina is the secret to wooing women into bed: "This brother told me a secret on how to get more chicks / Put a little medina in your glass and the girls will come real quick. It's better than any alcohol or aphrodisiac / A couple of sips of this love potion and she'll be on your lap." An implicit lesson of the song is that the medina, and by implication male sexuality, should be conserved and regulated so that men do not lose control (of their bodies, money, sexual freedom, etc.). But the most troubling implications of the song is that women should be made as passive as possible—as they are placed under a spell by the medina—so that men can retain control over male/female sexual relationships.

Framed as they are by the misogynistic undertones of the lyrics, the women in the video tend to dance sexily toward Loc or gesture provocatively toward the camera. At the beginning of the video, one woman in particular is presented through close-ups of her legs, mid-section, and face in ways that fragment and objectify her body. One male spectator observes her by pulling his sunglasses to the tip of his nose and surveying her up and down, offering a classic example of the "male gaze." Loc also observes several women in this fashion, lending added weight to the structures of the "male gaze" within the video. Loc's homophobic reference to a shocking encounter he had when he mistakenly fed the medina to a man, and his contempt for a woman who would go so far as to expect a marital commitment from him, further flesh out a portrait of Loc and his world as sexist and defensive about masculinity.

Part of Loc's persona, however, is his light-heartedness and sense of humor, which account for the accusation that he is not "hard-core" enough (Tannenbaum 31). His constant "mugging" for the camera and playful smiles offer up cues that the story about the medina, and its effects, are not to be taken too seriously. The final shot of the video, which matches the last abrupt beat of the music, emphasizes a happy-go-lucky tone by framing Loc in close-up as he gives a wink and an "A-OK" sign to the camera. While the light-heartedness with which Loc is able to sing about his attempts to trick women into catering to his desires indicates the more problematic aspects of music video (its escapism and blasé attitude), the humorous tone also signals to its MTV audience that such a story about male omnipotence and sexual prowess is not to be taken too seriously.

In addition, a sequence occurs toward the end of the video in which Loc is turned down by every woman he approaches in the nightclub. As he nears each one, a cartoon bubble conveying her thoughts appears over her head. One woman is thinking, "Tone who?" Another reacts to him with the thoughts, "Say what?" And the last woman's thoughts simply read "Kapoww!" as she strikes him in the face with her fist. The centralization of these women's subjectivities in relation to Loc—that is, their indifference to him and their resistance to his "magic formula"—offers an important counterpoint to the female characters who decoratively dance around Loc or serve as mere spectacle for the men in the bar.

One of Davis's videos for the D.O.C. and N.W.A. (which stands for "Niggaz with Attitude") leaves even less room for feminist commentary. "It's Funky Enough" is governed by a simple narrative spine inspired by the song's lyrics in which the D.O.C. must prove to N.W.A. that his rap is "funky enough." Its premise is that N.W.A.'s Eazy E is listening to the D.O.C.'s song on cassette tape as he rides in his limousine. Shot in stark black and white, the video randomly connects images of the D.O.C. directly addressing the camera with visuals of railroad tracks, tunnels, alleyways, and an abandoned landscape alongside a bridge underpass (probably the same location as that of MC Lyte's video). The series of settings, in conjunction with the eerie undercurrent of the song's downbeat, create a mood of loss and desolation that is counterpointed, to some extent, once the D.O.C. and N.W.A. join at the end of the video in what becomes a party-like atmosphere.

Central to "It's Funky Enough" is experimentation with light and the juxtaposition of low-key shadows. For example, one repeated shot shows the hood of a car as it drives through a tunnel toward the light at the other end. The light ahead casts a reflection on the car's hood and brings the hood ornament into shadow. The overall image of light and shadow becomes doubled, with one half of the image inverted, as the car drives closer to the tunnel's end. Another shot occurs in the tunnel and involves a spotlight that is directed onto the ground in front of the D.O.C. in such a way that, as he sings, the light looks like a record album. The spotlight is seen again jerkingly dancing across the D.O.C.'s face in a close-up. It appears that Davis attempted to extend the modest tools of the video's premise—Eazy E riding in a car, the D.O.C. trying to prove himself—to design unique and complicated visual images. The play of light on black-and-white video also adds a bleakness to the already barren settings that convey the idea that the D.O.C.'s ambition to be "funky enough" to achieve musical success is bound by his hopes to either escape the depressing landscape around him or change it.

As the D.O.C. and N.W.A. join together, the mood of the video becomes lighter with all the band members dancing, lipsynching, and playing "scratch" around a turntable on a city street. A group of women dancing in scant, Caribbean outfits avert their eyes from the camera. The camera shows their hips and waists in close up as the women rock and sway. They serve as decorative spectacle in ways that are similar to the women at the beginning of Tone Loc's "Funky Cold Medina." Davis may be able to reverse the structuring devices that frame women as objects for male consumption by placing the men in positions of spectacle for MC Lyte's videos, but she is not able to escape such devices altogether. This conclusion is not surprising in light of the heavy weight placed on the spectacle of the female body (especially through fragmenting close-ups) within the conventional codes of music video.

The objectification of the women in "It's Funky Enough" is also predictable given the background of the D.O.C. and N.W.A. These rappers have been attacked by feminists (from various racial positionings) for voicing lyrics that denigrate women and glamorize male brutality, and rightly so. But the criticism against hardcore "gansta rap" is complicated by racist denunciations that stereotype it as promoting "cop killing" and gang violence. Such blanket denunciations by popular press gloss over the reasons why urban African Americans might find gratification in the music of N.W.A. and the D.O.C.; and they deny the facts that in many cases the music is indeed "funky enough" to party to and that rural white teenagers have always been major consumers of hip-hop. In 1989, when Davis shot this video, N.W.A. enjoyed a certain amount of support from cultural critics who avoided those areas of concern and did not want to see hip-hop censored. (N.W.A.'s video "Straight Outta Compton" was banned from MTV for glamorizing gang violence.) However, the racial and class issues raised by the music of the D.O.C. and N.W.A. do not excuse their sexism. The D.O.C.'s lyrics in "It's Funky Enough" claim the rapper's right to be heard and respected in wider mainstream culture ("I am not illiterate / Not even a little bit / Nothing like an idiot"). But the song's celebration of African American male bravado and superiority eventually comes at the expense of the women (specifically women of color) who are forced to subordinate themselves visually to the male singers around them.

This brief comparison of female-centered and male-centered videos demonstrates some ways that the fragmentary, ambiguous, and multi-layered nature of music video does not guarantee MTV directors free range for cultural critique or political commentary. Not only were Davis's directorial decisions determined by the concerns of the marketplace but they were also formidably shaped by the interests and reputations of the performers. Davis's video for MC Lyte shows an early concern over issues of racial and gender difference, which becomes increasingly defined and sophisticated as Davis gained experience in the industry.

Davis shows a great deal of dexterity in borrowing the platform of alternative rock video to make a statement about female power and inequitable gender relations in her short film *No Alternative Girls*, which appeared on Polygram Video's program *No Alternative: A Benefit for AIDS Education and Relief* (1994). Geared toward raising awareness about AIDS, HIV, and safe sex, this program featured a collection of film shorts directed by independents such as Hal Hartley, Jennie Livingston, and Derek Jarman, and it included vocal performances by alternative artists such as Smashing Pumpkins and the Breeders. *No Alternative Girls* exists as a "female counterpoint" to the other shorts in the film, most of which appear devoid of any interest in the specificity of women's and girls' experience with safe sex or sexuality in general.

In *No Alternative Girls*, Davis juxtaposes random black-and-white and drained color images with interviews with grunge and rock performers Courtney Love, Luscious Jackson, Free Kitten, Huggy Bear, and Bikini Kill. While many unique images mingle in the short film, one shot is repeatedly inserted: a bleached out, faded yellow and green image of several women in a park seated around a turntable. Their positions around the turntable coincide with the lyric "revolutionary," yoking together music and politics.

The short emphasizes the female performers' common respect for one another and their mutual need to see other women articulating positions of power, even as they voice perspectives that are incongruent with one another. Most overtly, *No Alternative Girls* transforms the debate about safe sex into an issue of teenage girls' right to "say no" when faced with a sexual situation. The short becomes a reassurance that a girl has a right to her own body, to adorn her body in the way she chooses, and to share her body with whom she chooses. Rather than shouldering young girls with the burden of responsibility of sexuality, this congregation of female rockers ultimately empowers them with the right to abstain or to choose safe sex. *No Alternative Girls* clearly enabled Davis to explore feminist politics in a more direct and slightly less commercial way than many of her music videos had.

Tamra Davis's music video work places her squarely in the realm of youth culture. She defines one of the marks of her "authorial signature" as her appeal to female audiences under the age of thirty and her immersion in the world of popular culture. As we will see, her feature film *Guncrazy* exhibits this connection to young, "hip" audiences and should be viewed, in part, as an extension of her video work. She activates deeply complicated issues of contemporary feminism because her work emerges at the intersection of late capitalism and what some have called "postfeminism," a response to the second wave that both incorporates and erases feminist politics at the same time.[3] Davis's involvement in youth-oriented pop culture deserves to be considered in a feminist light. Her participation in what Lisa Lewis calls "female-adolescent discourse" engages in "the much needed work of acknowledging the fact that oppressed women begin their lives as oppressed girls" (Lewis 224). Therefore, it would be wrong to categorize Davis as "postfeminist," but appropriate, I think, to understand that her feminism is destined to continually face compromise because of the popular sphere in which she gained her foothold.

190

One of the central feminist questions Davis puts to her adolescent-female audience involves the issue of violence. Both *Guncrazy* and (her version of) *Bad Girls* advocate violence if activated in the face of oppression, particularly male oppression. She dramatizes the extent of this oppression by demonstrating the lengths her female characters will go to escape it. Without being didactic or providing any definitive answers, Davis invites a new audience, that of young teens, into rhetorical conversations about the legitimacy of violence as a means of gaining autonomy and/or political freedom. Her most specific interest concerns the ways in which any victim who is controlled through violence might "learn" that control mechanism so well that he or she turns it around on the oppressor.

GUNCRAZY

While Davis boasts a background in MTV, her first feature film was made independently on the relatively low budget of $900,000. *Guncrazy*, which took six years for Davis to make, first made the rounds at film festivals, including Cannes. While the film garnered minimal exhibitor interest, a number of festival critics rallied around the film and helped to spread word of mouth. Even though Pauline Kael–style "rescuing" of films that might otherwise fade into obscurity tends to occur less in the 1990s, *Guncrazy*'s success provides evidence that it still does happen. Based on the "buzz" created at festivals, various distribution rights were sold to the Showtime cable station and Academy Entertainment home video, allowing the producers to recuperate the film's production cost (Nichols C22). Reception at the Toronto Film Festival was particularly enthusiastic, and it was there that a Los Angeles film consultant, Ray Price, approached producers Zane W. Levitt and Diane Firestone in hopes of organizing a theatrical release. After *Guncrazy* was screened in several New York and Los Angeles "art house" cinemas, word of mouth began to spread and theaters in other cities expressed interest in exhibition. Theatrical distribution practically doubled the film's gross proceeds: it earned another $125,000 in four weeks. It was while the film established a platform in these larger cities that it was also released on home video by Academy and on cable by Showtime.

The three-pronged distribution approach with *Guncrazy* (theater, cable, video) is obviously quite rare and was only successful because video rental stores refrained from heavy publicity during the weeks that theaters exhibited it (C22). The simultaneity of distribution avenues actually encouraged word of mouth and reinforced the film's popularity. Diverging from the typically linear route from theater to video and/or cable represented a risky distribution strategy; but such non-traditional circulation paid off in this instance precisely because of the momentum built by word of mouth and critical acclaim. In general, rental videos and cable stations have provided women directors with more outlets for their work, as have the increasing number of both mainstream and counter-cinema festivals.

Although *Guncrazy* combines a glossy visual style with a straightforward narrative, the film also incorporates a feminist morality and a philosophical discussion of violence, suggesting that highly accessible films are not necessarily devoid of political content. *Guncrazy* has been criticized for glamorizing violence in the face of social adversity, partially because of its visual shimmer; however, the female protagonist's experiences are repeatedly foregrounded in a way that invites deeper questions about gender inequality and class immobility.

A basic tension structured *Guncrazy*'s reception upon its release. Critics either accused the film of promoting violence for violence's sake or they applauded it for re-vamping the film noir genre to provide a tragic commentary on the state of its main characters, Anita (Drew Barrymore) and Howard (James Le Gros). For instance, Graham Fuller of *Interview* lamented that the "post-MTV grunge" film is driven by "its own pointless momentum" and provides "a savvy study of nihilism" (Jan. 1993: 47). Similarly, *New York*'s David Denby emphasized the film's "unthinking fatalism made hip by extreme violence," claiming that it congratulates and romanticizes the protagonists' helplessness (22 Feb. 1993: 61).

On the other hand, Vincent Canby of *The New York Times* applauded the manner in which this "very accomplished, cruelly entertaining new movie . . . pays homage to its predecessors while also sending them up" (27 Jan. 1993: C17). In *The Independent*, Laurie Ouillette affirmed: "Violence and sexual promiscuity permeate the film, but the social origins and gendered connotations of Anita's troubled behavior are always emphasized" (Apr. 1995: 30). The latter arguments, to me, prove more valid, especially considering the sense that these characters are already "doomed" from the start of the film. This sense of doom invites the viewer to understand their problems within a socio-economic perspective and to try to envision what their futures, particularly Anita's, would have been had they been born without the physical abuse and economic exploitation that pervades most facets of their existence.

When I asked Tamra Davis how she viewed this debate about violence and what her intentions had been in developing the film's message, she explained:

> My goal was simply to get a reaction. When we test-screened it, some people laughed while others cried. But at least their reaction was extreme. I

wanted to say something about how our society abuses people and yet gives them violent possibilities to turn that abuse back onto society. I was interested in offending people about that. (author's interview)

While Davis dislikes the notion of prescribing a singular response to *Guncrazy*, she reiterated her own interest in what she calls "female abuse issues" (author's interview). She conducted extensive research into teenage girls' responses to sexual abuse in an attempt to understand patterns of dress, school performance, and social interaction. Davis set out to accentuate Anita's motivation as an abused girl, particularly Anita's desire to "be liked" and approved of.

The complaint that the film was too violent and superficial was no doubt elicited, in part, by *Guncrazy*'s glossy, hyper-conscious artistic style. Perhaps the visuals "distracted" some from the film's political content. Along similar lines, its heightened stylization would most likely be seen by feminist critics as a move away from women's counter cinema of the 1970s, which emphasized distanciation and a "destabilized" viewer. Lisa Rinzler's cinematography deploys odd angles, unique perspectives, and richly textured color motifs that are more about visual acrobatics and a demonstration of cinematic mastery than an attempt to distance the viewer. Unlike the static camera, minimal editing, and the interruptions of a directorial presence, which characterized films such as Coolidge's *Not a Pretty Picture* and Bigelow's *The Loveless*, Davis's direction and Rinzler's cinematography stretch the limits of "low-budget" filmmaking into a complex choreography of shots, cuts, and sound.

Working almost exclusively in music video and independent counter cinema, Rinzler has developed a reputation for mobile camerawork, slow motion film speed, and intricate use of lighting to create chiaroscuro effects and intense patterns of saturated colors (especially blues and reds in *Menace II Society* and browns and golds in *Dead Presidents*). *Guncrazy*'s style includes a great deal of camera mobility—a freeing up of the camera within performer space—and color imagery, particularly utilizing the blues and blacks that suggest film noir. Rinzler's presence, judging by her previous and subsequent films, is quite visible in *Guncrazy*. Davis credits Rinzler as "a true artist . . . she's a genius," asserting the importance of the cinematographer to the film (author's interview). At the same time, Davis enunciates a similar visual style to Rinzler because of her background in music video (which also emphasizes mobile camerawork and saturated colors). The fact that both women collaborated on a number of music videos prior to *Guncrazy* suggests their shared visual preferences and the degree to which their cooperative labor created the overall aesthetic of *Guncrazy*.

The blue and black tones, enhanced by shadows and low-key lighting, saturate the images and create the appearance of a hard "surface" to the film's colors, much like those in *I Like It Like That;* they seem to hint at the violence that is always just beneath the surface of character interaction.[4] The work performed by set design, the framing of the images, and the lighting underscores the main characters' preoccupations with power and symbols of violence. At the same time, the cinematography and setting suggest the characters' bleak, dystopian environment: multiple fades to black occur frequently at the film's start, there are close-ups of animal prey preserved through taxidermy, and non-diegetic sound prompts. By helping to create an ominous world, one that steps out of the mise-en-scène and acknowledges itself *as* ill-fated, these elements indicate that the characters cannot control the world they inhabit—and will not survive it either.

Several scenes are visually stunning. One example is the scene of Howard's parole hearing, which is framed in one shot from a high angle through the ceiling air vent. Also notable is the heavily edited, cinema-verité sequence of Anita and Howard eating their way through a convenience store, a scene that plays like a mini-music video. Perhaps most striking is a scene in which Howard and Anita are framed in gray silhouette against a dull blue sky; Howard shovels dirt from a grave directly into the camera, and the scene ends when the dirt buries the lens. In these instances, the cinematography reinforces the depressed and inequitable plight of *Guncrazy*'s characters and implies our own complicit position as voyeurs of that plight—we watch through a dirty lens. It also tests the acceptable limits of camera and light placement for mainstream narrative filmmaking.

Again, the style created by Davis and Rinzler might be defined as mere flash and self-flattery if it did not also function as an experimentation in representing Anita's subjectivity. For example, an early scene in which Anita complies to have sex with two "good-old boy" schoolmates provides an over-the-shoulder shot from Anita's point of view within a large gutter pipe. Steeped in darkness, the shot "from within" reinforces her helpless and passive position as these men tower over her, making false promises of friendship and acceptance. The sexual exploitation she experiences is framed so that she retains the camera's command, a framing that also occurs when Anita is raped by her mother's ex-boyfriend, Hank (Joe Dallesandro), and her feelings of repulsion are conveyed through close-ups of her face from a side angle. (In this latter scene, the camera grants her more space and authority than her abuser, without glamorizing her pain.) *Bad Girls* was to have a similar visual structure, opening a scene in which one of the heroines is being gang-raped with a tight shot on her face and then shifting to her point of view (Johnston 60).

While *Guncrazy* is presumably a story about a couple who meet, find they share a common fascination with guns, and then initiate a shooting spree, the film privileges Anita and centralizes her narrative trajectory over Howard's. The first twenty-minute act of *Guncrazy* features Anita almost exclusively and positions her as the film's primary agent—she first contacts Howard by mail, she finds him a job that leads to his prison release, and she acquires the guns that set the two of them down their destructive path. Davis makes it clear that it was her intention to privilege Anita's subjectivity—her own identification with the character was so strong that, in the initial stages of the development, Davis had planned to play Anita herself (author's interview). Drew Barrymore's star presence in her portrayal of Anita also heightens the character's importance, especially considering that this was one of her first "come-back" adult roles after an enduring career as a child star.

In fact, one of the major characteristics of film noir—the femme fatale being purged at narrative's end in order to restore order—is reversed in this film by having Howard sacrifice his life so that Anita may be found innocent of the crimes they both perpetrated. Anita is, thus, allowed to transgress and still survive the narrative.

As in Bigelow's *Blue Steel*, the symbolic status of guns in this film assumes a significant role in relation to characters. However, the power of the gun in *Guncrazy* seems to signify the possibility of class and geographical mobility more so than the desire to re-codify gender relations. Yes, Anita turns the gun Hank trained her to use against him in order to climb out of a sexually abusive situation, but the more significant relationship between Anita, the gun, and Howard is devoid of gender power imbalances.

Howard represents little threat to Anita, in part because he remains sexually impotent for most of the film. His impotence helps to realign her power position—she has been socialized to gain love and affirmation through sex and now she learns to relate to him as an emotional equal. In fact, the couple comes together across the ground of their "shared impotence"; when Howard reveals his inability to perform sexually, Anita discloses that she was raped by Hank. The fact that they feel closest when they murder someone else suggests that the act of sex has been replaced by their repeated declarations of social power, the potency they feel when empowered by weapons. One reviewer felt let down by the elimination of the sexual attraction in the film, arguing that such a maneuver makes it "less thrilling" (McCarthy, 1 June 1992: 68). However, I have to wonder whether the displacement was a tactical strategy on the part of Davis and screenwriter Matthew Bright to avoid compromising Anita by refusing to continually place her in sexual contexts.

The reason I suggest that the gun symbolizes class and geographical

In *Guncrazy* (1993), Drew Barrymore plays it her stepfather's
way just long enough to learn how to fight back. (Zeta
Entertainment, Inc.)

mobility is because each time Anita and Howard murder they are pro-
pelled closer to their (ultimately unreachable) goal of achieving the stability of a suburban, middle-class family lifestyle. Upon leaving Anita's
rural California trailer community, Howard helps Anita search for her
mother in Fresno. Anita perpetually attempts to match other people's
accounts of her mother (prostitute, liar, freeloader) with her own romantic image of her; but eventually she leaves the maternal search behind.
The maternal theme is underdeveloped, most likely because *Guncrazy*
refuses to invest in consoling images of an "ideal family" or a nostalgic
reunion.

The film's understanding of how sociological systems have failed
Anita becomes most clear once she and Howard steal into the empty
home of a vacationing, well-off family. Anita and Howard enjoy a night
of domestic bliss as they view photographic slides of the "happy" nuclear
family whose home they have temporarily invaded. The breach between
the characters and the slides they watch hints at the unattainability of

such social and economic stability. The fact that Howard finally overcomes his impotence in the bedroom of this house shores up the argument that the couple might have had a chance at "healthy" normalcy had they benefitted from class mobility. It also suggests that this "normalcy" would have included a restoration of patriarchal power, in the form of Howard's returned sexual potency.

However, *Guncrazy* does not invest too heavily in this brand of normalcy. The sheer fact that Anita and Howard have commandeered the house for a night suggests the fragility of the facade of a safe domestic haven. As Howard confronts his own death, making himself vulnerable to a barrage of gunfire, he does so descending the stairway of this idealized home. His final descent—the climax of the film—occurs on the precious, primary threshold of this family's domestic space. The final romantic night between Anita and Howard has been as illusory as the house's projection of safety and stability.

Guncrazy maintains strong links to *Bad Girls*, the film developed and initiated by Davis and then handed over to Kaplan. Both films feature exploited characters who are preoccupied with confiscating other people's power in an effort to balance out social differences, whether gender- or class-based. Women's relation to weapons of power, that is, their desire to appropriate signifiers that will stabilize and enfranchise them, is the subject of both films. Their right to violence is justified by the inequities of the social system in which they live. Also, according to industry reports, *Bad Girls* would have had a visual style similar to that of *Guncrazy*—mining low-budget technology to combine "art-house" style with a hyper-conscious, MTV look (Garey and Hruska 74). Although the second feature film directed by Davis, *CB4*, may seem worlds apart from both *Guncrazy* and *Bad Girls*, the Chris Rock vehicle articulates similar politics, an analogous aesthetic, and a corresponding immersion in youth and popular culture.

CB4

CB4 was conceptualized by comedian Chris Rock (formerly of *Saturday Night Live*) and music critic Nelson George as "a rap *Spinal Tap*" (1995: 136). They spent several years developing the project inspired by Rob Reiner's 1984 pseudo-documentary that featured an aging British rock group. Rock and George's goal was to spoof rap culture, particularly the paradox that many African American rappers who donned the persona of a tough, violent street-fighters "were really just middle-class kids" (137). Although George originally envisioned Reginald Hudlin, Kevin Hooks, or Bill Duke as *CB4*'s director, and Rock had Ben Stiller in mind, they eventually lobbied for Tamra Davis, whom George knew through the music industry (146).

Davis's status as a "director-for-hire," and not a "writer-director," makes it even more difficult to theorize her authorship. (Writer-directors are more likely to be considered auteurs because it is assumed that they have more control over the final product and more involvement in the conceptualization process.) Davis characterizes her career as often "falling into projects which I have not developed myself," an experience that is frequently the hard reality of studio directing and an important antidote to auteurism's "cult of the artist" (author's interview). While *CB4*'s writers and producers spent more time working on the film than she did, Davis reinforced their ideas by bringing to the film her MTV aesthetic and her intimate knowledge of the politics of rap.

An interesting link between Davis and Darnell Martin occurred in the development of *CB4*. George asked Martin, whom he knew through her work in music video and her stint at New York University, to create a demonstration reel for pitching the film to executives. Martin's short film, which boasted the pseudo-documentary aesthetic Rock and George originally envisioned, was well received. When I asked Martin if her reel looked anything like Davis's final product, she could not even remember its content, suggesting the high volume of projects she has directed and the fleeting nature of industry labor.

By the time Davis was attached to *CB4*, Rock and George (and co-writer Robert LoCash) had built creative momentum and cultivated a long history with producers Sean Daniel, an independent producer and liaison to Universal Studios who co-financed the film, and Brian Grazer, of Imagine Entertainment (142). One of the keys to Davis's hire was that George knew her, wanted her to direct, and fought to give her the opportunity. While he was in favor of hiring an African American director, George felt that the film required someone immersed in rap culture but not necessarily invested in black identity politics: he asserts that *CB4* was "more a rap film than a black one" (145). Davis's forte in directing rap videos aided her here, and executives ended up choosing between her and Rupert Wainwright, a white male rap video director.

Wainwright was actually chosen first by executives, but the job went to Davis when he turned it down (152). During this decision-making process, George realized that Davis was "facing an age-old problem: she was a girl" at the table with almost all white men (152). George reflects: "Rupert was a burly, big-voiced, take-charge kind of guy. In other words, he seemed more 'directorial' and you could feel the white men in the room respond to that quality" (152). In addition to these initial difficulties, when Davis did accept the position (and with it her first opportunity to direct a studio film), she consented to handling a number of obstacles and being paid a relatively low salary. Some of those hardships included an extremely tight shooting schedule, governed by Chris Rock's summer hiatus from *Saturday Night Live*, less-than-ideal weather conditions (Panorama City in the San Fernando Valley during 100-degree days), and a number of script cuts (167, 180).

Davis actually reflects positively on her experience with *CB4* executives. She characterizes Daniel and Grazer as "two of the best producers

Tamra Davis says it took time for her to realize that she (a young, white, petite woman) could exert her authority over a studio film. (Universal Pictures)

199

in Hollywood," indicating that she always felt she, and the integrity of the film, were fully represented in industry meetings (author's interview). When I asked Davis to compare making *CB4* with her independent *Guncrazy*, she explained, "It's just hard; it's like a war no matter what kind of film you make. The effort I put in is similar" (author's interview). Davis added that although *CB4* was a studio film, its content of rap culture was unfamiliar to most of the executives who would ordinarily define and influence that content. Because of *CB4*'s cultural specificity and narrow target market, these executives hung back.

Nelson George has articulated a "major contradiction" of the film that, he says, pervaded and troubled all stages of the filmmaking: "How do you make fun of something the majority of your audience will find appealing while still entertaining them and holding their interest?" (138). *CB4*'s target audience of young, African American male consumers might be offended by its parody of rap artists. This is ultimately a quandary of identity politics because the production team was hoping to capitalize on black urban identity and satirically joke about it at the same time, all the while pointing out the music industry's tendency to capitalize on that identity in the first place. *CB4* also challenged dominant Hollywood ideologies by choosing to centralize rap music at all, since rap has served as a projection screen for all of white America's worst fears about urban African Americans. The film, at least in intention, was to be "a nasty joke at the expense of street culture, conservatism, and extremism of various kinds" (George 165). Rock and George conceived it as a simultaneous political assault against the Moral Right Wing and the consumerist values of pop, "ghetto" culture.

One would imagine that Davis approached her position as a white woman engaged in this assault very gingerly. Her expertise in youth and popular cultures, and her interest in cross-cultural fertilization, empowered her to implement and guide the original conception. At the same time, the presence of the character A. White (Chris Eliot) in *CB4* allowed her to comment on her own narrational position. The rap group CB4 is introduced through a promotional "documentary" made by a white filmmaker whose "whiteness" is parodied throughout the film. Eliot's tendency to stereotype the middle-class rappers as gang-oriented street boys from the hood, and his own artistic aspirations, are sent up in a way that conveys Davis's self-reflexivity about her status as a white director. While A. White was in the script long before Davis took on the film, this character seems an obvious outlet for Davis to make fun of white biases.

CB4 maintains a highly fluid structure, often taking detours into flashbacks, dream sequences, and musical stagings. This format serves the comic effects of Chris Rock (who plays Albert) and his rap counter-

CB4 (1992) functions as a light parody of urban, African American masculinity. (Universal Pictures)

parts Euripides (Allen Payne) and Otis (Deezer D). The film is a bit uneven and misguided, partially because of struggles in development (in terms of a confused tension between documentary, music video, and classical story) and partly because of its contradictory messages. Nevertheless, Davis capitalizes on *CB4*'s excursive tendencies by locating certain segments that are ripe for social commentary. One sequence that Davis engineered, according to George, involves a parody of a "Spike Lee" technique that appears in *Do the Right Thing*, *Jungle Fever* (1991), and *Malcolm X* (1992).

In the spoof, Albert undergoes a moral transformation, questioning why he is disrespecting his mother and tagging women as "bitches" and "hos." Against the backdrop of a twilight sky, he "walks" along the sidewalk of his neighborhood; the Lee technique, however, involves having Chris Rock's Albert on the same dolly as the camera, making the character appear to glide with the camera as the sky recedes into the background. The wide angle lens positions Albert in the frame in a way that is reminiscent of many shots in Lee's films; his style, which is suggestive of previous films by "auteurs" such as Rainer Fassbinder, is both imitated and sent up. Jump cuts also disrupt the sequence, calling into question the purpose of the moving camera at all. According to Nelson George, Davis conceived of this parody—what he calls "one of the films smartest jokes"—as they were re-shooting certain components of the third act (183). The fact that Albert's speech consists of a critique of the way he has disrespectfully treated women might be seen as an additional jab at Lee, who has been criticized for his cinematic treatment of women.

While *CB4* is difficult to categorize, its major conflict involves the identity crisis faced by Albert after he confiscates the name and experiences of a tough criminal named Gusto (Charlie Murphy). Albert, Euripides, and Otis don the facade of street hustling rappers until Albert is forced to own up to his middle-class–well-educated upbringing. His father (played by Arthur Evans) teaches him, "You ain't from the street. I'm from the street. And only someone that wasn't would think it's something to glorify." Embedded in this lesson is a critical analysis of the rap industry, traditionally run by white men, which exploits African American urban experiences and manufactures "bad boy" identities for many of its artists.

Like *I Like It Like That*, *CB4* brings into relief the hypocrisy of the music industry. However, because *CB4* is structured by such randomness, and because it, at times, capitalizes on the very sexist and homophobic ideologies it at other times exposes, no clear political message emerges. This lack of clarity seems to be a direct result of the film's basic contradiction, which George identified as its attempt to satirically comment on the very audience it hopes to attract. Nevertheless, *CB4* exists as an informative document about the irony of trying to entertain critically—to ask an audience to respond to film analytically and politically within the context of escapist, mass culture—which relates to broader feminist debates in film theory.

Because *CB4* was aimed at a rather narrow target audience, its distribution resembled that of many independent films—it depended largely on word of mouth and grass roots campaigning. *CB4*'s soundtrack was circulated to radio stations well in advance of the film's release, promotional postcards were distributed while the film was still in production, and a rough cut trailer was leaked early to record companies and trade press (George 185–86).[5] While studio films are less likely to employ a niche marketing approach than are independent companies, this decision clearly served the narrowcast *CB4* (187). The film placed number one at the box office during its opening week, garnering $6.12 million on its premiere weekend. Its commercial success placed Davis in the position to be asked to direct similar comedic projects such as *Billy Madison* (1994) starring *Saturday Night Live*'s Adam Sandler and *Half-Baked* (1998) starring Dave Schappelle and Jim Bruer.

BAD GIRLS

Firing Davis

The original screenplay for *Bad Girls*, written by Davis's close friend Becky Johnston, featured a great deal of input from Davis before she lobbied for New Line Cinema to buy it and place her in the director's chair (author's interview).[6] After the project became a negative pick up (that is, a production abandoned after partial purchase), Twentieth Century-Fox decided to finance it, putting producers Al Ruddy and Andre Morgan in charge. Several weeks into production, the studio fired the producers, Davis, cinematographer Rinzler, and (eventually) seventeen actors, thereafter deciding to quickly hire producer Lynda Obst, director Jonathan Kaplan, and script doctor Ken Friedman to reconceptualize the film (Garey and Hruska 74, 90). It's ironic that the first project, commercial or otherwise, Davis could have boasted having had a strong hand in developing was wrestled from her. From Obst's book, *Hello, He Lied*, several trade-magazine articles, and Davis's own account, details emerged that suggest Davis was placed in an impossible position by Twentieth Century-Fox executives and producers, and that the content of the feminist Western set the stage for a number of battles that speak volumes about the politics of contemporary Hollywood.

Bad Girls, in all of its conceptions, was to be a story about a band of women prostitutes in the 1870s who were able to wield guns and rescue themselves—just like traditional, that is, male, western heroes. By all accounts, both the original screenplay and the film version work by virtue of the opportunity for commentary facilitated by the centralization of female characters and women's experiences within the typically "male" genre of the Western. I will compare the original with the final product later; it is clear from this synopsis, however, that various allegiances to

203

feminist politics and conventional representations of women within the male-dominant traditions of both Hollywood and the "wild west" were at stake in the production of *Bad Girls*.

Davis held a very precarious directorial position. Replacement producer Lynda Obst suggests that the film was too "top-heavy" in terms of its star package, and that Davis was relatively unsupported by producers both on the set and in executive meetings. Obst explained:

> I think that the picture's collapse was foreshadowed by the fact that each actress was being paid almost ten times more than its neophyte female director, Tamra Davis, who was making her first studio movie [actually her second]. . . . The pressure of being badly produced and inexperienced with major movie stars had toppled the director from the helm of *Bad Girls*. (1996: 78, 79)

In line with this assessment, it has also been reported that difficult competition existed between the film's four major stars, Madeleine Stowe, Mary Stewart Masterson, Drew Barrymore, and Andie MacDowell, and that Stowe and Masterson became dissatisfied with Davis (Garey and Hruska 74). If Davis's approach to the actresses had been supported by on-set producers, these quarrels might have been ameliorated, even in the face of the actresses' star power.

In addition to these complications, a disparity in aesthetic and, by extension, budgetary goals arose between two factions: Davis, Rinzler, and Johnston on one side, and Ruddy, Morgan, and Twentieth Century-Fox on the other. The former group had envisioned an "artsy," "edgy," "low-budget" style that would foreground the political themes of the Western. This look would have been fiscally reasonable considering that the estimated twenty-million-dollar budget provided by Fox later became depleted by the high salaries of the film's stars. However, the studio and producers began to call for a "sexier aesthetic," one that would provide glamour for the big-budget stars (Garey and Hruska 74).

Not only did the studio's request contradict the feminist content of the original screenplay, but it came into direct conflict with the production budget they had allotted. As Garey and Hruska relate: "According to Davis, the producers were scrimping so much on production that Rinzler didn't have the right equipment to do the job. 'If the original DP had been a guy,' says Davis, 'they wouldn't have done to him what they did to Lisa. They gave the new DP all the equipment he needed' " (74). As it was, Tom Jacobson, president of production at Twentieth Century-Fox, viewed the first few days of footage, saw that it "was not the film we wanted to make," and fired Rinzler, thereby precipitating a number of firings down the line (90).

Having worked almost exclusively in independent films and music

An image from Jonathan Kaplan's *Bad Girls* (1994). One is left
to wonder what Davis's film would have looked like. (Twentieth
Century-Fox)

video, Rinzler did not take well to a studio setting. Davis regrets her own
attempts to coax Rinzler into this position as studio cinematographer.
Davis remarks, "I tried to take her into a studio world with me but it
wasn't right for me to do that" (author's interview). Although Rinzler
was certainly accustomed to working under considerable constraints in
independent film, she must have been quite debilitated by the double
bind the studio placed her in when it gave her a compromised budget but
insisted upon a "big-budget" look. Frustrating, too, was the executives'
dissatisfaction with dailies.

Lynda Obst points to a number of other factors, in addition to Fox's
problems with Rinzler, that made Davis's an "impossible" situation. For
example, there was "no portable telephone transmission on location,"
leaving no way for emergency phone calls to get through (Obst 211).
The screening facilities for dailies were not working correctly (211). The
set had no "movable walls," which compromised shooting, and the hair
and makeup artists of each female star were arguing amongst each other

(212). Each of these complications points to the weaknesses and incompetencies of on-set producers Ruddy and Morgan. They also crystallize the fact that Davis was not merely fighting an ideological battle about the feminist vision of *Bad Girls*. She was up against a number of industrial, material, and "everyday life" constraints that prevented her from being able to carry out her supposedly empowered role as director. To what extent these latter constraints reflected a larger discontent with the film's feminist message on the part of Fox is unclear. It is more likely that the double bind faced by Davis stemmed from the studio's desire for a big-budget, glamorously styled film on a relatively low, ill-planned budget.

Kaplan was then hired to revamp *Bad Girls* to fit the vision of the studio. The script was entirely rewritten to emphasize movement and speed over character backstory development and expository dialogue. Kaplan's film style created exorbitant gloss in both long-shot action sequences and star-dictated close-ups. Revealing that he preferred the hiring of a female producer for rather stereotypical reasons, Kaplan remarks that he requested Obst "because I know nothing about wardrobe and hairstyles and stuff like that" (Garey and Hruska 90). Indeed, Obst saw her major role as that of contributing a sense of sexuality and play to the costumes and production design (Obst 80). The costumer (Susie DeSanto) who adapted to this newly defined style prospered, while the production designer, who disagreed, ended up quitting (80–81).

The costume style in the *Bad Girls* film blends 1990's "hip" youth fashion such as lace, denim, and kaleidoscopically busy fabrics with the traditional Western style of cowboy boots, leather, and spurs. It tends to enhance the characters' femininity and their status as sexual objects. Unlike the film, the screenplay attempted to critique this very objectification. In one scene, Lilly points out the uncomfortable tightness of the corsets required by Victorian mores (29). The women eventually liberate themselves by slicing off the bottom of their long skirts so that they can more easily operate the guns they are learning to shoot (79). Their liberation is completed later when they break into the general store and don male attire—quick cuts were supposed to show them putting on pants, vests, cowboy boots, and gun belts, among other male clothing (94). Whereas dress became a site for protest in the Johnston screenplay, it served as an uncontested site for feminine beauty and self-commodification in the final version.

The replacement of Davis with Kaplan would probably be considered a politically correct move by executives because Kaplan has a history of "feminist" films, including *The Accused* (1988), a film about a woman (Jodie Foster) who juridically avenges men who incited her rapists. Furthermore, Kaplan had a reputation for working well with female stars in the films *Unlawful Entry* and *Immediate Family* (1989). While Kaplan directed a cycle of "rape revenge films" early in his career, he also made exploitation films such as *Student Teachers* (1973) and *Night School Nurses* (1974). His background in music video means that he shares something of a common heritage with Davis and, in fact, Davis reportedly gave him her blessing when he replaced her on *Bad Girls* (Garey and Hruska 90). It would, therefore, be a mistake to place these two directors in stark contrast with one another—they have actually demonstrated similar interests and skills through their film work.

It would be reductive, indeed ludicrous, to tease out the "feminist" aspects of *Bad Girls* and then attribute them to Davis. Instead, my approach seeks to understand, with the help of the original Becky Johnston screenplay, how and where an originally feminist conception became altered by the replacement team of producers, director, writer, and cinematographer in order to boost market value and to better suit studio taste.[7] Is there a "Tamra Davis" ("Johnston," "Rinzler") in the final film *Bad Girls*? How can her (their) authorial signature(s) be traced in a text that, due to the studio mode of production and, in this case, executive overhaul, is inescapably fractured and multiply owned?

Two Versions of *Bad Girls*

The Davis and the Kaplan versions of *Bad Girls* share a similar plot trajectory. Both involve a group of prostitutes who must escape town and then overcome a handful of male bandits in order to regain their stolen money. The characters' reasons for running away differ slightly, though. In the Davis version, the women's pimp (Bart) discovers that they have been hiding some of their earnings from him and, when he threatens never to release any of them, Cyclone (Cody in the film) shoots him. In the Kaplan version, Cody (Madeleine Stowe) shoots a disrespecting customer when he physically threatens Lilly's (Drew Barrymore) life.

One of the major plot differences in the Kaplan film involves a bounty that is placed on the women's heads by the widow of the customer shot by Cody. This bounty means that the characters are forced to remain in hiding and on the run because they are being followed. However, one of the film's largest flaws results from this additional plotline—it may seem to raise the stakes initially, but it winds up being dropped entirely in the third act, despite the fact that the bounty hunters are still on the women's trail.

In addition, one of the major differences between the two versions involves character. When the new production team came on board, they fired not only lots of creative talent but two of the screenplay's African American characters as well, one of whom played a major role. Cynda

Williams, of *One False Move* (1991), had been cast as a fifth prostitute named Rosebud. The part of Bluetone, Cyclone's long-time confidante who accompanies the women for half of their journey was also cut. These characters functioned, in part, to highlight the oppression of people of color in conjunction with that of women. For example, there is a scene in which a hotel clerk turns the women away because Rosebud is a "colored" (39). (The other women, of course, refuse to stand for this prejudice.) By eliminating these scenes, the film's potential to link sexism to racism, or other kinds of discrimination, is decidedly decreased, as is its ability to represent any experiences other than those of white characters.

While the termination of these actors might indicate an underlying racism in that it implies that the African American characters were the most disposable, the conscious and subconscious reasons for these choices may never be clear. What is clear is that the elimination of these characters serves as an example of a broader trend followed by the replacement team that sacrificed character depth and dimensionality for action and image. The film places heavy emphasis on the women riding horses, escaping enemies, rescuing each other, and shooting villains, and does so in a way that facilitates a great many close-up glamour shots of the central stars. Obst explains that one of the changes the new team enforced was that "The piece is now more action-oriented. There's less sitting around and talking" (29).

Without slow-paced time for dialogue, however, character motivation and development is severely curtailed, providing little backbone to carry us from scene to scene and minimal investment in the protagonists. The superficial treatment of their individual desires and drives, combined with disinterest in their interactions with one another, means that this film is forced to ride on the glamour-power of its stars and the intensity of its action. While the characters slightly resemble their incarnations in Johnston's script, they are much more distinct in the original: Cyclone is a rebellious outlaw, Lilly is a Western show stuntwoman, Anita (Masterson) is a widow still grieving over the loss of her husband, and Eileen is a former New Orleans socialite who has not yet shed her sweet Southern manner. Rosebud has told the women that she escaped a moralizing preacherman father; however, it is eventually revealed that she has been disowned by her white father. In fact, it is these kinds of secrets, which are slowly and calculatedly disclosed in Johnston's script, that are perhaps that screenplay's greatest strength and a keen answer to the problems of character transparency in the final version.

Whereas each character's "label" works stereotypically in the film, it serves as a vehicle for backstory that adds dimensionality to the characters in Johnston's screenplay. Her version enables more depth because the women do not fully know each other and their pasts are revealed

208

slowly throughout the story. In the example of Rosebud, the slow disclosure of information about her father creates a story line that requires her to develop the courage to remain in the same town as her father despite his anger and disownment. (As might be expected, her father comes around and eventually saves her life in exchange for his own.)

Cyclone's backstory is also much more complicated in the original screenplay. A flashback, in addition to several dialogues with Bluetone, reveal that Kid Jarett (named Billy in Johnston's script, played by James Russo in the film) is not merely a former love interest. He is indeed the man who rescued Cyclone from a demeaning job as a stripper, renamed her from the meek "Anna Lee Rose," and trained her into becoming a vicious outlaw. The fact that Cyclone must now battle him and his dynastic family in order to regain the five thousand dollars they stole from the "bad girls" is made much more emotional, the stakes duly heightened. Here, she must dare to return to the man who both helped make her who she is and drove her away due to his violence.

Eileen's character is also more fleshed out in the Johnston screenplay. Lured away from her upper-middle-class New Orleans family by Bart's (the pimp) false promises that she could find a well-to-do husband in the Wild West, Eileen is both stereotypically feminine and unconventionally calculating. Her classism is critiqued much more overtly in the original through her scenes with Tosher, a working-class waiter in the hotel. Cyclone chastises Eileen for treating Tosher miserably mid-way through the screenplay and, by the third act, Eileen has fully learned her lesson by falling in love with him (42, 84). In the Kaplan film, the Tosher character, named William Tucker (James Le Gros), is a naive farm boy; however, the class dynamic is much less obvious, without any sense that Eileen is redeeming herself by confronting her own prejudices.

The feminist discourses in the two versions of *Bad Girls* differ greatly. In Kaplan's film, for example, the women are already "bad girls" ("bad dudes" if they were men) at the outset; Davis and Johnston, however, trace the women's journey from relative helplessness to raised consciousness and physical transformation. As evidence of this, the Johnston screenplay begins with the women escaping from their brothel in a carriage pulled by six horses and steered by Bluetone. It is not until the turning point in act three that they take the initiative to ride on horseback, which is also the point at which they learn to handle weapons. Thus, Kaplan has the women start out with all the knowledge they will ever have, and he deprives the audience of the enjoyment of watching them grow from passive passengers to active agents.

The two versions also differ in terms of their representation of victims, heroes, and codes of honor. In order for the women in the film to be painted as heroines, they must be seen as victims, first and foremost, so that the film can excuse their outlaw behavior. The characters' brand of feminism is about a code of honor—their ties outweigh all others, they watch each others' backs, and they remain loyal to their established goal of settling Anita's land once they regain their money. This code of honor, while feminist in nature, translates into their always being above reproach, always remaining fully justified in their anti-male actions. At the same time that these women demonstrate a strict, almost absurd morality, they remain humble. In the film's final scene, after the women have re-appropriated their money, done away with the villains, and saved one or two of their male love interests, Cody insists, "Aw, we ain't heroes."

In Davis's version, Cyclone shoots Bart after he has revealed that he has no intention of letting Anita or any of the others get out of the profession. Bart quietly pulls a gun on Cyclone while her back is turned, presumably without her knowing, and then she whirls around and kills him with one shot. Because Cyclone does not actually see Bart draw his gun, her shooting of him is perhaps less "justified" in the eyes of the feminist discourse of the final film, because she is less of a victim. Thus, the film fails to present this murder as the feminist gesture it should be. Rape seems to be one of the few defenses for women's violence in Kaplan's version; but there are many more in Davis's. The overwhelming reliance on rape as a plot device in Kaplan's version also suggests that his film is more influenced by classical Hollywood conventions of sexualized violence against women.

In the original *Bad Girls*, Cyclone's shooting of Bart also occurs in a context of male privilege and patriarchal ownership, which the screenplay has taken the time to illuminate. The Cyclone/Bart stand-off opens with Bart in the Roundup Saloon, which has "guns, spurs, sombreros, cattle prods, and branding irons displayed on the wall, each with the owner's name written on a label" (8). The setting, then, accentuates the pervasiveness of male power and territorialism, thereby implying that women, unfortunately, lack rights to property and weaponry. As Bart complains that he has been betrayed by the women, he says, "As of today, I only truck with whores that got a big 'Bart Jacobs' branded on their hindquarters. It don't pay if you don't own them" (9). This scene helps to foreground an omnipresent social order that disempowers women and perpetuates male socio-economic hegemony. In this way, the women do not need individual, kernel "excuses" for their desire to be bad girls, as they do in Kaplan's version. Their actions are fully justified and logical given the male-dominated climate in which they live.

Within this overall context of male power, the women's decision to unite in a mission to recuperate their stolen money becomes more of a feminist act than the fashion statement it seems to be in the film. Just

210

when they have lost hope and are about to go their separate ways, they change their minds, in part out of anger that Cyclone has just been raped by Billy and his gang. Anita declares:

> Comes a time when it's wrong to turn the cheek like we keep doing. All we get is slapped to the ground and kicked over and over again. I'm sick and tired of getting bruised. I'm sick and tired of people treating us with disrespect. . . . Committing hate on our persons then walking away with impunity. What they did to Cyclone, they'd do to all of us. And we got to show them that they can't. (72–73)

The rape-revenge theme is fully articulated here but it goes beyond one individual rescuing another. The theme becomes that of collective feminist action, of eradicating not just rape but the male privilege that feeds a rape culture.

Anita is given a second-act "feminist diatribe" in the Kaplan version as well. Her speech serves to highlight the economy of male ownership governing women's lives in the 1870s. When a male lawyer (Mark Carlton) tells Anita that her property deed is worthless because the only legitimate owner, her husband, is dead, Anita rails against him. Jerome Lurie, the attorney, says, "Ma'am, I'm sorry, but it's the law. Surely you understand that." Anita replies:

> Yes, I understand that. I was worthless till I was married so now I guess I'm worthless as a widow. Funny, I had some value as a whore. . . . If your laws don't include me, then they just don't apply to me either.

Anita's declaration functions as a dramatic beat in which she addresses the right of women to own their own property and manage their own bodies and sexuality without incrimination from male institutions. Interestingly, as the scene plays out (in a standard medium shot/reverse shot pattern), an African American woman can be seen cleaning the furniture in an office behind the lawyer. Barely visible in the background, this figure functions as a subtle reminder of the material and physical effects of a legal system that works against not only women, but people of color and lower classes as well.

Anita's speech might be seen as a remnant of the original screenplay, especially because of its political message and its multi-cultural implications. This scene, notably, also resembles Davis's short *No Alternative Girls*, in which teenage girls are reassured of their right to safe sex *and* to their sexuality.

Within the diegetic world of the characters in Johnston's script, the only avenue toward not "getting bruised" involves becoming more male. Eileen responds to Anita's speech by saying, "Anita . . . we're not made to fight like them" (73). Anita replies, "Time I learned. Time we all learned" (73). This logic, while it is somewhat binary because it implies that women cannot remain women if they take on male attributes of agency and aggression, seems reminiscent of the rhetorical strategies of Borden's *Born in Flames*. Like that avant-garde polemic, Johnston's screenplay advocates direct action, even violence, in the face of male oppression. The women of the original *Bad Girls* falsely seduce men in order to steal from or entrap them, they appropriate weapons and artillery, and they take a no-holds-barred approach to overturning phallic power.

The most obvious example of this approach occurs when Anita entices Billy's outlaw father, Rudyard (Frank Jarett in the film, played by Robert Loggia), into a hotel room, pulls down his pants and, off-screen, bites his penis (87). Because the women's goal is to kidnap Rudyard so that they can bargain with his son, the penis assault is not driven by the plot. Rather, it is purely symbolic and, according to Davis, intended as a humorous moment (author's interview). The castration symbolism disturbed Twentieth Century-Fox executives so much they demanded the scene be deleted; Davis describes that meeting as an absurd rehearsal of Hollywood male power. The 1993 trial of Lorena Bobbitt (who cut off her husband's penis in retaliation for years of alleged abuse) would have made such a moment in the film quite culturally resonant in 1994. This resonance most certainly fed the fears of studio executives. The Kaplan version swung so far from such an assault on Frank (Rudyard) that he was actually portrayed as a concerned patriarch who watched over Cody to the extent that he could.

Judging from the Johnston screenplay, the Davis version would have commented unrelentingly on the women's lack of agency by framing them in relation to phallic power—that is, a specifically male power that must be forcefully wrested back into women's control. Another, more humorous, example of this focus on the phallus occurs when Lilly declares "I gotta pee" in front of Josh McCoy (played by Dermot Mulroney in the film) after he has just joined the women on their journey to Echo City: "The women glance at McCoy in the coach, then all together, stand up and form a circle around Lilly. They hold out their full skirts, creating a wall around Lilly. Hear the SOUND of a WICKED PISS from behind the wall of skirts" (29). If Josh's presence functions as a reminder of the supposedly superior "male" proclivity for peeing while standing up, then perhaps Lilly's "wicked piss" lightheartedly challenges such "superiority." This brief moment serves to foreshadow the larger and more meaningful reappropriations of male signifiers that the women will enact later in the story.

Also involved in the women's reclamation of male power is the issue of male assistance. In the Johnston screenplay, Eileen responds to Anita's call to action by admitting, "it would comfort me to know we had some men to back us up." Rosebud replies, "If you ain't figured it out yet, it's the men who always put you in trouble. We gotta fight our own battles" (73). While McCoy ends up helping prepare the women by training them to shoot guns and ignite bombs, it is only after this discussion of women's tendency to depend on male strength, a discussion that lends reflexivity to the script but never takes place in the final film. This original version also has the bad girls reunite (with the exception of Anita who has died) with each other (with Tosher, Eileen's fiancé, off in the margins), so that the celebration of their victory is wholly theirs (106).

These feminist issues of overturning phallic power and resisting male assistance are also linked to lesbian discourses regarding separatism and radical politics. In fact, it has been suggested that Kaplan's film betrays a lesbian subtext, through the implied romances between Eileen/ Lilly and Cody/Anita, which Davis's film might have elaborated on if it had come to fruition. A reviewer in *Sight and Sound* sees a kiss between Eileen and Lilly and the latter's jealousy of Eileen's new fiancé as "the faintest tinges of anything remotely Sapphic" that might represent "remnants of the original script" (Sharman 38). In actuality, the lesbian aspects of the women's friendships are not much more fully developed in Johnston's screenplay, although they are implied in a similarly subtextual manner. Rather than Eileen and Lilly, it is Eileen and Anita whose relationship progressively takes on a romantic dimension. For example, Eileen rescues Lilly from a wild horse and Anita "wraps her arms around Lilly in eternal gratitude" (24). Eileen then declares, "Lilly, you are a true marvel. If I were a man, I would kiss you" (25). When Anita eventually dies, she winds up breathing her last breath in Eileen's arms. Anita manages to utter, "Bye, Lilly . . . love . . ." (104). Like the Kaplan version, these potentially lesbian moments remain implicit rather than explicit.

One of the most distinguishing features of the Davis version is the way in which it capitalizes on background female characters, women we never come to know and who never even meet the protagonists; they represent a site from which women's place in the conventional genre is questioned. For example, the film would have opened with the credits rolling on a calico print that, when the camera pulls back, reveals itself to be a simple dress worn by "a sturdily built pioneer woman" (1). After several establishing shots of the prairie land, an exterior shot of a graveyard shows that a "group of women are digging a grave in a fenced off cemetery on the prairie. Rows of crosses and tombstones, neatly lined up. Each surrounded by a picket fence. To keep out wolves" (1). After the graveyard shots, there is an exterior shot of a shack with children playing and their mother cooking dinner over an open campfire as she holds a newborn baby. According to the screenplay, "She is in her early thirties, but exposure and hard work have irrevocably aged her" (1). This opening sequence introduces the audience to traditional women's labor: the physical labor of caretaking, even that of grave tending. In the context provided by these peripheral female figures, the bad girls' battles take on significance not just in terms of struggling for male power, but also in terms of creating new alternatives to the limited life options available to 19th-century middle- and working-class women.

In keeping with this theme, the first spectator to witness the aftermath of the final fight is a townswoman whom we have never seen before: "[The street] is littered with dead bodies. A frightened woman opens a window, peers out at the carnage and gasps." Like those caretaking women in the opening sequence, this character bears the burden of emotionally understanding the painful consequences of the battle that has just been waged. The screenplay opens up a rare site from which to examine the *effects* of a Western standoff from a female point of view. Similarly, as Cyclone and Billy stare each other down in the climactic confrontation, there is a "sound of a BABY CRYING inside a house. A MOTHER nervously shushes it" (96). The women and children who have no control over this miniature war are shown to have lives that are affected by it nevertheless.

Once the bad girls have finished off the enemy and made it safe for those women and children to reenter the streets, the celebration of their female power becomes a collective movement. The script reads, "They put their arms around each other and hold one another up. We see the shutters and doors being timidly opened up and down the street. Townspeople cautiously make their way outside and silently watch the heroines" (106) As the women proceed to walk through the town's center, "Housewives and local women stand tall and proud, watching the gunwomen in awe" (107).

A tone of feminist reawakening is created by the gradual opening of shudders and the gathering of proud townswomen. Reinforcing the theme of collective female action initiated by Anita's speech earlier in the screenplay, this scene underscores that the entire social climate of the town has changed because of the strength and organization demonstrated by the band of women.

This comparison of the two versions of *Bad Girls* suggests that Davis's version would have been much better equipped to critique racism and classism and to portray its female characters as three-dimensional, complicated women who grow with their experiences. The characters of Johnston's screenplay were more interested in placing their individual experiences of male oppression within a political context and linking their experiences with those of other women, even women barely shown on screen. According to visual cues in the screenplay and anticipated reports about Rinzler's cinematography, the "gritty" aesthetic of the film would have concentrated on the rituals of women's traditional labor and brought women typically held in the periphery into the foreground.

The major themes and conflicts, then, which could not translate into the studio film version, had to do with contextualizing gender oppression and linking it to racial and class oppression. It is also clear that the re-placement team did not find it important to cinematically represent the *process* of consciousness-raising. Whether it was their belief that such a process would not sell well (although it found a market with *Thelma and Louise*, 1991, directed by Ridley Scott) or that it was simply not a core element, the themes of feminist consciousness-raising in Johnston's screenplay were dismantled.

In contrast to the gritty visual perspective intended by Davis and Rinzler, Kaplan's *Bad Girls* demonstrates a directorial style reminiscent of Sam Peckinpah's *The Wild Bunch* (1970) or *The Getaway* (1972). It consists of a roving eye that often starts out in long shot and then rapidly zooms in to isolate a movement (or, often, a ravishing female face). Cine-matographer Ralph Bode employs sepia earth tones to enhance the film's Western flavor and carefully orchestrated lighting to accentuate the lead-ing ladies' beauty. As Terrence Rafferty of *The New Yorker* argues, the film merely plugs women into Western generic conventions rather than taking the opportunity to comment on the way in which the genre has traditionally excluded women or been driven by the "insanity of mascu-linity" (9 May 1994: 99).

There is a great deal of evidence to suggest that, when the replace-ment team came in, the target audience shifted from a primarily female or feminist market to a young male target market, particularly consider-ing the intensifying of action scenes and the exploitation of stars. Unlike many of Kathryn Bigelow's films, which critique generic constraints of narratives aimed at male audiences, Kaplan's *Bad Girls* simply represents another product for that audience. This is not to say that such a shift in target audience is inevitable when a female director loses a film to a man or when a project originally bought by New Line Cinema becomes an acquisition of Twentieth Century-Fox. This was simply a phenomenon that occurred under specific constraints and circumstances.

Reviewers tended to complain about *Bad Girls'* superficial style and big-budget aesthetic. *Variety's* Todd McCarthy lamented its "squeaky-clean" production values while Rafferty called it a "hasty package of something-for-everyone" (25 Apr. 1994: 30; 99). Janet Maslin rejected its "Cowpoke Barbie" style as too much of a "fashion statement" that "busily works endless corsets, bloomers, chaps, gun belts and cute hats into an otherwise entirely uninvolving plot" (22 Apr. 1994: C8). While the making of *Bad Girls* was fraught with numerous ironies, perhaps this is the greatest one: critics faulted the film for its super-high production value and glossy showcasing of popular female stars, the very re-configuration performed by the second team who replaced Davis's crew. Davis's original vision of a gritty, "alternative" aesthetic might have serviced plot and theme over style and star, and thus, it might have enabled the film to better succeed commercially and critically. In effect, the vision that studio executives and several producers fought so hard to ensure was met with public indifference.

I hope that this examination has demonstrated the difficulty of ascribing authorship. As the test case of *Bad Girls* implies, authorship is neither monological nor easy to detect, despite the assumptions of traditional auteur theory. If *Bad Girls* had been directed by Davis, it would not have been fully her vision—screenwriter Johnson had conceptual input, cinematographer Rinzler was developing an aesthetic for the film, stars were engaging in reinterpretation and interpersonal negotiations, producers were adding their requests to those from Twentieth Century-Fox. Likewise, when *Bad Girls* was directed by Kaplan, it was not solely his. Not only was his film influenced by the above kinds of collaborators but it also evidences traces of Davis's contribution—her anticipation of 1870s heroines who battled sexist preconceptions, the buried lesbian subtext between female characters, and the decision to forgo punishing transgressive characters so three of them could ride off into the sunset toward their goal of owning land together.

CONCLUSION

THE LEGACY OF AUTEURISM

DIRECTORS HAVE BEEN ELEVATED to the status of "auteur" for a number of reasons. Alfred Hitchcock has been congratulated for integrating recurrent themes regarding the moral ambiguities and family dysfunction involved in a problematic social order into most of his films (Spoto 1983, Wood 1989). Because his work takes full advantage of the tools of film, Hitchcock has also been celebrated for commenting on the cinematic medium and the spectatorial process (Rothman 1982). Howard Hawks achieved auteur status for managing to instill his two principle preoccupations, the individual's place within larger society and the ludicrousness of certain prescribed social roles (through role reversals), into the variety of genres in which he worked (Wollen 1972: 81–91). Analogously, John Ford has been applauded for the ways in which he deployed the motif of the binary opposition "wilderness versus garden" in order to work through various components of the "American Dream," even within the commercial medium of Hollywood cinema (96, 110). Most of these classical directors were not recognized in their own time as auteurs, however, since there was no such thing. They were elevated by auteur theorists in the 1960s who discussed their respective bodies of work in terms of common themes and unities. This phenomenon suggests the historical and contextual nature of auteurism: directors could not be labeled auteurs until a conception of the "auteur" came into play.

It has been argued, however, that the thematic unities of these direc-

217

tors' films had little to do with their critical success. Robert E. Kapsis makes a strong case for understanding the ways in which auteurs achieved their heightened status through complex processes of reputation-building, self-promotion, and the approval of certain media gatekeepers, such as producers, curators, and critics (1992). As evidence for his argument, Kapsis demonstrates that when a film by Hitchcock failed to fit into his pre-existing body of work—when it strayed from the reputation already established by the director and his promoters—it failed commercially and, often, critically, as with *Vertigo* (1958) and *Marnie* (1964) (52–53, 64–68).

While Kapsis limits his study to Hitchcock and a handful of other directors, his argument easily applies to contemporary directors such as Spike Lee or Quentin Tarantino. These figures have engaged in reputation-building and self-promotion by acting in their films and establishing "pop culture" personas in forums such as talk shows, television commercials, and print journalism. (Indeed, Lee's and Tarantino's acting roles have enabled them to further establish an authorial "presence" in their films.) Clearly, until women directors, whether in Hollywood or independent filmmaking, develop the financial resources, cultural capital, and media collateral to promote themselves outside of their films and to build reputations that are widely circulated and relatively accessible, they will continue to be disregarded as auteurs (as defined in the contemporary, which is to say commercial, sense).

Another way in which the women directors in this study do not fit into an auteurist framework has to do with the general notion that an auteur succeeds because she or he develops a target audience, enters into a contract (of filmic expectations) with that audience, and maintains a relationship with them over time. Directors who move from women's counter cinema to mainstream film inevitably confront a shift in target audiences. Whereas Borden hoped to reach her *Born in Flames* audience with *Love Crimes*, her producers had the goal of appealing to young men. Bigelow's *Point Break* might have appealed to those who had seen *The Loveless* nine years before, but not everyone targeted by *Point Break* would have felt addressed by that earlier film. These women directors confront continually shifting contracts with target audiences that change relatively often. Without the resources to strengthen and shape a reputation, they (with the exception of Bigelow) lack the ability to develop a long-term, cumulative relationship with a familiar audience.

While aspects of auteurism continue to be criticized by film theorists and critics, auteurist biases often prevail in both academic and popular circles. Because this mode of categorization enables Hollywood participants to assign credit to particular contributors and commodify film products with ease, a popularized, commercialized ideology of the auteur

218

permeates the industry, from executive offices to the stalls of below-the-line laborers.[1] What began to interest me as I conducted interviews with the women in this study is the manner in which these directors both internalize and struggle against the tenets of auteurism at the same time. They express a keen awareness of the limitations of such an ideology, understanding that it is a set of biased beliefs, and they respond by negotiating their own formulations of authorship in provocative and illustrative ways. They often critique the elitism of auteur theory while simultaneously searching out role models within the industry whose cinematic and thematic interests they can learn from and emulate. Notably, the women's arguments against auteurism generally involve its hierarchical nature rather than its tendency to facilitate unified readings of a director's work, indicating that poststructuralist debates receive little attention within commercial film industries.

In her assessment of auteurism, Lizzie Borden first acknowledges that the term "auteur" is problematic because it reflects the French New Wave's male bias. But she goes on to say that, if forced to choose a great director, she believes "Jane Campion is the ultimate auteur. Even though *The Piano* was a collaborative effort, Campion leaves an indelible stamp and a series of memorable moments that stay with you long after you leave the theater" (author's interview). Darnell Martin, although she acknowledges the problems associated with sweeping "genius" statements, argues that a great director must deal with "humanity." Martin declares, "One director who has not received enough attention is [Stanley] Kubrick, someone who does deal with humanity. Look at *A Clockwork Orange* (1971) or *Dr. Strangelove* (1963) as films that seem polished and yet underneath they still deal with these very human questions of the moment" (author's interview).

Borden and Martin express reservations about romanticizing directors; Bigelow and Coolidge, however, articulate slightly more conservative conceptions of auteurism. Bigelow pays tribute to Andrew Sarris for his contributions to theories of the auteur, ideas she learned firsthand from him at Columbia University. Bigelow names her favorite directors as "[Walter] Hill, John Ford, Howard Hawks, Sam Peckinpah, Akira Kurosawa, Oliver Stone, James Cameron, Martin Scorsese" (Peary 11 Mar. 1990: 93). Her reasons for celebrating these "auteurs" (who all happen to be men) go as follows: "They're high impact filmmakers, and they draw characters with whom one can have strong emotional investment" (93). So Bigelow's criteria involve an ability to exploit the visceral qualities of the cinema and an adeptness at character-based drama. The fact that Bigelow has been situated as an auteur (or near-auteur) by the popular press might reflect her own adherence to auteurism, as demonstrated in her willingness to be considered according to auteurist precepts.

Coolidge attempts to diffuse the ideological hold of auteurism by claiming, "I believe that all directors are auteurs." But then she goes on to create a new category (above auteur) for those directors who should be canonized. Coolidge continues:

> But if you are a good director, you're a visionary. It doesn't matter whether you write the script or not. You find material about which you have a vision. What should we learn from independent filmmaking? All filmmaking is personal. The great directors know that. Francis Ford Coppola knows that. You work from out of yourself. (author's interview)

Coolidge, like Bigelow, lists male directors as those she would put in the "visionary canon": Woody Allen, Adrian Lyne, Sam Peckinpah ("I may not agree with his films, but there is no question he has a point of view"), and James Cameron. She uses Cameron to reiterate her point about personal filmmaking, saying, "Cameron leaves a mark on every movie he makes. He tells personal stories in giant settings" (author's interview).

In her discussion of auteurism, Coolidge makes an interesting point about how women directors might gain authorial control over their careers. Coolidge declares: "If a person is a writer-director, and she is talented, she is five legs up on a director. She has a huge benefit. You aren't out there looking for material for one thing" (author's interview). One of the biases of New Hollywood auteurism is that the more hyphens one can boast, the more likely one is to be perceived an auteur. In the postclassical era, directors-for-hire tend to be denied auteur status. While it is important to remain aware of these biases, the pragmatic reality of the constant search for material should not be forgotten. The case of Susan Seidelman is illustrative. She made a name for herself with *Desperately Seeking Susan*, but, as someone who does not write screenplays, she could not sustain that reputation because she found herself at the mercy of the material that was open to her (Ferncase 53). The less popular a director becomes, the more limited the pool of projects that is open to her, which means that a director's degree of agency and control can spiral downward.

Seidelman reveals a relatively pragmatic view of authorship within Hollywood. She explains: "Film is a strange art form because it is so commercial and, unlike painting or poetry or even fiction, you need other people to do it with you. So the challenge for someone who wants to direct with a personal point of view is to fight for that at the same time that you are being financially responsible." She goes on: "There are so many people within the system itself whose job it is to mediate the script. The goal [for a director] is to establish a name and a point of view so that people won't try to second-guess you when they approach you for a job" (author's interview). Seidelman tries to walk an even line, hoping to make an imprint on the commercial film and television industries without their economic interests causing her to become a "director-for-hire."

Of all the directors, Tamra Davis de-romanticizes the "auteur" the most, strenuously observing the industrial context of film direction. Davis suggests that a great director "walks the line between being versatile and yet still maintaining a distinctive style" (author's interview). She points out that because commercial filmmaking is so industrialized, one has to be open to working with many kinds of people, located within many divisions of labor, under various kinds of material conditions. About herself, Davis declares, "I am very much a collaborator. I try to stay on line with the writer. Yet I try to ensure that my style comes through no matter what form I work in. Part of that style concerns my reputation as a young woman well versed in the pop culture market" (author's interview). Her comments point to the ways in which the independent market has become increasingly profit-driven. A generation younger than those who helped establish women's counter cinema in the 1970s, Davis articulates a practical and business-like approach to the medium. She also expresses a weariness regarding the elitism of auteur theory. Because she dislikes the idea of hierarchizing directors, she refrained from naming anyone she might consider an "auteur."

The responses of these women suggest their intensely ambivalent reactions to the ideological power auteurism continues to hold within the Hollywood industry. The complex ways in which they negotiate their relations to auteurism point to their desire to create ideals and incentives while still finding room to criticize the exclusive nature of auteur theory. The intensity of their ambivalence is also structured by the fact that their work has straddled the worlds of independent and studio film: in the former, artisinal values are assigned to the director (who supposedly exercises more artistic control); in the latter, collaboration and labor divisions take precedence. The simultaneous subscription to and rejection of auteurism symbolizes how these women operate within the existing power structure, which is governed by multiple centers of sometimes contradictory ideologies. They are, to varying degrees, invested in auteurism, yet they resist its more oppressive implications. These directors hang onto certain threads (Campion leaves an "indelible stamp," Kubrick deals with very "human questions of the moment") and leave others to dangle.

It would be easy to interpret these women's reactions as internalized sexism or industry co-optation; but I think they point to the lack of available alternatives to the concept of auteurism in both industrial Hollywood and academic discourses. In sifting through the strands of auteurism to find those that "work" and those that do not in the evaluation of women directors' films, I too have devoted little time to the project of constructing a new theory of authorship. Instead my interest has centered around auteur theory's hold on the field of film studies. Auteurism has been productive for this study because it is preoccupied with the search for thematic interests, genre concerns, and social commentary across the trajectory of a director's films. The search has revealed, however, that the process of assigning continuities to any range of films involves imposing, or reading, unity in disparate elements; and some of those elements may not come from the director's efforts.

What is evident from this study in relation to auteur theory is that auteurism pretends to derive meaning from directorial themes and social messages, but its criteria are, more often than not, governed by the commercial and critical reputation a director is able to garner. The extent to which she is able to cultivate a "star" persona, through the fostering of a commercial identity, determines the degree to which she will be judged by auteurist criteria; media visibility also shapes the range of choices open to her as her career moves through independent and Hollywood spheres.[2] Kathryn Bigelow is the only director in this study to be positioned as "star," due, in part, to her status as "spectacle." She is also the director most likely to be designated an auteur (and, relatedly, a genre director) by the popular press. Although these women directors have developed authorial control, they still lack power in the realm of commercial identity, which means that they maintain minimal control over how their product is received in relation to their own Hollywood reputations.

REFRAMING COUNTER-CINEMA DEBATES

One of the main conclusions to emerge from this look at women directors is that no facile dichotomy exists between mainstream and counter-cinema films. Based on the interviews conducted and the films analyzed, any hasty judgments about studio forces being "all bad" and independent factions "totally good" seem ridiculous. Lizzie Borden had high praise for Harvey and Bob Weinstein of Miramax after making *Love Crimes*, and Tamra Davis felt fully supported by producers at Imagine Entertainment and Universal Studios during the production of *CB4*. On the other hand, Borden had difficult experiences with producers of her short in the independent collection *Erotique*, and Davis spent six challenging years trying to launch and then distribute the low-budget *Guncrazy*.

The dissolution of the boundaries between mainstream and independent is evident in a number of ways. For one thing, many directors move back and forth between studio projects and independent productions. Coolidge feels a keen alliance with independent filmmaking, celebrating the Independent Feature Project Awards more enthusiastically than the Academy Awards. She helped assemble the board of the Independent Film Channel even as she directs relatively high-budget, studio films. Likewise, Borden made her short for *Erotique* after *Love Crimes* and looks forward to directing independent, narrowcast films. Davis continues her work in music video, and she directed the film short *No Alternative Girls* the same year she made *Billy Madison* (1994). Seidelman has incorporated "art film" values into the situation comedy *Sex in the City*. Martin, highlighting the economic imperative of remaining flexible, stresses that she will direct in whichever mode—studio or independent—will provide her with a job and a reasonable degree of freedom. These directors should be seen in relation to male directors who move in and out of both realms—such as Spike Lee, Quentin Tarantino, Philip Kaufman—or those who return to the independent scene after becoming disenchanted with Hollywood—such as Mike Figgis (*One Night Stand*, 1997; *Leaving Las Vegas*, 1995; *Mr. Jones*, 1990; *Stormy Monday*, UK, 1988).

From the 1970s to the 1990s, counter-cinema techniques have become much more common in studio films. Self-conscious or reflexive narration has emerged as a "trendy" characteristic of those big-budget and/or classically plotted films that cater to highly film-literate audiences and those spectators who are willing to be tested in a mass entertainment setting. Because of this, easy assumptions such as "static camera equals feminist politics" or "intensity of editing equals patriarchal manipulation" made by some 1970s feminist theorists are more difficult to support today. Overt stylistic techniques like a sweepingly mobile camera or rapid editing have been exploited by directors (as growing budgets have allowed) in order to convey a social message or reinforce narrative meaning. Martin's Steadicam shots of Lisette's neighborhood in *I Like It Like That* or Davis's mini-music video sequence of Anita and Howard stealing food in a convenience store in *Guncrazy* provide evidence against the notion that static camerawork or minimal cutting is "more feminist" because it does not engage in the typical, and unwarranted, manipulation of Hollywood style.

At a time when avant-garde techniques have become more popularized—when films such as *I Like It Like That* and *Guncrazy* bridge the gap between mainstream and counter-cinema audiences—the point could be made that they are becoming less political. When these techniques are deployed within the context of a commercial, mainstream film, they might not work as they would in an "independent" or art-house context (even as these contexts are admittedly blurring). Because classical narrative, psychological editing, and self-effacing camerawork have "the weight of the culture" behind them—that is, they are the expected norm—counter techniques within a studio context may have little effect. They may simply embody an interest in "flavor of the day" or go unnoticed at all.

It is difficult, therefore, to argue that distancing techniques, when deployed in commercial cinema, will always distance effectively. This is one reason why I have relied on the concept of multiple logics within the film system. I have attempted to highlight these kinds of avant-garde or counter-cinema techniques and to suggest that these oppositional logics run alongside more classical or dominant logics within a film. By tracing continuities across a variety of independent-to-studio trajectories, I point out the stakes that these women have had in challenging dominant modes of representation and eliciting a critical, socially aware spectator even as they operate within Hollywood. In other words, alternative techniques that appear in mainstream film function through the "both/and" logic advocated by Mayne. They offer up a trendy, differentiated product *and* a challenge to the status quo.

The future of the relationship between studio and independent cinemas has yet to be seen. What seems apparent is that women's contributions and political concerns will continue to be erased and squashed so long as a backlash against feminism occurs in the broader socio-political climate in which industry changes take place. Predictably, women have been edged out of independent cinema as it has gained more momentum and economic power. While women helped to initiate and build the independent film sector in the 1970s, they have faced increasing exclusion and degradation as the sector has taken off. Furthermore, independent films, which have become more oriented around classical narrative and more technologically sophisticated, seem to depict overt feminist politics or radical points of view less often. At the same time, the increasing number of positions open to women within the realm of Hollywood studios is not necessarily promising. Lizzie Borden notes that, although Hollywood has grown to include more women in directorial or executive positions, the industry seems to release very few films that explicitly espouse feminism (author's interview). Borden's "more women, less feminism" hypothesis indicates that the backlash against feminism discussed by Susan Faludi and Suzanna Danuta Walters is not likely to go away with Hollywood's recent "embrace" of both women and independent filmmakers.

From the work of women directors, it is also clear that "genre" represents one of the major avenues for critiquing studio conventions within a studio context. Whether the directors have revised "male" genres (such as Bigelow with *Point Break* or Davis with *Guncrazy* and, potentially, *Bad Girls*), worked within "women's" genres to more closely examine women's experiences (Coolidge with *Rambling Rose* and *Angie*), or capitalized on the gender tensions of generic conventions (Borden with the female psychothriller *Love Crimes*, Bigelow with *Blue Steel*), their films testify to a preoccupation with the traditional narrative formulas and storytelling patterns of classical Hollywood. Because genres are guided by "systems of expectation," these women directors have, whether consciously or not, taken advantage of how these systems work and how they guide audience expectations, particularly in terms of gender norms (Neale 160). As Teresa de Lauretis describes, when women "go narrative," they often go narrative "with a vengeance," insisting on politically playing out story conventions to their logical conclusions.

These directors' focus on genre might be explained by their independent origins. Working from an independent perspective first, they undoubtedly developed a critical attitude toward Hollywood storytelling as well as a complex understanding of how its formulas work—that is, how genre films effect narrative tension and activate impossible cultural contradictions. Their distance from Hollywood better enabled these directors to foresee how genres might be revived, exploited, and critiqued—how they might be utilized to comment on already-told stories and to express new ones. While Bigelow is the only one in these case studies to actually be labeled a "genre director" by press accounts, almost all of the directors have demonstrated refined and intimate knowledge of generic conventions, whether or not that knowledge is conscious.

Darnell Martin is unique in that she is the most adamant about avoiding genre altogether. Her interest in Italian and French cinemas resulted in a resistance to those who would label *I Like It Like That* a "romantic comedy." This predilection also led to her insistence on ambiguous story structure even in the face of studio intervention. While Martin is less preoccupied with genre and enjoys experimenting with story, she still celebrates narrative. In commending Kubrick as a model filmmaker, she states, "*Clockwork Orange* is about drama and catharsis. I don't think we've found something better than what the Greeks did a long time ago" (author's interview). In favoring films that touch "humanity," perhaps best defined as everyday experiences of pain and conflict, Martin reinforces the importance of classical narrative. While she plays around with deviations and ambiguities of story structure, she is also clearly invested in typical conventions of character psychology, conflict, and realism. Again, her immersion in European art cinema and independent filmmaking help her to better comprehend those conventions and their potential effects on an audience.

But for those women whose works are explicitly concerned with genre, there is a great deal of evidence that part of their project involves making certain genres more historically relevant. Although it is difficult to separate the degree to which these films are products of a particular historical moment from the degree to which they are extensions of the feminist consciousness of an individual director, films such as *Rambling Rose, Angie, Blue Steel, Point Break, Love Crimes,* and *Guncrazy* frame their protagonists and conventions in terms that could not have been conceptualized in quite the same way before the 1970s feminist movement. Leo Braudy comments on how

> the methods of the western, the musical, the detective film, or the science-fiction film are . . . reminiscent of the way Shakespeare infuses old stories with new characters to express the tension between past and present. . . . The ongoing genre subject therefore always involves a complex relation between the compulsions of the past and the freedoms of the present, an essential part of the film experience. (415)

The "genre" films of these women directors tend to deploy generic conventions in order to bring into relief the ways in which past narrative structures have failed and to point out possible directions those structures might take.

The ways in which these directors have updated genres (and revised classical narrative in general) as they move into Hollywood suggest that they are gearing their films toward a newly emerging spectator position—one that is informed by second-wave feminist discourses. Elizabeth Ellsworth's study of the critical reception of *Personal Best* (1984) indicates that the second-wave feminist movement has led to a current historical moment in which many spectators are engaging with a "feminist discursive self-production" (46). That is, she proposes that the film prompted viewers to participate in a particular production of the self, to begin to see their "private" film-viewing activity as part of a larger, collective process of feminist identity politics.

Like *Personal Best*, the more commercial films by Seidelman, Coolidge, Bigelow, Borden, Martin, and Davis may address a spectator not by evoking collective, political activity per se, but rather by coaxing out an agency associated with the ongoing feminist processes of self-definition as it occurs through the negotiation of relations between self, discourse, and community. That spectator position is certainly not taken up in the same way by each audience member. But the period between the 1970s and the 1990s constitutes a historical moment that has seen a shift in material, economic, and social conditions whereby cinematic institutions, in conjunction with ideological institutions, are redefining sites of female identity, ideals of femininity, and definitions of what it means to be political. The development of feminist film theory, its popularization within the mainstream, and its intersection with women's film production, has contributed immeasurably to this shift.[3]

This examination of women's independent and studio films has served, in part, as an attempt to reinscribe women's authorship into Hollywood film. While acknowledging the limits of auteur theory, I have illuminated ways in which women directors can and do comment on social inequities through narrational and narrative devices. The numerous ways in which they have engaged in "revision"—encouraging identification with female characters through subjective camerawork, reflexively foregrounding women's relation to their own artistic representation, parodying signifiers of conventional masculinity, or refusing the heterosexual possibilities of a text—imply their ability to critically examine both classical Hollywood conventions and various politics of gender (or race, or class, or sexual preference) at the same time. They have faced disheartening challenges within the commercial, mainstream industry, such as Lizzie Borden's loss of authority in her attempt to ensure that Dana's subjectivity made it to the screen in *Love Crimes*, or Darnell Martin's struggle to accurately and fairly market *I Like It Like That*, or Davis's firing from *Bad Girls*. However, women directors have also re-appropriated, subverted, and stretched classical conventions in ways that bring feminist identities and conversations into the Hollywood fold. Their attempts to do so are best elucidated when their mainstream films are seen in relation to their independent work, in which their concerns with feminist "revision" are so apparent.

One of the most promising findings of my interview research is the heightened awareness that women directors convey about the contribution of each other's work and their own precarious status within a male-dominated industry. In press accounts, they often refer to their contemporaries or their female predecessors who paved the way for their entrance into Hollywood. Frequently in my interviews, the conversation would lead to the question of "who else was I interviewing?"—and, before I could answer, the director would launch a string of possible names, from both independent and mainstream spheres, which inevitably included those in this study. Most of the directors featured here know of each other, some have worked with each other in various capacities, and many have conversed with other women directors about the very issues raised in this book. While it is important not to romanticize that awareness, their knowledge does provide evidence that a counterpoint to the Hollywood "old boys' network," one that emphasizes collaboration and connection over competition and isolation, is slowly emerging.[4] In her dictionary of *Women Film Directors*, Gwendolyn Audrey Foster bemoans the fact that most women directors remain invisible to the public "and maybe, equally important, to one another" (1995: xii). While this is true, especially when filmmaking is considered within a global context, we might celebrate the knowledge expressed by the women directors in this book—knowledge that they are not alone and that their feminist politics are indeed quite visible . . . even in Hollywood.

227

NOTES

INTRODUCTION

1. This term, as de Lauretis points out, has a previous history—both as a name of an anthology edited by Mary Ann Doane, Patricia Mellencamp, and Linda Williams and in an essay by Adrienne Rich (1984; 1979). De Lauretis borrows the phrase "seeing difference differently" from Rich.

2. Examples of actresses who have become directors include: Barbra Streisand who performed in films and music for twenty years before directing herself in *Yentl* (1983); Penny Marshall (*Big* [1990], *A League of Their Own* [1994]) began as a television actress, directing several *Laverne and Shirley* episodes before going on to film; and Jodie Foster had a distinguished career as a child actress that led to her eventual directorial debut with *Little Man Tate* (1991). Dorothy Arzner (*Christopher Strong* [1934], *Dance Girl Dance* [1943]) became a director after working as a typist, then a cutter, then as an editor. (See Judith Mayne's *Directed by Dorothy Arzner*, 1994.) These women do not figure in this study because I am trying to make explicit connections between independent and mainstream cinema. With the exception, perhaps, of some of Foster's films, these women do not make "independent" films.

3. Gaining cultural capital as an actress, working one's way up through the secretarial or production ranks, and directing independent films are three major routes toward becoming a Hollywood director. Women have also found their way into the industry by directing television. Randa Haines directed episodes of *Hill Street Blues* before going on to make *Children of a Lesser God* (1986) and *The Doctor* (1991). After directing for *L.A. Law, China Beach*, and *ER*, Mimi Leder took the helm of the Dreamworks films *The Peacemaker* (1997) and *Deep Impact* (1998), which, respectively, carried $50 million and $75 million budgets.

Unfortunately, woman directors just as often find themselves directing television *after* enjoying a career directing mainstream films, when they can no longer find work in Hollywood. Claudia Weill has directed episodes of *thirtysomething* and *NYPD Blue* after making a string of films in the early 1980s. Donna Dietch has also directed for *NYPD Blue* after having made the first mainstream "lesbian" film, *Desert Hearts* (1986), and the television

229

miniseries *The Woman of Brewster Place* (1989). This is not to say that television is a "lesser" form than film, only to point out that women lose a certain amount of commercial power and "cachet" if they go from Hollywood to television directing. Despite this fact, Susan Seidelman says that she enjoys the creative control extended to her by cable television production (author's interview, 14 July 1998).

4. See Teresa de Lauretis's *The Practice of Love* for more on lesbian looking relations. She also provides a critique of Stacey's article.

5. Jackie Stacey's *Star-gazing* (1994) further complicates spectatorship by demonstrating through ethnographic research that viewers might be identifying with stars in ways that disregard textual systems entirely. These identificatory processes have more to do with expectations based on a star's range of films or on a star's public persona.

6. See Flitterman-Lewis's *To Desire Differently: Feminism and the French Cinema* (1990) and Rabinovitz's *Points of Resistance: Women, Power & Politics in the New York Avant-garde Cinema, 1943–1971* (1991) for in-depth accounts of these and other women directors.

7. For a summary of the critiques of feminist documentary see Kuhn 1993 (chapter 8), and Kaplan 1983 (chapter 10).

8. Janet Bergstrom criticizes Johnston's thesis that feminists should focus on the "ruptures" of Hollywood cinema, arguing that Johnston assumes that every textual moment will affect every viewer in the same way. She also suggests that Johnston does not contextualize these ruptures within the larger signification process. See "Rereading the Work of Claire Johnston" in Penley's *Feminism and Film Theory* 1988.

9. See Hartsock 1990.

10. Martha Coolidge interprets this trend with optimism. She remarks, "If you think about it, adult men don't go flustering to the movies in groups. Women do!" (author's interview, 20 Nov. 1997). Coolidge values the possibilities of this adult female demographic and believes that "female films" have a preconstituted audience.

11. *Blue Steel* grossed over $2.8 million in its first week; *Point Break* grossed over $8.5 million; and *Strange Days* grossed over $3.6 million in its first week.

12. In a helpful explication of Foucault, Susan Hayward remarks that "as a product and producer of power, the individual is both a producer and a product of reality" (1996: 111). In other words, even women producers and executives who see themselves as struggling against the oppressive institutions of Hollywood can potentially reflect the more conservative beliefs of these institutions as they oversee projects, negotiate contracts, and build creative teams. The debate in both trade publications and critical pieces about whether executive Sherri Lansing (*Fatal Attraction, Indecent Proposal*) produces feminist work speaks to this concern.

13. Bazin comments on this strange phenomenon: "paradoxically, the supporters of the *politiques des auteurs* admire the American cinema, where the restrictions of production are heavier than anywhere else" (154).

14. Janet Staiger stresses that Sarris's canon "explicitly appealed to the rationale of evaluative standards for the cultural good" (1985: 11). His pantheon of visionaries was supposed to educate film students on "good taste."

15. Bazin foreshadowed this argument in 1963, insisting that "the cinema is an art which is both popular and industrial" (142).

16. One example of a "progressive auteur" would be Douglas Sirk. Paul Willeman has studied the way in which Sirk's melodramas put forward political critiques of capitalism. Tracing Sirk's past history, including his escape from Nazi Germany and his attention to Left politics after World War II, Willeman argues that Sirk's films incorporate techniques of distanciation (1991: 273–78). (He identifies the intensification of generic rules and a constant oscillation between closeness to and distance from the characters.) We might view Sirk's work, then, as an expression of a larger cultural response to the horrific

dangers of fascism and even the ensuing threat of post-World War II capitalist recuperation.

17. At the same time, it is important to note that such a classification has been criticized—categorizing one film as a critique and another as complicit with dominant ideology becomes very tricky. The designation between "E" films and other films, "A"–"D," the spectrum defined by Cahiers du Cinema, is never cut and dried.

18. *Points of Resistance* examines the women's avant-garde movement from 1943 to 1971. In *To Desire Differently*, Flitterman-Lewis interrogates the notion of a "feminine voice" in the work of Germaine Dulac, Marie Epstein, and Agnes Varda. *Woman at the Keyhole* is oriented toward feminist "re-invention" and re-writing of dominant cinema. And Fischer's *Shot/Countershot* considers women's counter cinema in relation to mainstream films that are close in genre or theme, asking what a "reverse shot" of Hollywood looks like.

19. Schatz uses Saussure's concepts of "langue" and "parole" to distinguish between the general rules governing the language system ("langue," or, analogously, the general characteristics of a film genre) and the "individual utterances" that are made based on those general rules ("parole," or an individual film). Individual utterances, particular films, can affect (or change the rules of) the systems they manifest (96).

20. See Stacey's "Desperately Seeking Difference" and Teresa de Lauretis's "Film and the Visible" and *The Practice of Love: Lesbian Sexuality and Perverse Desire*.

CHAPTER 1

1. The following is a complete filmography for Coolidge, to date: *David: Off and On* (1972), *More Than a School* (1974), *Old Fashioned Woman* (1974), *Not a Pretty Picture* (1976), *Bimbo* (1978), *Photoplay* (unfinished, 1978–1980), *Employment Discriminations: The Trouble Shooters* (1979), *Strawberries and Gold* (1980), *Valley Girl* (1983), *The City Girl* (1984), *Joy of Sex* (1984), *Real Genius* (1985), *Plain Clothes* (1988), *Plain Clothes Roughhouse* (1988), *That's Adequate* (1989), *Trenchcoat in Paradise* (1989), *Rambling Rose* (1991), *Lost in Yonkers* (1993), *Angie* (1994), *Three Wishes* (1995), *Out to Sea* (1997).

2. See Gwendolyn Audrey Foster's *Women Film Directors: An International Bio-Critical Dictionary*. Regarding contemporary women, see Larry Rohter's "Are Women Directors an Endangered Species?"

3. The status of women's films was different in the past. The *Los Angeles Times* comments that women's films of the 1930s and 1940s tended to be guaranteed commercial and critical successes. Sharon Bernstein reports, "About *Back Street*, one critic wrote: 'Swell romance, a little tear-jerking and a woman's picture—which means a money production' " (1990: 83).

4. See Bernstein (1990), Birns (1985), Cole and Dale (1993), and Corliss (1986) for discussions of Coolidge's feminism.

5. Coolidge's own ambivalence about identifying herself as "avant-garde" suggests her in-betweenness. She refuses any easy location within film movements.

6. See also Birns's interview in *Premiere* and Coolidge's article in *American Film*.

7. Dorothy Arzner was known for bringing films in under budget. More recently, Susan Seidelman's (*Desperately Seeking Susan*) and Amy Heckerling's low-cost films have brought in high proceeds. Heckerling's *National Lampoon's European Vacation* landed in the 1985's top ten grossing pictures category.

8. Because *Not a Pretty Picture* is currently out of distribution, I include an added degree of description about this film.

9. Thomas Schatz uses John Huston's discussion of "brushstrokes" in his course on "Narrative Strategies" at the University of Texas at Austin. I would like to thank him for

the ideas his discussion generated for me, particularly those relating to the ways in which "showing the brushstrokes" might be applied to women's experimental filmmaking.

10. Throughout this section, I refer to Martha when I mean the character representing Coolidge's early self, and to Coolidge to indicate the director.

11. Coolidge's interaction with Jim clearly suggests her feminist investment in performing consciousness-raising not only with women but with men too. I think this investment is echoed in her later film *Real Genius*, which many critics have suggested posits a progressive version of masculinity and a feminist perspective on male relationships (see, for example, Foster 1995).

12. Further complications arose when Harlin's and Dern's agents battled each other over a contingency fee without the knowledge of the actors. When Harlin's agent tried to freeze Dern out of the fee, Harlin fired him. To make matters more intense, the two agents were married to each other (Richardson 25). The family politics that set the groundwork for this film's production are contrasted by the stable, happy family presented on screen.

13. See Kathryn Shattuck's article, "The Marquee Is the Message," *New York Times*, 24 Sept. 1995, 24, on how movie marquees function as reflexive commentary.

14. Jenson has served as Coolidge's cinematographer on a number of films, including *Bare Essentials*, *Trenchcoat in Paradise* (a television movie), *Rambling Rose*, *Crazy in Love* (a television movie), *Lost in Yonkers*, and *Three Wishes*.

15. The screenplay version of *Angie* can be located in the Margaret Herrick Library at the Academy of Motion Picture Arts and Sciences.

CHAPTER 2

1. Bigelow also wanted access to equipment to edit the footage that would eventually become *Set-Up* (1978), her first attempt at moving from painting to film. The film will be described shortly.

2. Together, Comden and Green wrote, among others, *Singin' in the Rain* (1952), *Auntie Mame* (1958), and *The Bells Are Ringing* (1960). Gordon and Kanin wrote *A Double Life* (1948), *Adam's Rib* (1949), *The Marrying Kind* (1952), and *Pat and Mike* (1953). Goodrich and Hackett collaborated on *The Thin Man* (1934), *It's a Wonderful Life* (1946), and *Seven Brides for Seven Brothers* (1954).

3. Lisa Lewis discusses an "ideology of sexual favors" in relation to the pop music industry (1991: 61).

4. A 1989 *Gap* print advertisement also suggests Bigelow's cross-over status as both "star" and director, a generally necessary status in the labeling of an auteur.

5. For press accounts that single out Bigelow for tackling a "male" genre, see Denby (1990), Acker (1992), and Powers (1995).

6. Universal Studios has a long tradition of cultivating female directors, screenwriters, and editors; the case of Lois Weber serves as an early example. Cunard was invited by Universal and insisted on bringing Ford along as her collaborator.

7. While Cunard may be the only female action director to predate Bigelow, the women screenwriters who chose more violent genres also beg some attention. Burbridge found herself writing for the B-Western genre in the 1930s and 1940s following a brief stint as an actress and journalist. After being hired by a producer at Republic to doctor up *Law of the Rio Grande* (1931), she went on to write for Gene Autry and John Wayne. In accounts similar to those of Bigelow, Burbridge's attractive appearance was often commented on in the popular press, which recounted her success in this typically male genre (Francke 74).

Roberts (*Honky Tonk*, 1941, *True Grit*, 1969) developed a reputation at MGM as a "man's screenwriter" (particularly for Clark Gable), and she succeeded in the category of the Western. Originally, though, she was a journalist, intrigued by the crime news she covered, who experimented in crime fiction (77). In a career that spanned from *The Big Sleep* (1946) to *The Empire Strikes Back* (1980), Leigh Brackett also carved herself a niche in male-dominated genres, attributing her interest in crime and science fiction to an early disdain for "lady-like" behavior (82).

8. The problem of idealizing female characters is that they are then positioned only at the level of metaphor, where their experiences cannot be accounted for. Such an exaltation perpetuates, and is perpetuated by, the stereotypical Madonna/whore dichotomy so prevalent in Western culture. See Schatz's *Hollywood Genres*, 50–52.

9. I would like to thank Walter Metz for helping me with this formulation.

10. Cora Kaplan provides a compelling reading of *Blue Steel* as a meta-commentary on women's position within film theory, and more explicitly within feminist discourses. She contends, "What is new in Bigelow's film is a textualization of and interrogation of *theory*," and she further suggests that "Bigelow provides a kind of interpretative synopsis of feminism's entry into film theory" in her initial "simulation" sequence (53, 68n. 6). Through this reading, we see Megan's realization of the impossibility of her position in a male world as representing the recognition by feminist theorists of the restraints of classical Hollywood conventions.

11. The television program *Cagney and Lacey* represents one exception in that it examines female friendship within the context of the cop genre. See Julie D'Acci's *Defining Women: Television and the Case of Cagney and Lacey* (Chapel Hill: University of North Carolina Press), 1994.

12. In keeping with the argument I have developed in this chapter, the male fantasies transmitted by the wire trips are countered by only one instance of a "real" flashback: Mace remembers the difficult day when her husband was carted off to jail by Lenny, whom she did not know at the time.

The camerawork is similar to the steadicam mode of the wire-trip fantasies, with the major difference being that she is experiencing a dear memory while the fantasies are simulated performances that cater to a particular kind of hyper-conscious, action blockbuster audience. In this way, Mace's "logic"—one centered around black female subjectivity—might act as an internal critique of the voyeuristic white men in the film.

CHAPTER 3

1. Borden worked hard to incorporate new audiences into her screenings of *Born in Flames*, sending out mailings to numerous grass roots organizations (Friedberg 43).

2. Mary Ann Doane uses psychoanalytic theory to explain female spectatorship in terms of masquerade. According to Doane, masquerade is used to deny the "lack" implied by the symbolic possibility of castration. It is a process by which a female character or spectator "flaunts" her femininity with excess. Although Doane does not see this process as providing women with much agency, she remarks, "The masquerade's resistance to patriarchal positioning would therefore lie in its denial of the production of femininity as closeness, as presence-to-itself, as, precisely, imagistic" (1991: 25).

3. Borden went on to say: "I didn't even know that I could walk away which I maybe should have done. But I had so much invested that I thought the problems would solve themselves."

4. Borden was pressured to incorporate this element of childhood trauma and psychological flashbacks by executives who were cause-and-effect oriented. However, their presence in the film results in a somewhat interesting female Oedipal journey.

5. *Love Crimes* also explores the controversial topic of female fantasies of rape, at least psychological rape and emotional abuse, through Dana's desires to give over control to

Hanover. It might function then as a way of exploring the anxieties and fears women inevitably experience in a culture where rape occurs so frequently. Molly Haskell has suggested (in a well-known 1976 *Ms.* article) that women's rape fantasies represent not a wish to be sexually abused, but rather a coping mechanism within a "rape culture" through which women can imagine how they might react in such a situation (84–86).

6. Dana's termination from the district attorney's office is much like Megan Turner's discharge from the police force in *Blue Steel.* Dana is accused of being sloppy and unreliable despite the fact that she has brought the murderer to the police.

7. Maria accuses the police of sexism in this scene, arguing that if Dana was a man, her authority would not be questioned.

8. Borden would disagree with de Lauretis. She prefers to see the cinematic apparatus as inherently neutral (Jackson 1987).

CHAPTER 4

1. Dash's *Daughters of the Dust* was made on an $800,000 budget (Dash 52). For an overview of the successful marketing strategies of the film, see Jesse Algeron Rhines's *Black Films/White Money* (1996: 66–67). The KJM3 marketing firm was hired to find a core audience for the film by cross-referencing tastes, habits, and consumption patterns of potential African American viewers. They utilized cultural grass roots networks, black TV and radio stations, political organizations, and churches, working hard to spread word of mouth in New York urban communities. Before this all-out attempt, no clear method for marketing African American independent films to a wider audience had existed.

2. Leslie Harris's film *Just Another Girl* might have also fallen by the wayside after being financed by Nelson George, Michael Moore, and Terry McMillan because Harris could find no distribution financing. Miramax stepped in during post-production and decided to distribute it (Rhines 100–101).

3. For a profile on these women, see Greg Tate's "Cinematic Sisterhood."

4. Rhines explains that *House Party* might be categorized as the first "black blockbuster" because the Hudlin brothers, after studying distribution methods through their own Black Filmmakers Foundation, learned how to saturate the young black market (62).

5. See, for example, David Denby's "I Like It Like That," in which he proposes, "Martin may already possess the innate emotional coherence that has eluded Lee, whose films whirl about brilliantly without any center" (31 Oct. 1991: 96).

6. Martin's crediting of Dickerson as a creative influence offers a productive intervention into auteurism by privileging the cinematographer. About Spike Lee and her increased awareness regarding labor conditions, Martin explains: "Lee made me aware that there weren't any black faces in the unions, in the film industry. There were jobs that required a lot of lifting. These unions are not only very racist; they are also sexist. But they were more racist than sexist when it came to hard labor. There were more women camera assistants than there were black camera assistants (even though the job entailed heavy equipment). Lee forced the unions to hire people of color" (author's interview).

7. The term "Spike Lee discourse" comes from an article by Wahneema Lubiano, which will be discussed shortly.

8. The documentary practice of presenting "positive images" or "real experiences" has been discussed in chapters 1 and 2. This practice was popular in the 1970s but has since been critiqued for being overly invested in a naive realism. Many African American films have been judged by whether or not they present negative stereotypes rather than for how their representations work semiotically or historically (See Lola Young 8–12).

9. This is not to suggest that Martin did not deserve acceptance in NYU's program,

only to suggest the importance of professional networking, especially among disenfranchised groups.

10. This statistic reflects the year of 1995. Rhines adds that "most Blacks see movies—even Black movies—in suburban multiplexes, not in the inner cities where they live" (7).

11. Martin's association with practical jokes is reminiscent of Alfred Hitchcock's reputation for playing practical jokes (which were often perverse) on the set. This notoriety helped feed his status as a notable auteur. See Spoto's *The Dark Side of Genius: The Life of Alfred Hitchcock* (1983).

12. Andrea Stuart reports that co-stars Lauren Vélez and Jon Seda fabricated a rumor that a private rehearsal between them led to rape. In response, Martin arranged for a police car to arrive at a dance club when she knew Seda would be there. A woman jumped out of the squad car and fingered him for rape, at which point the police officer began an arrest and then explained that Martin was retaliating with her own joke. This account suggests that Martin refused to allow rape to be joked about without ramifications that signaled its seriousness.

13. In late 1996, soon after my interview with Martin, HBO hired her to direct several episodes of a series titled *Oz*, which portrays prison life within a science fiction noir world. She also directed an episode of NBC's *ER* in November 1997.

14. According to Rhines, studios are less likely to back films aimed at African Americans if those films do not feature black stars (89). In neglecting to market Vélez, Columbia indirectly contributed to the shortage of black stars, and hence, the shortage of movies targeted at black populations.

15. While work on black female spectatorship is sparse, there are two excellent studies by Jacqueline Bobo (1988) and Andrea Stuart (1989).

16. Also, Lisette chooses to spend her last bit of money to try to get this job, whereas Chino expects her to spend it on his lottery numbers. The film sides with Lisette's choice, supporting the notion that hard work should be more rewarded than luck.

17. In locating this trend, Gibson-Hudson specifically discusses Akoya Chenzira's *Hair Piece: A Film for Nappy-Headed People* (1984), Julie Dash's *Illusions* (1983), and Kathleen Collins's *Losing Ground* (1982).

18. See Gayle Rubin's "The Traffic in Women," Adrienne Rich's "Compulsory Heterosexuality and Lesbian Existence," and Nancy Tuana's *The Less Noble Sex*.

19. Anne Stockwell of *The Advocate* suggests that Alexis represents "the film's moral center" (1 Nov. 1994: 76). However, Stockwell also laments that the character "rings false" and is portrayed with "vague discomfort" (76).

20. It has already been mentioned that *Daughters of the Dust* and *House Party* approached African American target audiences in landmark ways. *Waiting to Exhale* (1994, directed by Forrest Whitaker) is another example of a film that successfully parlayed "niche" success into larger box office returns by orchestrating word-of-mouth publicity and, because it was first a best-selling novel by Terry McMillan, relying on an audience already informed about its product.

CHAPTER 5

1. This is not to say that producers are only interested in selling products. Many Hollywood producers see their role as bringing to the screen projects and visions that truly interest them.

2. A partial list of videos directed by Davis: "Pacer" by the Amps; "In Your Room" by the Bangles; "Beavis and Butthead with Cher"; Depeche Mode's "But Not Tonight";

the D.O.C./N.W.A.'s "The Doc and the Doctor" and "It's Funky Enough"; Hanson's "Mmmbop" and "Where's the Love?"; Etta James's "Beware"; Ben Lee's "Away with the Pixies"; Living Color's "Love Rears Its Ugly Head"; Tone Loc's "Wild Thing" and "Funky Cold Medina"; Luscious Jackson's "City Song"; New Kids on the Block's "Call It What You Want"; Veruca Salt's "All Hail Me"; Sonic Youth's "Dirty Boots," "Kool Thing," and "100%"; and Young MC's "Bust a Move" and "Principal's Office." Davis also directed the Indigo Girls' concert video *Live at the Uptown Lounge* (1990).

3. "Postfeminism," which carries a number of connotations, has been problematized by feminist scholars. While some critics argue that the word should not be deployed at all because it suggests that we have moved "beyond" the need for feminism, others use the term "postfeminists" to characterize (mostly young) women who enjoy many of the benefits of the 1970s second wave feminist movement, yet feel no need to identify as feminist.

For more on the debates surrounding postfeminism, see *Feminism and Postmodernism*, ed. Margaret Ferguson and Jennifer Wicke (Durham: Duke University Press), 1994. On postfeminism and "girl culture," see Shelagh Young's "Feminism and the Politics of Power: Whose Gaze Is It Anyway?" in *The Female Gaze: Women as Viewers of Popular Culture*, ed. Lorraine Gamman and Margaret Marshment (Seattle: The Real Comet Press, 1989), 173–88.

4. Here I am recalling again Thomas Elsaesser's interview with Douglas Sirk in which the director discusses a certain relationship between saturated colors and internal violence (350).

5. See George (183–86) for problems that he and other producers ran into regarding censorship of the various songs on the soundtrack and lyrics in the film. Because these were not battles fought specifically by Davis, I have not highlighted them here.

6. Before Becky Johnston substantially rewrote *Bad Girls*, Yolande Finch had written a previous draft. After Davis was fired, Ken Friedman was called in to re-write Johnston's version. The screenwriting credits on the final film version were assigned to Yolande Finch and Ken Friedman. Story credits were given to Albert S. Ruddy, Charles Finch, and Gray Frederickson.

Becky Johnston's screenwriting credits include *Under the Cherry Moon* (1986), *The Prince of Tides* (1991), and *Seven Years in Tibet* (1997).

7. I would like to thank Tamra Davis for generously providing me with the original screenplay for *Bad Girls*.

CONCLUSION

1. I was led down this line of inquiry when I spoke with a female director of development for an internationally renowned and highly commercial writer-director-producer. She spoke of him as an auteur and continually downplayed her role as gatekeeper and pre-production collaborator.

2. See Timothy Corrigan's *A Cinema without Walls: Movies and Culture after Vietnam* (1991: 101–36). In his chapter "The Commerce of Auteurism," Corrigan explains that the auteur "has re-materialized in the eighties and nineties as a commercial performance of *the business of being an auteur*" (his emphasis) (104).

3. Gledhill, for example, suggests the way in which feminist film theorists contribute to the possibilities for "feminist self-production" through the texts they choose to write about. She argues that critical analysis "generates new cycles of meaning production and negotiation" in journals, classrooms, distribution practices, etc. (74). She reminds us: "Thus critical activity itself participates in social negotiation of meaning, definition, and identity" (74).

4. Linda Seger's *When Women Call the Shots: The Developing Power and Influence of*

Women in Television and Film (1996) goes far in outlining the way in which this network is expanding. Seger expresses a great deal of optimism that a new consciousness is spreading throughout Hollywood, one that emphasizes collaboration and replaces hierarchy with horizontal power structures. One can only hope that this emerging "women's network" can find ways to escape rituals of exclusivity and to extend itself to women of color and working-class women.

WORKS CITED

Abel, Elizabeth. "Black Writing/White Reading: Race and the Politics of Feminist Interpretation." *Critical Inquiry* 19 (Spring 1993): 470–98.

Abramowitz, Rachel. "Geena Soars." *Premiere* Feb. 1994: 54–60.

Acker, Ally. "Arts: Women behind the Camera." *Ms.*, Mar.–Apr. 1992, 64–67.

Altman, Rick. "Dickens, Griffith, and Film Theory Today." *South Atlantic Quarterly* (Spring 1989): 321–59.

Andrew, Dudley. "The Unauthorized Auteur Today." In *Film Theory Goes to the Movies.* Ed. Jim Collins, Hilary Radner, and Ava Preacher Collins. New York: Routledge, 1993. 77–85.

Bartky, Sandra Lee. "Foucault, Feminism, and the Modernization of Patriarchal Power." In *Feminism and Foucault.* Ed. Irene Diamond and Lee Quinby. Boston: Northeastern University Press, 1988. 61–86.

Barton, Sabrina. "Your Self Storage: Female Investigation and Male Performativity in the Woman's Psychothriller." In *The New American Cinema.* Ed. Jon Lewis. Durham: Duke University Press, 1998. 187–216.

Bazin, André. "La Politiques des Auteurs." 1957. In *The New Wave.* Ed. Peter Graham. Garden City, NY: Doubleday and Co., 1968. 137–55.

Bergstrom, Janet, and Mary Ann Doane, eds. *Female Spectatrix.* Spec. issue of *Camera Obscura* 20.1 (May–Aug. 1989).

Bernstein, Sharon. "But Is There Hope for the Future?" *Los Angeles Times*, 11 Nov. 1990, 9, 82–83.

Bigelow, Kathryn. "Walk on the Wild Side." *Monthly Film Bulletin* (Nov. 1990): 312–13.

Birns, Debbie. "Close Up." *American Premiere*, Sept. 1985, 4.

Bobo, Jacqueline. "*The Color Purple:* Black Women as Cultural Readers." In *Female Spectators: Looking at Film and Television.* Ed. E. Diedre Pribram. London: Verso, 1990.

Bordwell, David, Janet Staiger, and Kristin Thompson. *The Classical Hollywood Cinema: Film Style and Mode of Production to 1960.* New York: Columbia University Press, 1985.

239

Bovenschen, Sylvia. "Is There a Feminine Aesthetic?" *New German Critique.* Trans. Beth Weckmueller (Winter 1977): 111–37.

Bowser, Pearl. "The Black Woman in Cinema." In *Black Cinema Aesthetics: Issues in Independent Black Filmmaking.* Ed. Gladstone L. Yearwood. Athens: Ohio University Afro-American Studies, 1982. 42–52.

Braudy, Leo. "From the World in a Frame. . . ." In *Film Theory and Criticism.* 3d ed. Ed. Gerald Mast and Marshall Cohen. New York: Oxford University Press, 1985. 411–33.

Brown, Georgia. "Electra Glide in Blue." *Village Voice,* 20 Mar. 1990, 62.

Brown, Mary Ellen, and John Fiske. "Romancing the Rock: Romance and Representation in Popular Music Videos." *One Two Three Four: A Rock 'n' Roll Quarterly* 5 (1987): 61–73.

Brunette, Peter. "Working Girls." *Film Quarterly* (Winter 1986): 54–56.

Byars, Jackie. "Feminism, Psychoanalysis, and Female-Oriented Melodramas of the 1950s." In *Multiple Voices in Feminist Film Criticism.* Ed. Linda Dittmar, Janice R. Welsch, and Diane Carson. Minneapolis: University of Minnesota Press, 1994. 93–108.

Cahiers du Cinema editors. "John Ford's *Young Mr. Lincoln.*" 1972. In *Movies and Methods.* Ed. Bill Nichols. Berkeley: University of California Press, 1976. 493–529.

Cameron, James. *Strange Days.* New York: Plume/Penguin Books, 1996.

Canby, Vincent. "Film Noir Still Has Life. . . ." *New York Times,* 27 Jan. 1993, sec. C, pp. 17, 21.

"Cinderella debut." *Black Collegian* 25.1 (Oct. 1994): 8–9.

Citron, Michele. "Women's Film Production: Going Mainstream." In *Female Spectators: Looking at Film and Television.* Ed. E. Diedre Pribram. London: Verso, 1990.

———., Julia Lesage, Judith Mayne, B. Ruby Rich, and Anna Marie Taylor. "Women and Film: A Discussion of Feminist Aesthetics." *New German Critique* (Winter 1978): 83–107.

Cole, Janis, and Holly Dale. *Calling the Shots: Profiles of Women Filmmakers.* Kingston, Ontario: Quarry Press, 1993.

Comolli, Jean-Louis, and Jean Narboni. "Cinema/Ideology/Criticism." *Screen* 12.1 (Spring 1971): 27–36.

Coolidge, Martha. "Dialogue on Film." *American Film,* Dec. 1988, 14–19.

———. "I've Made the Film, Now What Do I Do with It?" *American Film,* Apr. 1976a, 88–90.

———. "You Mean People Get Paid to Do That?" *American Film,* June 1976b, 68–70.

Cordero, Caroline King. "The Numbers Never Lie." *Premiere: Women in Hollywood,* Sept. 1993, 33–36.

Corliss, Richard. "Calling Their Own Shots." *Time,* 24 Mar. 1986, 82–83.

Corrigan, Timothy. *A Cinema without Walls: Movies and Culture after Vietnam.* New Brunswick, NJ: Rutgers University Press, 1991.

Cowie, Elizabeth. "Fantasia." *m/f* 9 (1984): 70–105.

Cripps, Thomas. *Black Film as Genre.* Bloomington: Indiana University Press, 1978.

D'Acci, Julie. *Defining Women: Television and the Case of Cagney and Lacey.* Chapel Hill: University of North Carolina Press, 1994.

Dash, Julie, with Toni Cade Bambara and bell hooks. *Daughters of the Dust: The Making of an African American Woman's Film.* New York: W. W. Norton, 1992.

Davis, Kathy, and Sue Fisher, eds. "Power and the Female Subject." *Negotiating at the Margins: The Gendered Discourses of Power and Resistance.* New Brunswick, NJ: Rutgers University Press, 1993. 3–20.

de Lauretis, Teresa. "Aesthetics and Feminist Theory: Rethinking Women's Cinema." In *Female Spectators: Looking at Film and TV.* Ed. E. Diedre Pribram. London: Verso, 1990.

Works Cited

———. *Alice Doesn't: Feminism, Semiotics, Cinema.* Bloomington: Indiana University Press, 1984.

———. "Film and the Visible." In *How Do I Look?: Queer Film and Video.* Ed. Bad Object Choices. Seattle: Bay Press, 1991. 223–71.

———. *The Practice of Love: Lesbian Sexuality and Perverse Desire.* Bloomington: Indiana University Press, 1994.

———. *Technologies of Gender: Essays on Film, Theory, and Fiction.* Bloomington: Indiana University Press, 1987.

Denby, David. "All in the Family." *New York,* 22 Feb. 1993, 60–61.

———. "Dirty Harriet." *New York,* 26 Mar. 1990, 76–77.

———. "I Like It Like That." *New York,* 31 Oct. 1994, 96.

"Desperately Seeking Susan." Press Kit, Orion Pictures, 1986.

Deutchman, Ira. "Independent Distribution and Marketing." In *The Movie Business Book.* 2nd ed. Ed. Jason Squires. New York: Fireside, 1992. 320–27.

Doane, Mary Ann. *The Desire to Desire: The Woman's Film of the 1940s.* Bloomington: Indiana University Press, 1987.

———. *Femmes Fatales: Feminism, Film Theory, Psychoanalysis.* New York: Routledge, 1991.

———., Patricia Mellencamp, and Linda Williams. *Revision: Essays in Feminist Film Criticism.* Frederick, MD: University Publications of America in association with American Film Institute, 1984.

"Domestic Box Office." *Variety,* 14 Oct. 1987, 12.

Doty, Alexander. *Making Things Perfectly Queer: Interpreting Mass Culture.* Minneapolis: University of Minnesota Press, 1993.

Drucker, Elizabeth. "Love Crimes." *American Film,* Aug. 1991, 49–50.

Ellsworth, Elizabeth. "Illicit Pleasures: Feminist Spectators and *Personal Best.*" *Wide Angle* 8.2 (1986): 45–56.

Elsaesser, Thomas. "Tales of Sound and Fury: Observations on the Family Melodrama." In *Film Genre Reader II.* Ed. Barry Keith Grant. Austin: University of Texas Press, 1995.

Erens, Patricia, ed. *Issues in Feminist Film Criticism.* Bloomington: Indiana University Press, 1990.

Faludi, Susan. *Backlash: The Undeclared War against American Women.* New York: Doubleday, 1991.

Ferguson, Margaret, and Jennifer Wicke, eds. *Feminism and Postmodernism.* Durham: Duke University Press, 1994.

Ferncase, Richard K. *Outsider Features: American Independent Films of the 1980s.* Westport, CT: Greenwood Press, 1996.

Feuer, Jane. "Genre Study and Television." In *Channels of Discourse, Reassembled.* Ed. Robert Allen. Chapel Hill: University of North Carolina Press, 1992. 138–60.

Fischer, Lucy. *Shot/Countershot: Film Tradition and Women's Cinema.* Princeton: Princeton University Press, 1989.

Flitterman-Lewis, Sandy. *To Desire Differently: Feminism and the French Cinema.* Urbana: University of Illinois Press, 1990.

Foster, Gwendolyn Audrey. *Women Film Directors: An International Bio-Critical Dictionary.* Westport, CT: Greenwood Press, 1995.

Foucault, Michel. *Discipline and Punish: The Birth of the Prison.* Trans. Alan Sheridan. New York: Pantheon, 1977.

———. *The History of Sexuality, Vol. I.* Trans. Robert Hurley. New York: Vintage Books, 1990.

Francke, Lizzie. "A Debut to Bank On." *The Guardian,* 30 Jan. 1995, 29.

———. *Script Girls: Women Screenwriters in Hollywood.* London: BFI Publishing, 1994.

Friedberg, Anne. "Cinema and the Postmodern Condition." In *Viewing Positions*. Ed. Linda Williams. New Brunswick, NJ: Rutgers University Press, 1995.

———. "An Interview with Filmmaker Lizzie Borden." *Women and Performance* 1.2 (Winter 1984): 37–45.

Fuchs, Cynthia. "The Buddy Politic." In *Screening the Male: Exploring Masculinities in Hollywood Cinema*. Ed. Steven Cohan and Ina Rae Hark. New York: Routledge, 1993. 194–210.

Fuller, Graham. "Shots in the Dark." *Interview*, Jan. 1993, 47.

Garey, Juliann, and Bronwen Hruska. "They Shoot Bad Girls, Don't They." *US*, May 1994, 74, 90.

Garvin, Tom. "Independents Find Moneys Available, for the Right Price." *Variety* 2–8 (Mar. 1998): 80.

George, Nelson. *Blackface: Reflections on African Americans and the Movies*. New York: Harper Perennial, 1995.

Gledhill, Christine. "Images and Voices: Approaches to Marxist-Feminist Criticism." In *Multiple Voices in Feminist Film Criticism*. Ed. Diane Carson et al. Minneapolis: University of Minnesota Press, 1994. 109–23.

———. "Pleasurable Negotiations." In *Female Spectators: Looking at Film and Television*. Ed. E. Diedre Pribram. London: Verso, 1990.

Goodwin, Andrew. Dancing in the Distraction Factory: Music Television and Popular Culture. Minneapolis: University of Minnesota Press, 1993.

———. "Music Video in the (Post) Modern World." *Screen* 28.3 (1987): 36–55.

Guevara, Nancy. "women writin' rappin' breakin.' " In *dropping science: essays on rap music and hip hop culture*. Ed. William Eric Perkins. Philadelphia: Temple University Press, 1996. 49–62.

Hall, Stuart. "Encoding/Decoding." In *Culture, Media Language*. Ed. Stuart Hall, Dorothy Hobson, Andrew Lowe, and Paul Willis. London: Hutchinson, 1980.

Hamburg, Victoria. "Dark by Design." *Interview*, Aug. 1989, 84–87.

Hartsock, Nancy. "Foucault on Power: A Theory for Women?" In *Feminism/Postmodernism*. Ed. Linda J. Nicholson. New York: Routledge, 1990. 157–75.

Haskell, Molly. "The 2,000-Year-Old Misunderstanding—Rape Fantasy." *Ms.*, Nov. 1976, 84–86, 92, 94, 96, 98.

Hayward, Susan. *Key Concepts in Cinema Studies*. New York: Routledge, 1996.

Heath, Stephen. "Comment on 'The Idea of Authorship.' " In *Theories of Authorship: A Reader*. Ed. John Caughie. London: Routledge and Kegan Paul, 1981. 214–20.

Heilbrun, Carolyn G. *Writing a Woman's Life*. New York: Ballantine Books, 1988.

Hillier, Jim. *The New Hollywood*. New York: Continuum, 1993.

Hollywood Creative Directory. Santa Monica: Aleks Horvat, Summer 1996.

Hoberman, J. "Making It." *Village Voice*, 18 Oct. 1994, 49.

Hoffman, Jan. "Mom Always Said, Don't Take the First $2 Million Offer." *New York Times*, 9 Oct. 1994, sec. H, p. 28.

hooks, bell. *Black Looks: Race and Representation*. Boston: South End Press, 1992.

———. *Reel to Real: Race, Sex, and Class at the Movies*. New York: Routledge, 1996.

Horton, Robert. "Connecticut Yankee." *Film Comment*, Sept.–Oct. 1991, 16–20.

Hulser, Kathleen. "Les Guerilleres." *Afterimage*, Jan. 1984, 14–15.

Huston, John. *An Open Book*. New York: Alfred A. Knopf, 1980.

Jackson, Devon. "As She Likes It." *Village Voice*, 18 Oct. 1994, 58.

Jackson, Lynne. "Labor Relations: An Interview with Lizzie Borden." *Cineaste* 15.3 (Fall 1987): 4–9.

Jameson, Frederic. "Reification and Utopia in Mass Culture." *Social Text* 1 (1979): 130–48.

Jeffords, Susan. *Hard Bodies: Hollywood Masculinity in the Reaganite Era*. New Brunswick, NJ: Rutgers University Press, 1994.

Works Cited

Johnston, Becky. *Bad Girls.* Beverly Hills, CA: Bad Girls Productions, 22 June 1993.

Johnston, Claire. "Women's Cinema as Counter Cinema." In *Movies and Methods.* Ed. Bill Nichols. Berkeley: University of California Press, 1976.

Kaplan, Cora. "Dirty Harriet/Blue Steel: Feminist Theory Goes to Hollywood." *Discourse* 16.1 (Fall 1993): 50–70.

Kaplan, E. Ann. "Mothering, Feminism and Representation." In *Home Is Where the Heart Is: Studies on Melodrama and the Woman's Film.* Ed. Christine Gledhill. London: BFI, 1987.

———. *Rocking around the Clock: Music, Television, Postmodernism and Consumer Culture.* New York: Methuen, 1987.

———. *Women and Film: Both Sides of the Camera.* New York: Methuen, 1983.

Kapsis, Robert E. *Hitchcock: The Making of a Reputation.* Chicago: University of Chicago Press, 1992.

Kelley, Robin D. G. "kickin' reality, kickin' ballistics: gangsta rap and postindustrial los angeles." In *dropping science: essays on rap music and hip hop culture.* Ed. William Eric Perkins. Philadelphia: Temple University Press, 1996. 117–58.

Kramer, Mimi. "Undressed for Success." *Vogue,* July 1987, 218–19, 272.

Kroll, Jack. "To Hollywood, Via the Bronx." *Newsweek,* 17 Oct. 1994, 79–80.

Kuhn, Annette. *Women's Pictures: Feminism and Cinema.* London: Verso, 1993.

Lapsley, Robert, and Michael Westlake. *Film Theory: An Introduction.* Manchester, Eng.: Manchester University Press, 1988.

Lewis, Lisa. *Gender Politics and MTV: Voicing the Difference.* Philadelphia: Temple University Press, 1990.

Lubiano, Wahneema. " 'But Compared to What?': Reading, Realism, Representation, and Essentialism in *School Daze, Do the Right Thing,* and the Spike Lee Discourse." *Black American Literature Forum* 25.2 (Summer 1991): 253–82.

Lucia, Cynthia. "Redefining Female Sexuality in the Cinema: An Interview with Lizzie Borden." *Cineaste* 19.2–3 (Feb. 1993): 6–10.

MacDonald, Scott. *A Critical Cinema: Interviews with Independent Filmmakers.* Berkeley: University of California Press, 1988.

Martin-Barbero, Jesus. *Communication, Culture and Hegemony: From the Media to Mediations.* Thousand Oaks, CA: Sage, 1993.

Maslin, Janet. " 'Bad Girls' Showing Off. . . ." *New York Times,* 22 Apr. 1994, sec. C, p. 8.

Mayne, Judith. *Cinema and Spectatorship.* New York: Routledge, 1993.

———. *Directed by Dorothy Arzner.* Bloomington: Indiana University Press, 1994.

———. "The Female Audience and the Feminist Critic." In *Women and Film.* Ed. Janet Todd. New York: Holmes and Meier, 1995.

———. *The Woman at the Keyhole: Feminism and Women's Cinema.* Bloomington: Indiana University Press, 1990.

———. "The Woman at the Keyhole: Women's Cinema and Feminist Criticism." In *Re-vision: Essays in Feminist Film Criticism.* Ed. Mary Ann Doane, Patricia Mellencamp, and Linda Williams. Frederick, MD: University Publications of America, 1984.

McCarthy, Todd. "Bad Girls." *Variety,* 25 Apr. 1994, 30.

Mellencamp, Patricia. *Indiscretions: Avant Garde Film, Video, and Feminism.* Bloomington: Indiana University Press, 1990.

Metz, Christian. "The Imaginary Signifier." *Screen* 16:2 (Summer 1975): 14–76.

Mills, Nancy. "Cameos: Lizzie Borden." *Premiere,* May 1991, 47–48.

———. "Blue Steel: Kathryn Bigelow in Action." *American Film,* Sept. 1989, 59.

Mizejewski, Linda. "Picturing the Female Dick: *The Silence of the Lambs* and *Blue Steel.*" *Journal of Film and Video* 45.2–3 (Summer–Fall 1994): 6–23.

Modleski, Tania. *Loving with a Vengeance: Mass-Produced Fantasies for Women.* New York: Methuen, 1984.

243

WORKS CITED

————. *The Women Who Knew Too Much*. New York: Methuen, 1988.

Morse, Margaret. "Postsynchronizing Rock Music and Television." *Journal of Communication Inquiry* 10.1 (1986): 306–8.

Mulvey, Laura. *Visual and Other Pleasures*. Bloomington: Indiana University Press, 1989.

————. "Visual Pleasure and Narrative Cinema." *Screen* 16.3 (1975): 6–18.

Murphy, Kathleen. "Black Arts." *Film Comment*, Sept.–Oct. 1995, 51–53.

Neale, Steve. *Genre*. London: British Film Institute, 1980.

————. "Questions of Genre." In *Film Genre Reader II*. Ed. Barry Keith Grant. Austin: University of Texas Press. 159–83.

Nichols, Peter M. "Home Video." *New York Times*, 25 Feb. 1993, sec. C, p. 22.

Obst, Lynda. *Hello, He Lied and Other Truths from the Hollywood Trenches*. New York: Little, Brown, 1996.

"An Open Invitation." *The Washington Post*, 25 Oct. 1995, sec. C, p. 9.

Ouillette, Laurie. "Reel Women: Feminism and Narrative Pleasure in New Women's Cinema." *The Independent Film and Video Monthly* 18.3 (1 Apr. 1995): 28–34.

Peary, Gerald. "Why Should Guys Have All the Fun?" *Boston Globe*, 11 Mar. 1990, 93–94.

Pener, Degan. "What Price 'Happiness'?" *Entertainment Weekly*, 30 Oct. 1998, 20–21.

Penley, Constance. *The Future of an Illusion: Film, Feminism and Psychoanalysis*. Minneapolis: University of Minnesota Press, 1989.

Perkins, William Eric, ed. *dropping science: essays on rap music and hip hop culture*. Philadelphia: Temple University Press, 1996. 117–58.

Perren, Alisa. "Indie, Inc: Miramax, Independent Film and the New Hollywood." Master's thesis, University of Texas, 1998.

"Plunge into a Vibrant. . . ." *New York Times*, 9 Oct. 1994, sec. H, p. 22.

Polan, Dana. "S/Z MTV." *Journal of Communication Inquiry* 10.1 (Winter 1986): 48–54.

Powers, John. "The Director Wore Black." *Vogue*, Oct. 1995, 194–96.

————. "Pressing Ahead." *American Film*, Apr. 1988, 49–50.

Quart, Barbara Koenig. *Women Directors: The Emergence of a New Cinema*. New York: Praeger, 1988.

Rabinovitz, Lauren. *Points of Resistance: Women, Power, and Politics in the New York Avant Garde, 1943–1971*. Chicago: University of Illinois Press, 1991.

Rabinow, Paul, ed. *The Foucault Reader*. New York: Pantheon, 1984.

Radway, Janice. *Reading the Romance: Women, Patriarchy and Popular Literature*. Chapel Hill: University of North Carolina Press, 1984.

Rafferty, Terrence. "Bad Girls." *New Yorker*, 9 May 1994, 98–99.

Rainey, Buck. *Those Fabulous Serial Heroines: Their Lives and Films*. Metuchen, NJ: Scarecrow Press, 1990.

Rhines, Jesse Algeron. *Black Films/White Money*. New Brunswick, NJ: Rutgers University Press, 1996.

Rich, Adrienne. "Compulsory Heterosexuality and Lesbian Existence." *Signs* 5 (Summer 1980): 631–60.

————. *On Lies, Secrets and Silence*. New York: Norton, 1979.

Richardson, John. "Love Bites." *Premiere*, Jan. 1991, 25.

Robinson, Jennifer. "Susan Seidelman Is Making Movies." *Columbia Film Review* 7.2–3 (Winter/Spring 1989): 3–6.

Rose, Tricia. *Black Noise: Rap Music and Black Culture in Contemporary America*. Hanover, NH: University Press of New England, 1994.

Rothman, William. *Hitchcock: The Murderous Gaze*. Cambridge, MA: Harvard University Press, 1982.

Rowe, Kathleen. *The Unruly Woman: Gender and the Genres of Laughter*. Austin: University of Texas Press, 1995.

Rubin, Gayle. "The Traffic in Women: Notes on the 'Political Economy' of Sex." In *Towards an Anthropology of Women*. Ed. Rayna Reiter. New York: Monthly Review Press, 1975. 157–210.

Sawicki, Jana. "Identity Politics and Sexual Freedom: Foucault and Feminism." In *Feminism and Foucault*. Ed. Irene Diamond and Lee Quinby. Boston: Northeastern University Press, 1988. 177–91.

Schatz, Thomas. *The Genius of the System: Hollywood Filmmaking in the Studio Era*. New York: Pantheon Books, 1986.

———. *Hollywood Genres: Formulas, Filmmaking, and the Studio System*. New York: Random House, 1981.

———. "The New Hollywood." In *Film Theory Goes to the Movies*. Ed. Jim Collins, Hilary Radner, and Ava Preacher Collins. New York: Routledge, 1993. 8–36.

———. "The Structural Influence: New Directions in Film Genre Study." In *Film Genre Reader II*. Ed. Barry Keith Grant. Austin: University of Texas Press, 1996. 91–101.

Schickel, Richard. "Hollywood's New Directions." *Time*, 14 Oct. 1991, 75, 78.

Schwichtenberg, Cathy. "Madonna's Postmodern Feminism": Strategies of Simulation and the Sexual Politics of Style." Paper presented at Culture and Communication Conference, 1989.

Seger, Linda. *When Women Call the Shots: The Developing Power and Influence of Women in Film and Television*. New York: Henry Holt and Company, 1996.

Sharkey, Betsy. "Kathryn Bigelow Practices the Art of the Kill." *New York Times*, 11 Mar. 1990, 17, 26.

Sharman, Leslie Felperin. "Bad Girls." *Sight and Sound* 4.7 (July 1994): 37–38.

Shattuck, Kathryn. "The Marquee Is the Message." *New York Times*, 24 Sept. 1995, 24.

Sherman, Betsy. "An Independent Woman." *The Boston Globe*, 30 Aug. 1992, sec. B, pp. 5, 8.

Silverman, Kaja. *The Acoustic Mirror: The Female Voice in Psychoanalysis and Cinema*. Bloomington: Indiana University Press, 1988.

Smith, Gavin. "Momentum and Design." *Film Comment*, Sept.–Oct. 1995, 46–50.

Smith, Valerie. "Reconstituting the Image: The Emergent Black Woman Director." *Callaloo: A Journal of Afro-American and African Arts and Letters* 11.4 (Fall 1988): 710–19.

Snead, James A. "Images of Blacks in Black Independent Films: A Brief Survey." *Blackframes: Critical Perspectives on Black Indepedent Cinema*. Boston: MIT Press and Celebration of Black Cinema, Inc., 1988.

Snitow, Ann. "Sex on the Job." *Ms.*, May 1987, 20–22.

Spoto, Donald. *The Dark Side of Genius: The Life of Alfred Hitchcock*. New York: Ballantine Books, 1983.

Stacey, Jackie. "Desperately Seeking Difference." In *The Female Gaze: Women as Viewers of Popular Culture*. Ed. Lorraine Gamman and Margaret Marshment. Seattle: The Real Comet Press, 1989. 112–29.

———. *Star-Gazing: Hollywood Cinema and Female Spectatorship*. New York: Routledge, 1994.

Staiger, Janet. *Interpreting Films: Studies in the Historical Reception of American Cinema*. Princeton: Princeton University Press, 1992.

Stockwell, Anne. "Bronx Cheer." *The Advocate*, 1 Nov. 1994, 75–76.

Stuart, Andrea. "From the Bronx to Bellisima." *Sight and Sound* (Mar. 1995): 22–23.

———. "*The Color Purple*: In Defence of Happy Endings." In *The Female Gaze: Women as Viewers of Popular Culture*. Ed. Lorraine Gamman and Margaret Marshment. Seattle: The Real Comet Press, 1989.

Sussler, Betsy. "Born in Flames." *Bomb*, Winter 1983, 27–29.

Suter, Jacqueline. "Feminine Discourse in *Christopher Strong*." *Camera Obscura* nos. 3–4 (1979): 135–50.

"Swayze, Patrick, Interview with." *Empire*, Dec. 1991, 70.

Tasker, Yvonne. *Spectacular Bodies: Gender, Genre and the Action Cinema*. New York: Routledge, 1993.

Tate, Greg. "Cinematic Sisterhood." *Village Voice*, 11 June 1991, 73–77.

Tetzlaff, David. "MTV and the Politics of Postmodern Pop." *Journal of Communication Inquiry* 10.1 (1986).

Travers, Peter. "Women on the Verge." *Rolling Stone*, 21 Sept. 1989, 47–48.

Tuana, Nancy. *The Less Noble Sex: Scientific, Religious, and Philosophical Conceptions of Women's Nature*. Bloomington: Indiana University Press, 1993.

Walters, Suzanna Danuta. *Material Girls: Making Sense of Feminist Cultural Theory*. Berkeley: University of California Press, 1995.

Weintraub, Bernard. "From Valley Girls to Sunshine Boys, a Deal on *Yonkers*." *New York Times*, 26 Apr. 1993, sec. C, p. 11.

Willeman, Paul. "Towards an Analysis of the Sirkian System." In *Imitation of Life*. Ed. Lucy Fischer. New Brunswick, NJ: Rutgers University Press, 1991. 273–78.

Williams, Linda. "Film Bodies: Gender, Genre and Excess." In *Film Genre Reader II*. Ed. Barry Keith Grant. Austin: University of Texas Press, 1995. 140–58.

———. "Something Else Besides a Mother: *Stella Dallas* and the Maternal Melodrama." In *Issues in Feminist Film Criticism*. Ed. Patricia Erens. Bloomington: Indiana University Press, 1990.

———., ed. *Viewing Positions*. New York: Routledge, 1995.

Wollen, Peter. *Signs and Meaning in the Cinema*. London: Secker and Warburg/British Film Institute, 1972.

———. "Ways of Thinking about Music Video and Postmodernism." *Critical Quarterly* 28. 1–2 (1986): 167–70.

Wood, Robin. *Hitchcock's Films Revisited*. New York: Columbia University Press, 1989.

Wyatt, Justin. "Economic Constraints/Economic Opportunities: Robert Altman as Auteur." *The Velvet Light Trap: A Critical Journal of Film and Television* 38 (Fall 1996): 51–67.

———. "From Roadshowing to Saturation Release: Majors, Independents, and Marketing/Distribution Innovations." In *The New American Cinema*. Ed. Jon Lewis. Durham: Duke University Press, 1998. 64–86.

Yearwood, Gladstone, ed. "Introduction: Issues in Independent Black Filmmaking." *Black Cinema Aesthetics: Issues in Independent Black Filmmaking*. Athens: Ohio University Afro-American Studies, 1982.

Young, Lola. *Fear of the Dark: "Race," Gender and Sexuality in the Cinema*. New York: Routledge, 1996.

Young, Shelagh. "Feminism and the Politics of Power: Whose Gaze Is It Anyway?" In *The Female Gaze: Women as Viewers of Popular Culture*. Ed. Lorraine Gamman and Margaret Marshment. Seattle: The Real Comet Press, 1989. 173–88.

251